CULTS, CUSTOMS AND SUPERSTITIONS OF INDIA

CULTS, CUSTOMS AND SUPERSTITIONS OF INDIA

JOHN CAMPBELL OMAN

GYAN

Published by

GYAN

Gyan Publishing House
5, Ansari Road
Daryaganj, New Delhi-110002
Phone: 011-47034999, 9811692060
E-mail: books@gyanbooks.com

Distribution Network
gyanbooks.com
India, USA, Canada, UK, Australia, France

ISBN: 978-81-212-9358-7 (PB)
First Published, 1908

2nd Impression 2023

Printed at: Gyan Press, Delhi.

CULTS, CUSTOMS AND SUPERSTITIONS OF INDIA

AUTHOR: JOHN CAMPBELL OMAN

CULTS, CUSTOMS AND SUPERSTITIONS OF INDIA

From a painting by an Indian artist

GURU GOVIND SINGH

Frontispiece

CULTS, CUSTOMS AND SUPERSTITIONS OF INDIA

BEING A REVISED AND ENLARGED EDITION OF
"INDIAN LIFE, RELIGIOUS AND SOCIAL"

Comprising Studies and Sketches of interesting peculiarities in the Beliefs, Festivals and Domestic Life of the Indian People; also of Witchcraft and Demoniacal Possession, as known amongst them

BY
JOHN CAMPBELL OMAN

FORMERLY PROFESSOR OF NATURAL SCIENCE IN THE GOVERNMENT COLLEGE, LAHORE

AUTHOR OF
"THE BRAHMANS, THEISTS, AND MUSLIMS OF INDIA,"
"THE MYSTICS, ASCETICS, AND SAINTS OF INDIA,"
ETC., ETC.

WITH ILLUSTRATIONS FROM PHOTOGRAPHS AND FROM DRAWINGS BY WILLIAM CAMPBELL OMAN, A.R.I.B.A.

LONDON
T. FISHER UNWIN
ADELPHI TERRACE
1908

Indian Life, Religious and Social, *first printed*, 1889
Second Edition (Cults, Customs and Superstitions of India), 1908

PREFACE

As in my other books, so in this one I have drawn largely upon my personal experiences, hoping thereby to bring the reader more into touch, as it were, with the people of India than would otherwise be possible. Facts of Indian life gathered from men and women directly concerned in each case, carefully sifted by me and punctually noted, occupy a considerable portion of the volume; while legends and stories have also a place in it. The illustrations are intended to elucidate the text, and will, I trust, be found to serve the end in view.

I have striven, to the best of my ability, to be scrupulously impartial in my judgments of the character and institutions of the interesting peoples about whom I have written. But I am well aware of the extreme difficulty, or even impossibility, of being impartial without giving offence in some quarter or other, and particularly so when dealing with India, for both Hindus and Muslims are very sensitive to and intolerant of criticism. However, the educated amongst them know full well that there are many objectionable features in the beliefs and practices connected with some of the more secret Hindu cults, and in certain prevailing customs both religious and social. Against these defects many strong protests have been made by native reformers. But there are Anglo-Indian members of Parliament who seem to be more sensitive to criticism of anything Indian than the Hindus themselves, and one of these gentlemen, in a little book which he has recently given to the public, displays a puritanical horror, bordering upon the ridiculous, at statements made by me in regard to secret rites practised by certain sectarians in connection with goddess-worship in Bengal; although the existence of shamefully indecent rites in certain forms of Tantric worship which are recognized as Hindu is perfectly well known, at any rate to students and investigators.

But the point to which I would now draw attention is this,—that no account of Indian life and religion can be anything but misleading unless it affords some glimpses at least of the objectionable forms in which, *under certain circumstances*, Hinduism, even at the present time, finds practical, if covert, expression; and, therefore, I have in other books, and in this one too, ventured reluctantly to lift, just a very little, the veil which shrouds these dark places of Hinduism from public knowledge, so that my readers may be able to form fairly accurate opinions with regard to the intellectual and moral condition of contemporary India.

Having in this volume detailed many strange beliefs, superstitions and popular delusions, I invite attention, in this connection, to the very backward state of India as respects the education of the people generally. The latest Census Report shows that out of a total of 214,683,915 persons *over ten years of age*, the "illiterate" number 199,611,382, the "literate" being all who can just read and write *any* language. Those of *all ages* who are "literate in English," *including Europeans and Eurasians*, number 1,125,231; and I need hardly add that the vast majority of persons returned as *literate in English* are by no means educated.

If we take account only of persons *over twenty years of age*, the Census Returns lead us to the striking result that in the whole of India and Burmah, out of a population of 294,364,056 souls, there are only 770,911 adult men and women (including Europeans and Eurasians) who are "literate in English"; a fact that should be kept steadily before the mind by every one who wishes to have a reasonable comprehension of the Indian political problems which have of late been so prominently before the world. The temptation to linger over these figures, to view them from different standpoints and to draw deductions from them is very great; but this is not a suitable opportunity for doing so, and I therefore pass on with the remark that if the reader will bear in mind the unsatisfactory, I might almost say deplorable, fact already pointed out, that there are in India to-day nearly 200,000,000 of persons over ten years of age who are quite unable to read or write their own or any other language, he will have no reason to be surprised at any of the strange ideas and practices of the Indian people recorded in this volume.

With respect to the plan of the book a word seems called for. It is divided into four parts. Part I is devoted to religious and sectarian matters, the several chapters (really separate studies or sketches) being arranged in a sort of chronological order commencing with Hindu asceticism, which is older than Buddhism, and ending with the Arya Samaj, a sect which has come into existence and attracted attention within quite recent years. Part II is devoted mainly to fairs and festivals; Part III to certain aspects of domestic life among the common people, and Part IV to curious beliefs and superstitions. The matter of the book and its arrangement will, I believe, justify the title now adopted for this much enlarged and illustrated reissue of "Indian Life, Religious and Social."

To my son, Mr. W. Campbell Oman, I am indebted for the drawings and many of the photographs which appear in this book, also for various helpful suggestions for the emendation of the text.

J. C. O.

MUSWELL HILL, LONDON, N.
21st *April*, 1908.

PREFACE TO THE FIRST EDITION

HAVING seen a great deal of India, from the Vale of Kashmir to the tropical uplands of Ceylon, from the historic borderland of the Indus to the forest-covered banks of the Brahmaputra, having resided in each of the Provinces of Northern India from Assam to the Punjab, and having done my best to understand the character and intellectual condition of the people of the country, I trust the sketches of Indian life which I have embodied in this volume may prove acceptable to readers who take an interest in the *two hundred and fifty millions* of Hindus and Muhammadans in India, so frequently alluded to in contemporary writings.

Of the inner life of a people who adhere to the rigid rules of *caste*, and keep their women in seclusion, it is not, perhaps, possible for an alien to form a just opinion; and this difficulty certainly exists in regard to the entire upper and middle classes of the Indian world, whether Hindu or Muslim. But the common people, more free and open in their domestic arrangements, afford better opportunities for observation, and I have not neglected the chances which have come in my way of gaining an insight into the mode of life and habits of thought of the humbler ranks of the community. In Part II of this volume I have recorded, from personal knowledge, many particulars connected with the somewhat peculiar domestic life of the lower orders, which may help English readers towards accurate conceptions regarding the lives and ideas of many millions of men and women in British India.

J. C. O.

LONDON,
10th January, 1889.

Photo by Lala Jadu Kishan

THE TEMPLE AT BUDDH GAYA

CONTENTS

PART IV—SUPERSTITIONS

CHAPTER I

WITCHCRAFT, DEMONIACAL POSSESSION, AND OTHER SUPERSTITIONS OF THE PEOPLE

CHAPTER II

EXPERIENCES WITH FORTUNE-TELLERS

LIST OF ILLUSTRATIONS

PART I.—RELIGIOUS

ERRATA

Page	55	line	28	*for*	primordeal	*read*	primordial
„	135	„	20	„	narcotic	„	narcotics
„	135	„	20	„	contributes	„	contribute
„	169	„	46	„	branches	„	branch
„	231	„	8	*omit*	who		

CULTS, CUSTOMS AND SUPERSTITIONS OF INDIA

CHAPTER I

YOGIS AND MAHATMAS, THE SAGES OF INDIA

" The brooding East with awe beheld
  Her impious younger world.
The Roman tempest swelled and swelled,
  And on her head was hurled.

The East bowed low before the blast,
  In patient, deep disdain :
She let the legions thunder past,
  And plunged in thought again."

MATTHEW ARNOLD.

A SWOLLEN river rushing brimful, with rapid and audible current, past town and hamlet, past field and forest, is a sight that has attractions for most people. And the old *Hydraôtes* of Greek geographers—the Ravi—big with the melted snows of the Himalayas and the rain of the wide plains of the Punjab, is as good a river to watch in flood as many another; so on a Sunday in July I took a drive from Lahore to see the rush of water by the bridge of boats, for I knew the river was pretty full at that time.

Passing the European cemetery and the Taksali gate of the city, my way lay behind the stately mosque of Aurangzeb, with its marble domes gleaming in the morning twilight. Beyond the mosque a well-metalled road, sheltered by trees and skirted by green fields of cotton and sugar-cane, traversed the open country to the river —and not to the river only, but, as the finger-post indicated, to distant Peshawar on the western frontier of the Indian Empire.

It was one of those sultry mornings so suggestive to the victim of an Indian summer of the pleasures of the bath, that with the idea in my own mind I had little difficulty in accounting to myself for the number of natives of both sexes on the road between the city and the river. As I proceeded, however, the scene became unusually animated. There was a holiday look about the people I met, and, before long, I discovered that the object of attraction was not merely the refreshing water, but a group of tents which had been pitched upon the open plain to the left of the trestle bridge which spans an old channel, now known as the *Chota Ravi*.

I drew up and approached the encampment, along with a stream of natives on their way to the bathing-place or the tents. A large enclosed space on the sandy river-bank was occupied by open pavilions. In the one nearest the direction of approach there were seated, round a smouldering fire, a number of *yogis* very much *un*dressed, and rubbed over from head to foot with mud and ashes. One of them was beating a gong. Towards the centre of the enclosure, on a slightly raised place, sat the principal yogi. I had seen yogis and other ascetics in different parts of India; but had never come across an encampment of yogis like the one before me. As for the leader of the party, there was about his appearance neither the emaciation of person one might expect to see in a professed ascetic, nor the absent, self-concentred look one would be prepared to find in a devotee given to severe and long-continued contemplation. He was apparently between thirty-five and forty years of age, in excellent condition, and apparently in vigorous health, with the commanding presence, easy carriage, and self-possessed manner of one accustomed to the homage of men. Round about him, in picturesque disorder, were groups of men, women, and children, seated on the ground as close to his feet as possible. Three yogis repeating some Sanskrit *Mantras*,[1] probably quite unintelligible to them-

[1] "Mantra—a hymn of invocation or form of prayer in the Sanskrit language. Mantras are used in the performance of every

Photo by W. Campbell Oman

A GROUP OF YOGIS, ONE MAN ENJOYING HIS *CHURRUS* PIPE

To face page 4

selves, were walking rapidly round the saint and then round the fire at which their companions were seated. A diminutive tent erected under the general canopy contained some Hindu idols—grotesque representations of their gods—which two men were fanning in a listless sort of way.

From time to time the *principal* yogi rose to his feet with all the pride of sanctity—pride often as overbearing and offensive as any other kind of pride. His rising was the signal for the devout to make their offerings, which they did with tokens of the most humble veneration. The men were respectful enough in their manner; as for the women, they, in the effusiveness of their nature, seemed literally to worship the yogi. I saw them dip their fingers into brass *lotas* of Ravi water (for they had approached the great man after their morning ablutions), rub their moist hands over the yogi's dirty feet and legs, and then apply the offscum to their eyelids and foreheads.

In return for their offerings the visitors received, as tokens of the saint's favour, a few flowers, which they would carry away as charms and talismans to be used in the cure of the sick, or to bring good fortune to their homes.

And who can tell what real or imagined benefit the sanctified trifles may have brought to many a sick-bed in Lahore! Indeed, I was afterwards told, by one who professed to speak from personal knowledge, of a remarkable cure effected by the yogi. A boy had been ill of fever for some time. All the usual remedies had been tried without success, when the mother had the sufferer carried into the presence of the yogi. The holy man touched him, and handing his mother a few *chillies*,

religious rite. They are of various sorts, invocatory, evocatory, deprecatory, conservatory. They are beneficent or hurtful, salutary or pernicious. By means of them, it is believed that great and various effects may be produced. Some are for casting out evil spirits, some inspiring love or hatred, for curing diseases or bringing them on, for causing death or averting it. Some are of a contrary nature to others, and counteract their effect: the stronger overcoming the influence of the weaker. Some are potent enough, it is said, to occasion the destruction of a whole army; while there are others which the gods themselves are constrained to obey."—Garrett's "Classical Dictionary of India."

directed her to give the patient one every morning. She did so, and in a very short time the boy was quite restored to health. Perhaps, as currently believed, faith works wonders; perhaps the excitement of the interview with the famous saint brought about a favourable change in the sick child's condition; or maybe the story is, after all, only one of those very doubtful ones which spring up and cluster round every religious teacher or famous ascetic.

I had taken up a convenient position just outside the enclosure when I overheard a native address another in English, evidently with the object of attracting my attention. I entered into conversation with him about the yogis, and gleaned the following particulars with regard to them. The chief man, the centre of attraction, was a native of Lahore, who had been away some twelve years, engaged, according to popular belief, in deep, ecstatic contemplation and the most impossible austerities. He had now come back to his native place with all the prestige of sainthood about him. Certainly the hardships he had voluntarily endured had left no trace upon his person. And perhaps this fact was, to his admirers, only a more convincing proof of his sanctity and power. In conversing with me my informant expressed his regret at the ignorance and superstition of the common people, as if to draw the line between himself and the vulgar herd. Superstition, however, is an Old Man of the Sea not to be easily shaken off, and I am very much mistaken if a threatened curse from the yogi he affected to contemn would not have reduced my loquacious friend to a state of abject terror; for every Indian knows how direful and irrevocable are maledictions proceeding from the mouth of one who has obtained superhuman power by the practice of austerities.

This remarkable and peculiarly Hindu notion, which deserves attention in connection with the subject of yogis, has been made familiar to the English reader by Southey, who, in his poem "The Curse of Kehama," has worked out the subject with much skill and force.

When the great yogi had his attention drawn to me he rose and approached the spot where I was standing, carrying in his hands a present, consisting of two mangoes and half a cocoa-nut. I accepted his gift with a *salaam*, but believing that the rules of Oriental etiquette required, in such a case, some return, however trifling, I told the saint that I had no money (" rupees ") with me to make a suitable requital for his courtesy. He put on a deprecating smile, raised his hands above his head, and, in an exceedingly natural and graceful attitude, gave me his benediction, observing, with reference to my remark, and in truly Oriental phrase, that " by my favour he was sufficiently rich." When I was about to withdraw, another yogi came up, with garlands of flowers taken off the saint's neck, and placed them in my hands. My casual visit to the yogi has, I have little doubt, been already exaggerated into a devout pilgrimage. Probably while I write this, stories are passing from mouth to mouth regarding the *Sahib* who came deliberately to pay his respects to the yogi and made him most valuable offerings. That I could have come that way merely for a morning drive, or for the pleasure of looking at the rushing river, did not, in all probability, occur to any soul present, and so the assembled crowd must, and most naturally too, have connected my presence there with the yogi's fame, while the little romance about valuable offerings would almost of necessity find a place in an Oriental account of my pilgrimage to the renowned ascetic.

Before I left the spot, three young yogis, with a large dog as companion, proceeded from the enclosure apparently on a begging expedition to the city. All three were well fed, in good condition, and full of animal spirits, as was evident from the brisk and boyish scamper with which they started on their pleasant and profitable errand.

On my return home the presents I had received from the yogi were begged for eagerly by my servants, to whom the *syce* (groom) had related my morning's adventure. One of them gave expression to the opinion, shared no doubt by his fellows, that my good luck was boundless in having been thus favoured by the great yogi, whose fame was spreading far and wide. So widely, indeed, had his fame extended, and so great had been his success, that he had, on more than one occasion, been able to feast a vast number of the city people, both *Hindus and Muhammadans*, on the open plain near his pavilion. I was told that several college students had partaken of the yogi's hospitality. Those who had done so did not relish my knowing the fact, but could not conceal from me that they secretly entertained a superstitious respect for the successful ascetic.

That the yogi had achieved a great reputation in Lahore was indisputable. Speaking of him, an educated native [1] remarked to me, that not the least "miraculous" act of the yogi was feeding the multitude when he had not a rupee to call his own. "Who," he asked, "could, without supernatural power, have induced the stingy *baniyás* and close-fisted *mahájans* to open their stores and supply him (as they certainly had done), without money and without price?" The obvious answer, from a European point of view, that superstitious dread of the yogi's power was quite sufficient to account for his success with the ignorant tradesfolk, did not find favour with my Hindu friend, who, with characteristic leaning towards the supernatural and mystical, preferred his own explanation of the yogi's influence in the bazaar.

To obviate the production of any false impression on the reader's mind by the foregoing narrative, I must state that there are hundreds of yogis in India very unlike those well-nourished and worldly-wise saints who treated me with so much courtesy on the banks of the Ravi. Indeed, there are yogis who have deliberately cut themselves off from all interest in the active pursuits of life. Seldom appearing in the busy haunts of men, these devotees practise rigid self-denial, undergo the most painful self-inflicted tortures, and spend their lives in solitary contemplation.

Every one who has seen much of India must have come across some of these ascetics, living skeletons, almost

[1] By the term *educated native* is meant, throughout this book, the native who has been educated in European learning and science through the medium of the English language, this being the meaning now universally attached to the term in India.

naked, and overlaid with dirt and ashes. Sometimes they are to be met with seated in the midst of five fires, four smouldering round them and the fifth—the sun—pouring its fierce rays upon their unclothed bodies, from a sky that looks like brass. In remote out-of-the-way places the traveller may occasionally see a yogi, with an arm, attenuated and quite rigid, upraised above his matted locks, or with hands so long closed that the growing nails have penetrated the lifeless flesh. These are certainly rare, though I have come across one or two in my time. If current belief is to be trusted, the solitudes of the jungle and the lone caverns of the Himalayas are tenanted by many earnest yogis, who have retired as far as possible from the world and its distractions.

To the ordinary European, whether resident or tourist, these ascetics are incomprehensible [1] and loathsome; [2] but the Indian sees them with very different eyes, and regards them with very different feelings. To the Hindu the yogi is both a saint and a philosopher. Indeed it may not be too much to say that a comprehension of the ideas which underlie the practices of the yogis is indispensable to the student of the spiritual and religious side, which is by far the most important side, of Indian life and character. Save in their voluntary penances and self-inflicted tortures, the yogis bear no resemblance to the Christian anchorites who, in the early centuries of our era, weighed down by a sense of their own unworthiness, and awed by the expected approaching destruction of the world, fled to the wilderness to mortify their flesh and humble themselves before God. Far from making any professions of humility or acknowledgment of unworthiness, the yogis put forward the most extravagant claims to knowledge and power, said to be obtained by following out a certain painful and difficult course of mental and physical discipline. "The adept acquires the knowledge of everything past and future, remote or

[1] "To me these men are living enigmas, and I look in vain for the sphinx who can or will give me the clue."—Baron Hübner's "Through the British Empire," vol. ii. pp. 173–174.

[2] ". . . for their reverence of such degraded, filthy, naked, and unclean beasts, as these fakirs, there is simply no excuse."—"Two Years in the Jungle," by William T. Hornaday, p. 86.

hidden; he divines the thoughts of others, gains the strength of an elephant, the courage of a lion, and the swiftness of the wind; flies in the air, floats in the water and dives into the earth, contemplates all worlds at one glance, and performs other strange feats."[1]

Ascetic practices are common all the world over, especially amongst peoples in a low stage of civilization, "for the purpose of bringing on those abnormal mental states which are supposed to imply either possession by spirits or communion with spirits;" or with the view of producing the maniacal excitement which is mistaken for inspiration.[2] The peculiarity in the case of the yogi is that he follows out an elaborate system of ascetic exercises, essentially Indian in conception, and framed to meet the requirements of a subtle school of philosophy, which has had, and still has, a potent influence upon the speculative conceptions and practical life of the people of India.

As might have been expected, the possessors of such powers as those ascribed to the yogis are objects of dread to the ignorant, who dare not so much as question them about their lives or past history;[3] but invent and believe the most ridiculous stories about them. An Indian, himself a believer in the yogis, writing about certain members of this order, says they are "objects of great reverence to the ignorant hill-tribes living in the neighbourhood, who fear that the yogis may assume the forms of tigers and eat them up."[4]

Amongst Hindus trained in European modes of thought, and more or less acquainted with the results of European science, many unhesitatingly reject the pretensions of the yogis. Some, while believing that the Yoga system is true, are persuaded that, in these degenerate times, no one is able to act up to it. But, on the other hand, many Hindus of marked ability profess undoubting belief in the reality of the so-called Yog-science and in the existence of adepts or *mahatmas* at the present

[1] Colebrook's "Essays," vol. i. p. 263.

[2] Mr. Herbert Spencer's 'Ecclesiastical Institutions,' in "Principles of Sociology," vol. ii. p. 759.

[3] "Theosophist," vol. i. pp. 90–92.

[4] Ibid. p. 92.

day. As for the ignorant millions, without knowledge of *yoga-vidya*, its objects, or its practices, they have an unfaltering faith in the power of the yogi, and venerate him accordingly, with the reverence that is born of dread. The system seems to have had its attractions for even so sceptical a mind as that of the great *Akbar*, regarding whom Professor H. H. Wilson says: "He wore his hair after their fashion, and anticipated the liberation of his soul by the fontanelle as they (the yogis) teach." [1] But it may be added that Akbar's admiration of the yoga system did not prevent his allowing a pitched battle in his presence between the rival sects of the Sanyasis and Yogis, which (notwithstanding their superhuman powers) ended in the complete discomfiture of the latter.[2]

Let us not, however, turn away from the yogi with contemptuous indifference on account of his preposterous pretensions, for naked, emaciated, and covered with ashes though he be, he represents, albeit in an unhealthy form, an important idea. In the grovelling world of polytheistic India, he stands forth a bold and ever-present asserter of man's inherent dignity and exalted position in the universe. Before the multitude cowering in abject terror at the altars of hideous and terrible idols, he appears as an embodiment of the belief that man, even though he be degraded and trammelled by his fleshly garment, can by his own exertions raise himself to divine heights of knowledge and power. The yogi is also highly interesting as a living exemplification of the attitude, since time immemorial, of the Indian mind towards life and nature; of the world weariness which has oppressed the East since ages before the dawn of European history, and caused her sons to fly from the struggles and pleasures of life to the quiet retreat of the jungle, and to seek in a living death an escape from the disquieting, and to them unbearable, activity of thought itself.

It was probably during the Macedonian invasion that the European world made its first direct and personal acquaintance with the Indian anchorites, when one of

[1] "Essays," vol. ii. p. 395.

[2] Sir H. Elliot's "Muhammadan Historians of India," edited by Dowson, vol. v. p. 318.

them, the naked Dandamis, reclining on his bed of leaves, treated with scornful indifference the haughty messengers of Alexander, bidding them go tell their master: "Dandamis has no need of aught that is yours, and therefore will not go to you, but if you want anything from Dandamis come you to him."[1] That event occurred more than two thousand years ago. But for centuries prior to the Macedonian invasion India had been *par excellence* the land of anchorites, and during the long interval, from the days of Alexander to the present time, has produced an abundant crop of hermits, misanthropes, and mystics. Some of the grandest figures in Indian epic poetry are the anchorites, who, according to the poets, were in their day a terror to the gods themselves.

Writing in the middle of the ninth century of our era, the Mussulman historian Abu Zaid said:

> "In India there are persons who, in accordance with their profession, wander in the woods and mountains, and rarely communicate with the rest of mankind. Sometimes they have nothing to eat but herbs and the fruits of the forest. . . . Some of them go about naked. Others stand naked with the face turned to the sun, having nothing on but a panther's skin. In my travels I saw a man in the position I have described; sixteen years afterwards I returned to that country and found him in the same posture. What astonished me was that he was not melted by the heat of the sun."[2].

Succeeding historians down to our own time have referred to or described the Indian ascetics, for they have ever been a noteworthy feature in the Indian world. Here is a modern picture which I present to the reader as of interest from more than one point of view:

> "Wolff went also with Mr. Wilson to see one of the celebrated Yoghees, who was lying in the sun in the street, the nails of whose hands were grown into his cheeks, and a bird's nest upon his head. Wolff asked him, 'How can one obtain the knowledge of God?' He replied, 'Do not ask me questions; you may look at me, for I am God.' Wolff indignantly said to him, 'You will go to hell if you speak in such a way.' The subtle pantheism of the ascetic absorbed into Vishnoo was beyond the Judæo-Christian dervish."[3]

---

[1] J. W. McCrindle's "Ancient India as Described by Megasthenes and Arrian," p. 126.

[2] Sir H. Elliot's "Muhammadan Historians of India," edited by Dowson, vol. i. p. 6.

[3] Dr. George Smith's "Life of Dr. Wilson," p. 74.

All, however, who practise austerities are not necessarily yogis; nor need they be actuated by the yogi's desire to attain utter unconsciousness of his individual existence by identification with the Universal Spirit.

Here and there, all over India, may be seen men who practise, or pretend that they have practised, austerities for their purification from guilt and the ultimate attainment of beatitude. And there are, no doubt, in the ranks of the ascetics many disappointed men for whom the battle of life has been too hot, and who have taken refuge in flight; the spirit of renunciation which lies at the root of true asceticism being only too much in harmony with the passive, desponding temper of the Indian mind.

The yogis, however, must not be confounded with other ascetics. They form a distinct order, hold peculiar doctrines, and go through, or pretend to go through, a prescribed course of discipline for the attainment of certain objects which they have in view.

The *yoga-vidya* is one of the six recognized systems of Hindu philosophy, and the text-book of the yogis is an old Sanskrit work, the yoga-Sûtras of Patan-jali,[1] which teaches that by contemplation, posturing, the suspension of the breath, and other practices, the ascetic can disengage his soul from its gross earthly connections and then be able to attain a full knowledge of the past and of the future, of the condition of this and of other worlds, and of the very thoughts of his fellow-men. Not only far-reaching knowledge, but power over man and nature of the most extraordinary and unlimited kind, is promised to the successful yogi.

It is certainly not, at the present day, easy for the Western mind to enter into the spirit of the so-called yoga philosophy; but the student of religious opinions is aware that, in the early centuries of our era, the Gnostics, Manichæans, and Neoplatonists, derived their peculiar tenets and practices from the *yoga-vidya* of India, and that, at a later date, the *Sufi* philosophy of Persia drew its most remarkable ideas from the same source.[2]

[1] This work has been translated into English by Dr. Rajendra Lala Mitra.

[2] Professor Weber's "Indian Literature" (English translation), p. 239.

The great historian of the Roman Empire refers to the subject in the following passage:

"The fakirs of India and the monks of the Oriental Church, were alike persuaded, that in total abstraction of the faculties of the mind and body, the purer spirit may ascend to the enjoyment and vision of the Deity. The opinion and practice of the monasteries of Mount Athos will be best represented in the words of an abbot, who flourished in the eleventh century. 'When thou art alone in thy cell,' says the ascetic teacher, 'shut thy door, and seat thyself in a corner; raise thy mind above all things vain and transitory; recline thy beard and chin on thy breast; turn thy eyes and thy thoughts towards the middle of thy belly, the region of the navel; and search the place of the heart, the seat of the soul. At first, all will be dark and comfortless; but if you persevere day and night, you will feel an ineffable joy; and no sooner has the soul discovered the place of the heart, than it is involved in a mystic and ethereal light.' This light, the production of a distempered fancy, the creature of an empty stomach and an empty brain, was adored by the Quietists as the pure and perfect essence of God himself."[1]

A system like that of the yogis, which has lasted so many centuries, which is still believed in, and which influenced the ideas and practices of ascetics in far distant lands, can hardly be undeserving of attention.

Without entering into unnecessary details—many of them are simply disgusting—I shall quote, as samples, a few of the rules of practice required to be followed by the would-be yogi in order to induce a state of *samadhi* —hypnotism or trance—which is the condition or state in which the yogi is to enjoy the promised privileges of yoga. The extracts are from a treatise on the yoga philosophy by Assistant-Surgeon Nobin Chander Paul.[2]

"Place the left foot upon the right thigh and the right foot upon the left thigh; hold with the right hand the right great toe and with the left hand the left great toe (the hands coming

---

"The principal points of contact, however, between Indian philosophy and Gnosticism may be regarded as common to both branches of the former. These are (1) the doctrine of the emanation of the world from the one absolute existence and of its final reabsorption into that existence; (2) the doctrine of the inherent evil, and at the same time of the unreality of matter; (3) the doctrine of the antagonism between spirit and matter, and the practical consequence, that the highest aim of religion is to free the soul from the contamination of matter and to raise it to a final absorption in the being of the absolute."—"Gnostic Heresies of the First and Second Centuries," by Dean Mansel, pp. 29–30.

[1] Gibbon's "Decline and Fall of the Roman Empire," chap. lxiii.

[2] Republished in the "Theosophist."

from behind the back and crossing each other); rest the chin on the interclavicular space and fix the sight on the tip of the nose.

* * * * * * *

"Inspire through the left nostril, fill the stomach with the inspired air by the act of deglutition, suspend the breath, and then expire through the right nostril. Next inspire through the right nostril, swallow the inspired air, suspend the breath, and finally expire through the left nostril.

* * * * * * *

"Be seated in a tranquil posture, and fix your sight on the tip of the nose for the space of ten minutes.

"Close the ears with the middle fingers, incline the head a little to the right side and listen with each ear attentively to the sound produced by the other ear, for the space of ten minutes.

"Pronounce inaudibly twelve thousand times the mystic syllable *Om*, and meditate upon it daily after deep inspirations.

"After a few forcible inspirations swallow the tongue, and thereby suspend the breath, and deglutate the saliva for two hours.

"Listen to the sounds within the right ear abstractedly for two hours, with the left ear.

* * * * * * *

"Repeat the mystic syllable *Om* 20,736,000 times in silence and meditate upon it.

"Suspend the respiratory movements for the period of twelve days, and you will be in a state of *samadhi*."

Such are a few of the rules of discipline prescribed by that system of yoga-vidya which is known as the *Hatha yog;* and although the reader may not, perhaps, feel surprised at the yogi's attaining *samadhi*, or anything else, after successfully performing feats of which the above are only samples, it can hardly fail to strike him, if he be at all acquainted with what has been improperly called the science of "animal magnetism," that the rules in question, however extravagant they may be, have, some of them at least, been framed with a practical knowledge, if not an intelligent appreciation, of the means by which self-hypnotization may be produced. I refer more especially to the rules requiring the yogi to fix his eyes on a near point, as the tip of his nose, and to concentrate his attention for a prolonged period upon a particular sound, as that supposed to be produced in the right or left ear.[1]

[1] On this subject I may cite the following: "On retrouve en Orient, et en particulier dans l'Inde, des états analogues à l'état hypnotique; pour les provoquer, les uns, comme les fakirs, regardent fixement le ciel, un objet lumineux ou le bout de leur nez; les autres, comme les moines du Mont Athos, contemplent leur nombril, d'où le nom d'Omphalopsyches qui leur a été donné."

Leaving out of consideration the crowning feat of yogaism—complete absorption into or identification with the Universal Spirit—an impartial account of the system and its results requires that mention should be made of some strange achievements of the yogis, for which at least there is ample testimony—whatever that testimony may be worth. Only two generations ago, if we are to credit the statements of several eye-witnesses, the yogi Haridas, after voluntarily falling into a self-induced trance in the presence of Mahárája Ranjít Singh, of the Punjab, and his court, was carefully buried in a garden outside the city of Lahore. For forty days strict watch was kept over the grave, and, at the expiration of that time, the yogi was exhumed, cold, stiff, and unconscious; but was gradually restored to animation by applying warmth to the head and friction to the body, while forcing air gently into the lungs. Granting the truth of the story, and the absence of any collusion or trickery, the only legitimate inference from the facts is, of course, that Haridas, in the practice of *yoga-vidya*, or otherwise, had acquired the art of suspending animation for a considerable period; an art not without interest from a physiological point of view, but one the acquisition of which Europeans are never likely to care for. As regards Haridas himself, it is said that he was a man of loose morals, against whom several complaints were made to Ranjít Singh; that he eloped with a Khatrany woman, made his way to the hills, died there, and was duly buried according to the custom of the country.[1]

Referring to the case of Haridas, the writer (W. F. K.) of the article 'Hybernation' in the "Encyclopædia Britannica" said:

"Long-continued suspension of consciousness in man, whether voluntary or otherwise, is rare in temperate climates, but it is more frequent in India, where some religious ascetics are stated, on unimpeachable authority, to possess the power of throwing themselves into a state closely resembling hybernation for an indefi-

—"Le Magnetisme Animal, étude critique et experimentale sur l'hypnotisme," par le Dr. Fernand Bottey, p. 211. Paris, 1884.

[1] See "Thirty-five Years in the East," by Dr. Honigberger, Physician to the Court of Lahore, pp. 126, 130. London, 1852.

nite period. Many curious cases have been recorded by Mr. Braid in his small treatise on 'Human Hybernation' published in 1850, the most celebrated of which is that of a fakir who was actually buried alive at Lahore in 1837 in the presence of Ranjít Singh and Sir Claude Wade, and who was dug up and restored to consciousness several months[1] afterwards, after every precaution had been taken to prevent any from disturbing the grave in the interval."

Besides the *Hatha yog* system, which I have briefly described above, there is another one, the *Raj yog*, according to which *samadhi* may be attained without severe bodily discipline, by the mere force of self-control and meditation, possibly combined with fixation of attention on some object (*e. g.* the nose) near enough to cause squinting. Whether this system owes its origin to the extreme difficulty, not to say impracticability, of acting up to the rules of the Hatha yog system, or whether, as I have been assured, it is older than that system, I do not pretend to say. But I should state here that some who claim to be authorities on the subject maintain that one could not attain *samadhi* through the Raj yog alone, unless, indeed, one had gone through the terrible discipline of the Hatha yog in a previous existence.[2]

The *Raj yog* philosophy, as expounded in English by the Madras yogi Sabhapaty Swami, with whom I had the pleasure of conversing on one occasion, teaches that man's existence, as distinct and separate from the Infinite Universal Spirit, is a mere delusion, which arises from the genesis of the so-called twelve faculties, due to the circulation of the Universal Spirit through the human body, in a triple set of hollow vessels, answering in some way to animal functions, mind, and soul—reminding one of Lytton's impressive description of the red, the azure, and the silvery light circulating through Margrave's prostrate frame, in the museum, under the power of Sir Philip Derval's spells. The position and course of these vessels is indicated in a fantastic diagram in the Madras yogi's pamphlet. In its passage through them the Infinite Spirit evolves, at different points, the several faculties, senses, and desires of men; but these, being entirely

[1] Dr. Honigberger, who was at Ranjít Singh's court at the time, says *forty days*.

[2] Swami Dyanand Saraswati in "Theosophist," vol. ii. p. 47.

gross and delusive, must be subdued and annihilated, if the soul in man is to gain its lost omniscience and serenity. For the attainment of this object Sabhapaty Swami—himself a professed adept who had been privileged to fly through the air to Kailas, the celestial mountain, and there to behold the Great God Siva employed in yoga practices—lays down detailed rules, having for their aim and object a gradual extinction of all the human faculties, senses, and desires, by means of arguments addressed to them separately; by a course of long-continued meditation with closed eyes in a secluded place; by drawing the spirit up and down through the triple channel of the *sikmana* (or Sashumna) *nadee*, and by the uttering of certain *mantras* or spells.

Addressing the neophyte, he observes :

"Remember . . . that you must be very cautious that the twelve faculties dead and buried should not give forth the bad effluvia of their putrification and annoy and disturb you at the time of your *samadhi*. I again warn you and say beware of those treacherous faculties, and become not again their servile, crouching, mean and ignoble slave and victim.

"If in this state you have any consciousness of seeing the Infinite Spirit, cancel that consciousness also. For who is it that sees, and what is that that is seen? In fact empty yourself from the consciousness of wisdom and duality; *you must become the Infinite Spirit without* the idea of becoming the Infinite Spirit."

Thus by the practice of Raj yog and the attainment of *samadhi* the devotee becomes unconscious of his existence as a man, and passes, as it were, into the full consciousness of divinity with all its attributes. But what becomes of the body? On this point the Madras yogi says that the *rishis* and yogis, after remaining, as long as they like, in the condition of absorption in the Infinite, metamorphose their bodies into lingams,[1] many of which may be seen in the *ashrums* (hermitages), and then enter into final reunion with the Universal Spirit. The Madras yogi goes on to say that many ancient rishis, stated to have died thousands of years ago, are still living, and are visited periodically by the yogis on the Neilgherry Hills,[2]

[1] The phallic emblem worshipped by the followers of the god Siva.

[2] A treatise on "Vedantic Raj Yoga Philosophy," by the Mahatma Giana Guroo Yogi Sabhapaty Swami. Edited by Siris Chandra Basu. Lahore, 1880.

Photo by Bhai Ram Singh

YOGIS IN MEDITATION

To face page 18

So congenial are marvels to the genius of the East, that possibly when Mr. Rider Haggard's powerful story "She" finds its way into the hands of Indian believers in *yoga-vidya*, they will pretend that the yogis had long since discovered the wonderful fire which is the Spirit of the World, the very life of Nature, and, bathing in its life-giving flames, had secured themselves against physical decay and death.

In one form or other the idea which underlies the doctrine of yoga, a doctrine of very great antiquity in India,[1] has a profound and abiding influence on the religious life of the entire Hindu race, and a fascination even for minds which have emancipated themselves, to a large degree, from hereditary and traditional influences. Yoga in its spiritual aspect, and in an Occidental disguise, is well presented by the late Babu Keshub Chunder Sen, "the Apostle of the New Dispensation," in the following interesting passage:

"What does yoga literally mean? Union. The English word which makes the nearest approach to it is Communion. The created soul, in its worldly and sinful condition, lives separate and estranged from the Supreme Soul. A reconciliation is needed; nay, more than mere reconciliation. A harmonious union is sought and realized. This union with Deity is the real secret of Hindu yoga. It is a spiritual unification, it is consciousness of two in one; duality in unity. To the philosophical and thoughtful Hindu this is the highest heaven. He pants for no other salvation; he seeks no other *mukti* or deliverance. Separation, disunion, estrangement, a sense of distinction, duality, the pride of the eye, this is to him the root of all sin and suffering; and the only heaven he aspires to is conscious union and oneness with Deity. He is ever struggling and striving to attain this blessed condition of divine humanity. Once in possession of it, he is above all sorrow and distraction, sin and impurity, and he feels all is serene and tranquil within. All his devotions and prayers, his rites and ceremonies, his meditations and his self-denials, are but means and methods which help him on to this heaven."[2]

It will be evident, after what has already been stated in this paper, that this yogaism of the *Brahmo* leader is not quite that of the orthodox *Hindu*, but, like Dr. Jen-

[1] "In this he (Buddha) merely conformed to the Hindu yoga—a method of attaining mystic union with the Deity—which, though not then formulated into a system, was already in vogue among the Brahmans."—Sir Monier Williams' "Buddhism," p. 32.

[2] "Yoga: Objective and Subjective." Calcutta: The Brahmo Tract Society, 1884.

kinson's Christianity in Mr. Mallock's "New Republic," is "really a new firm trading under an old name and trying to purchase the goodwill of the former establishment."

Some years ago the *yoga-vidya* system temporarily attracted an unusual amount of attention amongst the educated classes in India, owing to the fact that a Yankee colonel and a clever Russian lady went about the country openly professing their belief in the existence of yogi adepts and their extraordinary powers. The gallant colonel told a large audience of natives, in the most emphatic manner, that there were at the present time Indian adepts in *yoga-vidya* who could carry on conversation with one another, at any distance, without the cumbrous appliances (" poles, wires, and pots of chemicals ") of the European electric telegraph; omitting, however, to add that the wonderful occult telegraph system of the yogi—independent of poles, wires, and pots of chemicals —had not been of much use to the people of India, and that the vast knowledge of the secrets of nature possessed by these sages had not helped their compatriots to make life one whit more pleasant or endurable. As for the Russian lady, she took higher ground: for, although not an adept herself, she enjoyed the privilege of the friendship and countenance of one of the great yogis or *mahatmas* of the Himalayas, Koot Hoomi Lal Singh, whose mighty aid enabled her, it seems, to accomplish a few feats such as ordinary conjurors perform every day without the help of such highly-endowed patrons.[1]

Certain classes of the natives of India naturally hailed, with joy and pride, the advent of these new allies from

[1] "It is strange, by the way, that one never hears of Mahatmas in Ladak or in Tibet proper. The lamas know nothing of the mysterious beings who are supposed to dwell in their midst, and who, while disdaining to manifest themselves to their own people, apparently delight in carrying on a telepathic communication of a trivial, if miraculous, kind with their alien disciples in England and America. The nearest approach to a mahatma that one comes across in these regions is the skooshok; but I much doubt whether a European esoteric Buddhist would accept one of these incarnations as his spiritual master. Bower traversed Chinese Tibet from end to end, but found no signs of a mahatma."—"Where Three Empires Meet," by E. F. Knight, p. 131.

the advanced and civilized countries beyond the sea; allies who were never tired of flattering their national vanity, by telling them that their own yogi adepts, dwelling in remote parts of the Himalayas, had satisfactorily solved problems towards which European science was only just feebly groping its way. That many Hindus should, under the circumstances, become ardent followers of these apostles from the West, was only natural. But it has to be added that the clever lady and her colleague actually found believers and followers amongst the highest and best educated class of Europeans in India. Possibly a strong tincture of scepticism with regard to all ancient beliefs, combined with a leaning towards the Comtean *Religion of Humanity*, may have led these gentlemen to give a favourable reception to the idea of the existence of human-gods in the inaccessible mountains. But whether this surmise be correct or not, it is certain that several Europeans of good social position joined the Theosophical Society, and became humble disciples of Madame Blavatsky and the invisible but potent Koot Hoomi Lal Singh. One convert to the new religion wrote a very readable book on the occult world, in which he unfalteringly believed. Others gave what countenance and support they could to the new movement. A shrine of Koot Hoomi, with a lock and key, was set up, and many remarkable, if meaningless, phenomena took place there; for instance, fragments of a broken saucer were introduced into the shrine and the door locked. On opening it, a whole saucer was found inside. We were of course to believe that the whole saucer was made in some wonderful way by the presiding divinity out of the broken pieces put into the cabinet—though the sceptical have been wicked enough to suggest the existence of sliding backs and such-like things.[1]

In April 1883, I had the pleasure of listening to, and exchanging a few words with, one who professed to be

[1] For the story of Madame Blavatsky's mahatmas, their wisdom and manifestations, and also the exposure of the great mahatma hoax, the reader interested in such matters is referred to "Isis Very Much Unveiled," by Edmund Garrett, and "Madame Blavatsky, her Tricks and Dupes," published by The Christian Literature Society, Madras.

an advanced *chela*, or disciple, of the mahatmas of the Himalayas and Tibet, that dark borderland of mystery to the Indians of our days, as it was to their forefathers; who believed that on Mount Meru lived the Uttara Kurus, who reached the age of ten thousand years on the banks of streams which flowed in golden beds. His advent was thus publicly announced:

> "An advanced chela (on his way from the North) has condescended to attend the meeting, and to show certain test phenomena, in order to convince the people as to the reality of occult forces, and will also narrate his personal experiences in *yoga-vidya* as well as give an account of the mahatmas of the Theosophical Society."

The *chela* was a very spare, diminutive, dark-skinned man, evidently a Dravidian from Southern India, although, for obvious reasons, he declined to reveal his nationality. His dress was peculiar. On his head he wore a small skull-cap of orange-yellow cloth with a dark border, below which his long hair could be seen. A loose-sleeved robe of a brown material reached nearly to his ankles. Over it was a sleeveless vest of a gay pattern. Dark-coloured trousers and well-fitting English boots of untanned leather, laced up the front, completed this strange costume.

As for the "Mahatmas of the Theosophical Society," they are adepts in *yoga-vidya*, like the mythical Koot Hoomi Lal Singh, "whose comprehension of Nature and Humanity ranges," according to Mr. A. P. Sinnett, "so far beyond the science and philosophy of Europe, that only the broadest-minded representatives of either will be able to realize the existence of such powers in Man as those he constantly exercises."[1] These are the words of a European, but we shall better understand what the people of India think about such matters by letting the *chela* enlighten us on the subject.

Addressing his audience in English, he said that when quite a little child, only seven or eight years of age, a yogi appeared before him unexpectedly. A radiance streamed from the person of the holy man, and so sur-

[1] "The Occult World," by A. P. Sinnett; Dedication. Trübner and Co., 1881.

prised and awed him that he fell down and worshipped his visitor, regarding him as a god, "for," added the *chela*, naïvely, "in those days I believed in a God, in fact in many gods." The yogi taught the child some signs, which he learned, later on, were *masonic* signs, and then vanished. After this visit the child became thoughtful, gave up the companionship of his young playmates, refused food, and did nothing but long for the reappearance of the wonderful yogi. His parents thought that he had gone mad, and were sore distressed on his account. At length he became possessed—I forget how—of a talisman, by means of which he could constrain the yogi to appear before him. He exercised his power, and the yogi, who was really a mahatma of exalted wisdom and sanctity, came and carried him off, apparently without the knowledge and consent of his parents. He subjected the boy to a very severe course of discipline. For instance, if the *chela* had to proceed to a village one mile away, his master would order him to go there by a circuitous route of seven miles. If he lay down to rest in any spot, the yogi would, in a most arbitrary way, order him to rise and lie down somewhere else, and all this simply to test his pupil's capacity for implicit obedience. The yogi eventually, however, rewarded his disciple's devotion by instructing him in occult science. He then wandered through many countries, Assam, Bengal, the Himalayas, and Tibet, living in the forests in great physical discomfort, often obliged to climb up a tree and tie himself at night to its branches for security against wild beasts. Once in traversing a pathless jungle he found himself suddenly upon the verge of a stupendous precipice. He hesitated to retrace his steps, because he was superstitious and thought that such a course would be inauspicious, so he prayed earnestly to his *guru* (spiritual guide), who suddenly made his appearance, and bade him follow him. He did so. Before him no pathway was visible, and, as he proceeded, there was none behind, but *between* himself and his guide there was a distinct and well-marked pathway. "Let science explain this if it can!" said the *chela*, triumphantly. In this strain was he proceeding, when voices in the audience (all present except myself were natives) suggested that as darkness was closing in upon us, the exhibition of the promised test phenomena should not be delayed. Well, they were at last arrived at, and proved to be simple enough. To establish the truth of *yoga-vidya* and the reality of the hidden forces in which the so-called *occultists* profess belief, the "advanced *chela*" offered to allow one of his fingers to be cut; asserting that no blood would flow from it, and that if that member were amputated entirely, it would be miraculously restored. I examined the particular finger which was thus ready to bear the heavy burden of occultism. It was a thin, fleshless, skinny finger, but resembled in these respects its fellows on the same hand. A ring encircled this finger. An educated and highly-respectable native gentleman of good position examined the ring critically, remarking to me that he knew a certain talisman, and wished to see if this was the same, apparently prepared to find the finger fully protected from the knife by the virtue of the charmed circlet. In reply to an inquiry, the *chela* said he would not object to another finger being experimented upon, provided the ring were transferred to it, thus admitting or declaring the potency of the ring.

Mr. Sinnett, already quoted, wrote as follows:

> "Ask any cultivated Hindoo if he has ever heard of mahatmas and *yoga-vidya*, or occult science, and it is a hundred to one that you will find he has—and, unless he happens to be one of the hybrid products of Anglo-Indian Universities, that he fully believes in the reality of the powers ascribed to yoga."

This statement I am prepared to endorse. And on the occasion I refer to, there were present many "cultivated Hindoos" of the type approved of by Mr. Sinnett, and also several of the "hybrid products of Anglo-Indian Universities," whose scepticism regarding the truth of *yoga-vidya* was apparent in their eagerness to put the *chela's* pretensions to the test.

In response to the *chela's* challenge, one young man came forward to cut the finger. Several applauded him; others cried shame! The president vetoed the proceeding, saying, that the amputation or cutting of the finger would be regarded by the law as a case of causing grievous hurt, duly punishable under the penal code. The maintenance of order was now impossible. Everybody pressed forward to see what was going on. An animated dispute was being carried on round the *chela*. Two of the three kerosene lamps on the table had been extinguished, whether by accident or otherwise I could not tell. The affair had become, literally, a *screaming farce*, and I thought it time to withdraw.

But the matter did not end here. The *chela* and his supporters were followed to their lodgings. The fulfilment of the proposed test was pressed home, with the result that a young student in the Government College sliced off a portion of the flesh from the end of the *chela's* finger, followed of course by a copious flow of blood. The facts of the case were stated to me by the man who performed the operation; and the incident may be taken as a fair sample of the uncompromising struggle which may be looked for in India, between the deeply-rooted time-honoured superstitions of the East and the modern ideas imported from the West.

In his "Biographical Essays," p. 177, Professor Max Müller remarked that the yogi hermits living in the forests of the Himalayas would be the last to claim any mysterious knowledge beyond what the *sastras* supply. I do not know what authority the learned Professor may have had for this statement; but as far as my experience goes, yogaism in the eyes even of men who have had the privilege of instruction in Western science is, without doubt, a system of strange, extraordinary, and mysterious knowledge, giving its possessor very extensive power over men and natural phenomena. Not so many years ago a graduate of an Indian University thought it worth while to publish a treatise on *yoga-vidya*, embodying such puerilities as the following:

"In a lonely place let a student of yoga stand with his back towards the sun or moon. Let him fix his eyes on the throat of the shadow he throws and repeat the mantra, *Om Kram para brahmane mansah* for one hundred and eight times, standing in the same position. Let him see into the sky. In this practice let him persevere for six months. He shall see the great light, and obtain powers over those who walk on earth. The subject is a very extensive one. There are many other advantages in this practice. If it is carried on for two years, past as well as future becomes present to the man."[1]

The passage just cited refers, I believe, to the fact that if you stare intently for some time at your own shadow in bright sunshine and then look up at the sky, you will see your shadow-image reproduced there. This after-image Indian mystics call the *astral body*, and they declare that it is possible to establish familiar intercourse with it, to induce it to converse freely and to get it to render assistance in the affairs of life. Thus upon a fact well known to scientific men, and easily explainable, the exuberant Oriental imagination has built up an airy fabric of mystery and delusion.

The ethical system of the yogi is simple enough. He has apparently no duties to perform in regard to his fellow-men, though he is required to abstain from slaughter, falsehood, theft, incontinence and avarice.[2] His object in life is to withdraw, as far as possible, from human society, from its business, its troubles, its aspirations, and, in silent solitude, to deliberately annihilate every faculty and attribute of his manhood. The world of humanity may go its way while the yogi is lost in the Universal Spirit. With a strange want of appreciation of the legitimate powers and functions of the healthy human mind, without even a glimmering of the beauty and interest of the infinitely varied phenomena which science has brought within its ken, the yogi shuts his eyes to the sensible world around him, and expects universal knowledge from idle self-contemplation.

The root idea of the yoga philosophy and practice must be looked for in that pantheism which has ever been the esoteric creed of Brahmanic India and of Asia generally. Since man is really and essentially a part of the Universal Deity (the all-God), consisting of both spiritual and material elements, it is surely possible, argued the Brahman, for the intelligent part of him to attain to a consciousness of its oneness with Deity, or rather the Universal Spirit, and in doing so to become possessed of all the attributes

[1] "The Science of Breath," by Pandit Rama Prasad Kasyapa, B.A.

[2] "Hindu Philosophy," by Ram Chandra Bose, M.A., p. 175.

of godhood. The real difficulty in the way was the body, with its senses, its appetites, and its passions. If these could be subdued the desired object would be secured.[1] In a state of trance the bodily functions become suspended, and hence it seemed to the Brahman that the attainment of this condition should be the aim of any one who desired to be reunited with the Universal Spirit. And as already remarked, the practices enjoined by the rules of the *yoga-vidya* would seem to be such as the experience of the Hindus had found to be most conducive to the production of a state of hypnotism. Thus far we can follow the yogi. Beyond this comes dreamland, mental hallucination and deliberate imposture.

Although there are, and must at all times have been, honest yogis, yet the calling has, undoubtedly, its attractions for impostors. The disappointed man, disgusted with life, and willing to renounce it, turns for consolation to a system which promises complete release from the illusions of human hopes and the penalties of human infirmities. The ambitious enthusiast enters upon its practices to acquire the power he expects to attain by the proper observance of the prescribed conditions; whereas the knave, on his part, takes up the calling without any serious intention of abiding by the rules, but with the very sufficient object of imposing upon the credulous multitude, under the influence of the vague, indefinable terror inspired by the superhuman power he arrogantly lays claim to, and which the vulgar are only too ready to attribute to him.

Of the fact that some men who practise yog do honestly believe they acquire extraordinary power thereby, we had a curious instance at Lahore. A yogi, who believed himself possessed of a commanding influence over wild animals, in order to put his powers to the test, attempted some familiarities with the tiger in the Lahore Zoological Gardens, and got himself so mauled that his arm had to be amputated.

[1] The reader of Plato will not need to be reminded how Socrates taught that the body, with its eyes and ears and other organs of sense, was only a hindrance to the soul in the acquisition of the knowledge of existence ("Phædo").

Cases of deliberate imposture are numerous, and sometimes come before our law courts.

Some years ago the following story went the round of the Anglo-Indian newspapers :—A yogi predicted that on a certain important occasion an idol would emerge from the ground at Bithooria in Jodhpore. In due time an idol rose gradually above the surface of the earth, and immediately became an object of worship to tens of thousands, who flocked to lay their offerings before the god who had thus miraculously made his appearance in the world. The place was taken under the Mahárája's protection, and yielded a considerable revenue, though probably only for a brief period, as the idol retreated into the earth, as slowly and mysteriously as it had come forth. The explanation of the mystery was that the prophet had dug a deep but narrow pit, and filled it, almost to the brim, with *gram*. On this foundation he placed the idol and covered it up. He then allowed a sufficient supply of water to reach the gram, which in swelling in the narrow pit raised the idol above the ground. When, subsequently, the gram was allowed to dry or rot the idol subsided with it, and was lost to the anxious gaze of its worshippers.

A philosophy of quietism is natural to the indolence and enervation of an Indian life. While European writers are never tired of insisting that *action* is the object of man's existence—or as Carlyle put it, "the end of Man is an Action and not a Thought, though it were the noblest"—the Hindu philosopher deprecates action, believing rather in quiet contemplation. Hence yogaism flourishes and has flourished for ages in India, and the question naturally presents itself : What has been the practical outcome of the system? The question may not be easy to answer, but this much at least may be said without hesitation, that the best minds have been withdrawn, through yogaism, from the pursuit of practical objects, and drowned in a dull lethargic sleep, unprofitable alike to themselves and their country; while upon the masses, unacquainted with the subtle doctrines of pantheism and so-called yoga philosophy, the effect of having before them the idle yogi as an ideal of excellence and a

Photo by Bhai Ram Singh

A PARTY OF WANDERING YOGIS

pattern for imitation, cannot have been otherwise than injurious, even though at the same time these ascetics undoubtedly provided the religiously-minded with living examples of unworldliness and contempt of riches. How long the ascetic, who, disregarding every duty and obligation to family or society, sits absorbed in the contemplation of the tip of his own nose, or wanders about the country living upon the credulity and fears of the ignorant, shall remain an object of veneration to the people, must depend upon the many and various influences now at work in modifying the ideas and character of the natives of India. Of course it is the heroic, and not the obviously repulsive, side of asceticism which, in the case of the yogi or any other anchorite, commands, in the first instance, the admiration of the people. The ascetic's self-denial, his contempt of the world and worldly pleasures, his self-inflicted penances and mortifications, are indications of will-force, determination, tenacity of purpose and self-sufficiency, which attract and overawe the multitude. The ascetic, by his scornful renunciation of all they hold most valuable, asserts his superiority to and commands the homage of the vulgar, which in the case of the yogi is enhanced by dread of his supposed power. After making allowances, however, for whatever of good there may be in yogaism and in the yogis themselves, it will be admitted, at any rate by Europeans, that until these uncouth idols are dethroned, the Indian mind will not rise to a just appreciation of real (as distinguished from ceremonial) cleanliness, manly energy, and public spirit.

Happily there are already signs which indicate that even such educated natives as cannot emancipate themselves from a belief in *yoga-vidya*—national beliefs die hard—are beginning to be ashamed of the indolent, and oftentimes repulsive mendicants who perambulate the country, and, for the credit of the so-called yog-science, pretend that the *real* yogis are very different from these unsightly objects of popular veneration.

With the spread of Western ideas, and with the growth of new objects of ambition, such as wealth and political power, created by intimate contact with the restless industrial civilization and democratic ideals of the Western world, the yogi and his system will necessarily occupy a diminishing place in the thoughts and in the hearts of the people of India; but so thoroughly suited is *yoga-vidya* to the genius of the East, that probably very many generations, perhaps very many centuries, will pass away before it is numbered with the extinct systems of a vanished state of society.

CHAPTER II

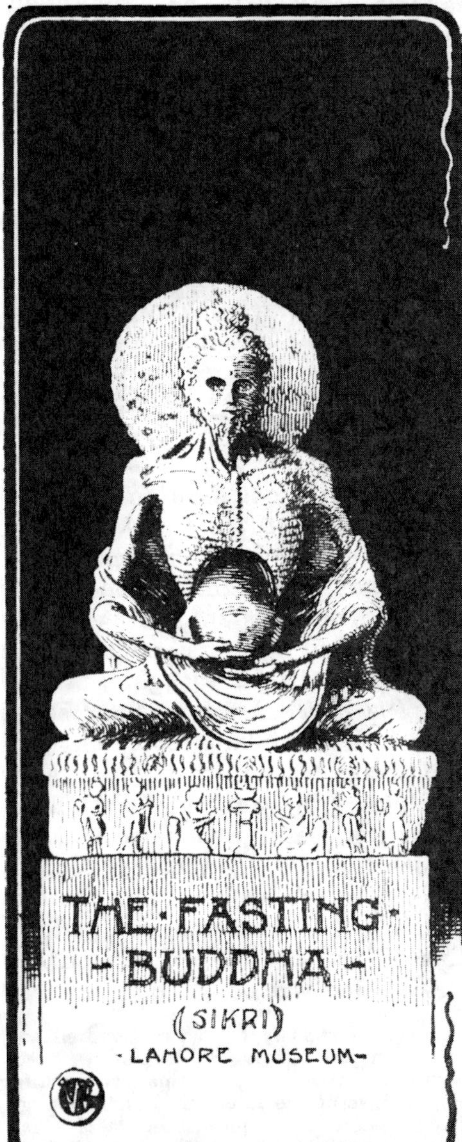

THE MOST SACRED SPOT ON EARTH; OR, BUDDH GAYA AND BUDDHISM

SECTION I.—BUDDH GAYA AND ITS ASSOCIATIONS

IF it were possible to ascertain, by any means, what particular spot on earth is the most sacred in the opinion of mankind, there is reason to think that the majority of votes would be given in favour of Buddh Gaya, which is held in high veneration by both Buddhists and Hindus. Such a spot is certainly worth a visit.

Leaving the busy town of Bankipore one afternoon in April, I travelled some fifty-seven miles to Gaya, by the branch railway, over a level uninteresting looking country, unredeemed in its drear monotony except by picturesque groups of slender palm trees, which, always and everywhere, lend grace and beauty to the landscape they adorn.

I arrived at Gaya after dark. It was quite an early hour; but the town, with its population of 76,000 souls, was already beginning to retire to rest. The atmosphere was oppressive, and the dimly-lighted streets, which were being turned into dormitories for the night, presented anything but agreeable pictures. Here and there a perspiring half-clad *halwái*, who had not yielded to the early-closing movement, squatted listlessly in his "fly-swarmed sweetmeat shop" behind a few trays of uninviting confectionery; or a drowsy *baniyá*, with his knees drawn up to his chin, dozed over his uncovered heaps of rice, *dál*, *átá*, and *ghi*. These half-awake shopmen were apparently the principal, if not the only, representatives of trade in Gaya at that hour. *Charpoys* in scores were already occupying the main thoroughfare in very unpicturesque disorder. On some of these rickety beds, unprovided with mattresses or pillows, the owners were stretched full-length; on others, two or three almost naked men sat silently fanning themselves in a drowsy way with little palm-leaf fans, or with the free ends of their *dhotis*. What was the burden of their thoughts, as they sat there on those charpoys in the hot and dusty street of the sacred city? Were they thinking, as so many of their national sages had thought before them, that, after all, life was not worth living? or were they performing that act of cogitation on the merits and defects of the British Government which the late Sir Richard Temple, sometime Governor of Bombay, seemed to think the two hundred and fifty millions of the Indian people perform every day?[1] Not being able to divine their thoughts, I can only say that my own mind was occupied with a sort

[1] "It is difficult to summarize concisely what two hundred and fifty millions of people are presumably saying to themselves every day. But probably the sum of their thoughts amounts to this, that they are by the will of an inscrutable fate living under foreign rule; that they are ineffably better, nicer, pleasanter people than their rulers; that they have a purity of descent, a grandeur of tradition, an antiquity of system, with which a European nation has nothing to compare; that, despite their union, socially and morally, they cannot hold together politically, etc."—"Fortnightly Review," January 1883.

of vague anxiety as to whether I should be able to get accommodation for the night in the Government bungalow for travellers, as Gaya did not contain a single hotel.

Fortunately I found a vacant room in the travellers' bungalow, where I passed a most uncomfortable night under the *punkah*. The furniture of the room consisted of the usual table, a couple of chairs, and a bed; but there were two photographs of the great Buddh Gaya temple on the wall at the foot of my bed, which attracted my attention and somehow mingled in a most fantastic and disagreeable manner with all my dreams during that restless night.

Long before daybreak next morning I started for Buddh Gaya in a one-horse carriage, a sort of cab with double seats and sliding doors.

The dim twilight of approaching dawn revealed street scenes even more unlovely than those I had witnessed the night before. People sleeping out in the dirty road upon cots or mats, but more frequently upon the bare sand or mud. Cows and oxen calmly reposing in the middle of the highway; goats also and poultry, quite at home upon the streets, under the open canopy of heaven. In the hot sweltry atmosphere men and women lay asleep, contorted in every ungainly position imaginable. From some the light covering had slipped away, and left them almost if not quite naked. I had often been through Indian towns at a very early hour of the morning, but had never before seen such a combination of squalor and repulsiveness. There was just light enough to show the hideous nightmare spectacle in all its ugliness, a spectacle so disagreeable in every way as not to be easily forgotten. The return through the same streets some hours later was more pleasant. Glorious sunlight gilded the mean huts and dirty alleys of the town—what would the East be without its sunshine?—the people were astir, all more or less clothed according to Indian fashions, which depend but little either upon modiste or tailor.

The town of Gaya is situated near some low, barren, but not unpicturesque hills, and is associated with the ever-memorable life and work of the founder of the Buddhist religion; it is also a famous place of Hindu pilgrimage. An extravagant Hindu legend connects the little hills of Gaya with the history of a giant no less than 576 miles high, who by the power derived from the performance of austerities became, as usual, a terror to the gods. Taking a mean advantage of the giant's piety, the wily divinities, with Brahma at their head, induced him to allow his sinless body to be used as the altar for a great sacrifice. This prostrate position gave them the opportunity they sought. Upon his huge head they placed a sacred stone, and literally sat upon it; while Vishnu belaboured the poor giant with his terrible mace until he became motionless. In his extremity the blameless monster, thus overreached by the unscrupulous gods, merely asked, as a favour, that the place where he lay —or rather I should say where his head lay—should ever afterwards be associated with his name, Gaya, and that on this spot "should abide for the good of mankind all the sacred pools on the earth, where persons by bathing and offering of oblations of water and funeral cakes may obtain high merit for themselves, and translate their ancestors, blessed with all that is desirable, and salvation, to the region of Brahma." [1] This foolish and unedifying legend is, we are told by Dr. Rajendra Lala Mitra, implicitly believed by the people; but the learned gentleman himself sees in it *an allegorical reference to the overthrow, by artifice and force, of the religion of Buddha by the Brahmanical priesthood.* Any way, the far-sighted and never-to-be-conquered Brahmans have in this case, as in many another one, succeeded in appropriating to their own glory and profit places held sacred by heretical seceders from the fold of Hinduism, and Gaya is now a favourite place of Hindu pilgrimage, where hundreds of thousands flock annually to the Vishnupada Temple, to prostrate themselves before the footprints of the god and to perform the funeral ceremonies of their dead relations.[2] This temple, surmounted by a dome and gilded pinnacle, stands on one of the ridges. The Temple

[1] Dr. Rajendra Lala Mitra's "Buddh Gaya," pp. 10–17.

[2] "The birth of that man is the occasion of satisfaction to his progenitors, who performs, at the due time, their obsequial rites at Gaya."—Prof. H. H. Wilson's translation of the "Vishnu Purana," book iii. chap. 16.

of the Sun, with its sacred tank, occupies the low ground within the town.

The principal object of my visit was, however, Buddh Gaya, where five hundred years before the birth of Christ the immortal founder of the Buddhist religion had obtained "enlightenment"—a spot considered one of the most sacred places on this earth of ours by perhaps a third of the entire human race. Even in this matter-of-fact age, which is supposed to have eyes and ears only for utilities, one may be pardoned for leaving the direct road to Calcutta in order to visit a spot round which so many memories cluster.

My way lay along a dusty road through open fields, and for some distance alongside the dry sandy bed of the river Phalgu. The country through which I passed presented this April morning a very different appearance, no doubt, from what it wears during the brief winter which succeeds the rainy season in India. Under the mild winter sky, man and beast, field and forest, seem to revive a little, and the European tourist flits through the verdant country, charmed with the mild sunshine of these favoured climes. And if he writes a book of his travels, its pages reflect the lovely blue sky and the soft, mild climate he has been enjoying. In April it is otherwise, as the resident in India knows only too well. As I proceeded on my way, a carved stone here and another there on the roadside, or built into a mud hut, served to indicate my approach to Buddh Gaya and its ancient temple.

A drive of about six miles from the Government Dák Bungalow brought me to a large group of buildings enclosed within a high masonry wall, which the driver of my cab seemed to think must be the object of my visit. It was a Hindu monastery, situated in a garden on the riverside. I went in through the wide-open gateway, accompanied by my coachman. On the terraced roof of a building of some three or four storeys, the Mahant or Abbot—Maharaj they styled him—was taking his ease, and after being informed by my loquacious coachman, who knew nothing whatever about me, that I was a visitor from Calcutta, directed his servants to show me over the place. Later on he expressed a wish to make my acquaintance. He asked many inquisitive questions about myself and about the object of my visit, and showed me, with much pride, a copy of Dr. Mitra's book on Buddh Gaya, which had been presented to him by the Government of Bengal. He could not read English, and seemed to care little for the Buddhist temple, but he could appreciate the compliment paid him by the British authorities, and I dare say found pleasure in the big picture-book they had given him, which was in all probability the only illustrated volume in his possession.

The monastery over which this abbot presides was, according to Dr. Mitra, originally established in the early part of the eighteenth century by a Sanyasi mendicant of the order of Giri. A successor appropriated the then neglected Buddhist temple, which became a source of large income to him from the gifts of Hindu pilgrims to the sacred Bo-tree. In the course of time the society acquired considerable property, and Hindu temples sprang up in the neighbourhood.

A very short walk from the Hindu monastery brought me to the ancient temple I had come to see, the hoary relic of many fleeting centuries. As it stood there before me it looked quite *new*, and I must confess that a feeling of disappointment took possession of me as I contemplated the "restored" edifice, with the fresh stucco mouldings and Portland cement additions of the Department of Public Works. In my disappointment I could not help thinking that the renovated temple might, perhaps, bear as much resemblance to the original temple erected on the spot as the Buddhism of some recent European writers to the doctrines of Sâkya Muni.

In the belief of five hundred millions [1] of Buddhists, the site occupied by this temple is the identical one on which, seated in the shade of a spreading Bo-tree, Gau-

[1] As regards the number of either nominal or real Buddhists in the world at the present time we have no reliable statistics, though estimates or mere guesses give us figures ranging from one hundred millions to five hundred millions, the former being favoured by the late Sir Monier Williams. I have adopted the figures given by Prof. T. W. Rhys Davids' "Buddhism," p. 6.

tama—known also as Prince Siddârtha and Sâkya Muni —attained " enlightenment " some five hundred years before the Christian era; and although so remote in time, the event referred to still makes itself unmistakably felt, across the long intervening centuries, in the life and thought of many nations.

Some three hundred years later, the great Buddhist king Asoka erected a *vehara* here for the accommodation of Buddhist monks, which was replaced by a temple perhaps as far back as the first century B.C., when image-worship would appear to have already become a recognized feature of Buddhism. In A.D. 637 the Chinese pilgrim Hiuen Tsiang visited this temple, and his description of it shows that the building which attracts the modern traveller is substantially the same as that erected some eighteen or nineteen hundred years ago. There is evidence to show that, having fallen into decay, it was repaired by the Burmese in the early years of the fourteenth century. Notwithstanding partial attention and repairs, the corroding breath of five hundred years again reduced the old building to a ruinous condition, when, in 1876, the Burmese came once more to the rescue of the dilapidated temple. Upon this the Government of Bengal, actuated by a proper regard for the venerable old-world monument which the vicissitudes of fortune had brought within its jurisdiction, resolved to have it carefully examined and thoroughly repaired. The result of this determination was before me; a sort of revised, abbreviated, and amended edition of the original temple of Buddh Gaya prepared by order of Government.

Defaced by time and the hand of man, transformed a good deal through well-meant restorations, the celebrated temple at Buddh Gaya, even in its modern disguised condition, with its nineteenth-century stucco about it and its brand-new gilt finial, is an imposing structure about one hundred and seventy feet high and fifty feet wide at its base. All things considered, it has certainly lasted remarkably well, the material of which it is constructed being only well-burnt brick cemented with mud. Stone has been used only in the door-frames and flooring. The building is plastered with lime-mortar. It is built in the form of a pyramid of nine storeys, embellished on the outer side with niches and mouldings. Facing the rising sun is the entrance doorway, and above it, at an elevation greater than the roof of the porch which once adorned the temple, there is a triangular opening to admit the morning glory to fall upon the image in the sanctuary.

Around the base of this ancient structure the *débris* of centuries had entirely covered, to a depth of nearly twenty feet, a host of interesting shrines and memorials which the excavations carried out by the Government have brought to light—votive relic-shrines, known as *Stupas*,[1] images of Buddha in different attitudes, and a substantial and ornamented stone railing as old as the time of Asoka. Within the shadow of the great temple many modern buildings are also to be seen—Hindu temples and the burial-place of the Hindu abbots of the neighbouring monastery;[2] while monuments seen by the early Chinese pilgrims have entirely disappeared. And where is the Bo-tree? Gone, like the olives of Gethsemane, centuries ago, with many a successor fabled to be a lineal descendant of that original Bo-tree whose trembling leaves were, in Buddhist belief, witnesses of the greatest events in the history of the world. A raised platform attached to the temple now supports a young and vigorous Peepul-tree (*Ficus religiosa*), a sort of sentimental representative of the Bo-tree of the sixth century before Christ, which in its day stood over the miraculous diamond throne, a structure as old as the world itself, nearly a hundred feet in circumference, and reaching down to the bottom of the earth. An attendant mentioned to me, not without a trace of dissatisfaction in his tone and manner, that the young tree before me was not even a descendant of its predecessor on the same spot,

[1] "Models or miniatures of tumuli and graves varying in size, at Buddh Gaya, from three inches to about three feet, the oldest being hemispherical, like a water-bubble."—Dr. Rajendra Lala Mitra's "Buddh Gaya."

[2] "The dead bodies of the monks, unlike those of other Hindus, are buried. . . . The body is buried in a sitting posture."—Idem, p. 4.

which had attained a great age, but had perished, he said, from ill-usage during the excavations. Its wood, he assured me, had for the most part been taken by the King of Burmah for the fashioning of images of the sage. Professor Sir Monier Williams, who visited the place, was told that the tree had been destroyed by the excessive devotion of Buddhist pilgrims, who watered its roots with Eau de Cologne.

However stately may be the venerable fane which has for so many centuries adorned Buddh Gaya, its real claims upon the attention of the traveller are due to the site on which it is built. On this spot near the old Narainjana of the Buddhist writers, and by those low, dreary hills, Gautama successfully defied the terrors and resisted the temptations of the Evil One. Here he attained *Buddha-hood*, and from this place he went forth to proclaim to the world that the way of deliverance from death was found.

For such as may be interested in the history or doctrines of Buddhism, an ample literature, gathered from many lands and translated from many different ancient and modern languages of Central and Eastern Asia, is now available—thanks to the researches and labours of the many learned Orientalists who have toiled in this fruitful field. Possibly, however, for the majority of even well-informed persons, the only source of Buddhist lore has been Sir Edwin Arnold's beautiful and charming poem, "The Light of Asia," which embodies in a refined, Europeanized form, but with glowing Oriental imagery and rich local colouring, such an outline of the Buddhistic legend as cannot but be acceptable to every lover of the beautiful in language or sentiment. But it must be confessed, however reluctantly, that the Prince Siddârtha with whose person, life, and thoughts we have of late grown familiar, is, for the most part, a creation of European literature and scholarship.

The legend, as preserved in various countries, though not in identical forms, relates that Buddha had no earthly father; but in the fulness of time descended of his own accord from the celestial regions to help the world, and was born on earth as the son of Mya, the wife of Suddhodana, King of Kapelavastu. The universe thrilled with joy to its very core at these auspicious events, and signs and wonders in heaven and earth attended the conception and birth of this saviour of mankind, who, on entering the world, stepped boldly forward, proclaiming in a loud voice that he was the chief of the world, and that this was his last birth. When a few days later he was presented at the temple, the Hindu gods did obeisance to him. After this it will not surprise any one to learn that, while still a mere infant, being on one occasion left alone in the shade of a tree, he was found there some hours later sitting cross-legged in the posture appropriate to deep meditation, and that the shadow of the tree which protected him from the sun had kept its position over him, while the shadows of the other trees had moved, as usual, with the altered position of the sun in the heavens. To such a very precocious and favoured child no earthly teachers could well impart knowledge, and those appointed his tutors had naturally to own their immense inferiority to their young pupil in all the arts and sciences. In his home at Kapelavastu (in the modern district of Goruckpore), within view of the mighty Himālayas, the boy grew up thoughtful and religious, caring so little for martial pursuits as to call forth the taunts of his fellow nobles. But when put to the test he easily surpassed all competitors, performing the most wonderful and startling feats of daring and strength.

Although blessed with a dignified position amongst men, and in the enjoyment of every comfort, a vague dissatisfaction with life seems to have taken possession of the young prince, intensified by certain sights—or *visions*, as some say—which presented themselves to his view on a momentous occasion when out for a drive in his chariot. These were first a man in the decrepitude of old age, next an unfortunate overwhelmed by fell disease, then a festering corpse by the wayside, and lastly a placid hermit who had deliberately turned away from the vanities of this world. With these sights, or visions, in his mind Gautama, after the birth of his first son, resolved upon what has been called "the great renunciation," and abandoning his life of pleasure, went forth alone, at the fated hour, from his father's capital, to discover in the usual Indian way, by solitary contemplation, a remedy for the miseries of existence. Before and since the great renunciation of Gautama men have gone out into the wilderness in quest of peace or in search of knowledge. Before and since Gautama's time nobles like St. Bernardo have, in a fit of piety, given up the pomps and vanities of a brilliant and luxurious world of chivalry and fashion for the solitude of the caves, and round them too the chronicler and poet have woven their glittering curtain of legend and romance. Such an event as the great renunciation afforded ample materials for a highly dramatic treatment, and good use has been made of the situation by the Eastern poets. Even to this day millions of hearts melt with tender pity as they recall the scene in which the prince takes a last fond look at his lovely wife sleeping with her infant on her arm,[1] and steals through the lordly chambers of his sumptuous palace away into the silent moonlight, to find out in poverty and solitude a way of deliverance for mankind. But the deliverance of mankind was an object by no means acceptable to *Mara*, the Evil One, who, appearing in the sky, urged Gautama to give up his mission and accept universal sovereignty instead. Unmoved by the glittering offer of temporal power, the prince, burdened with the sorrow of the world, and with the thirst of the wilderness upon him, pursued his way from Kapelavastu to the little hills near Rajagriha, and there studied Hindu philosophy with the Brahman hermits in the caves. Having learnt what these wise men had to teach, he removed with five disciples to the neighbourhood of the place where the temple of Buddh Gaya now stands. What events occurred here; why this particular spot is regarded by a third part of the human race as the most sacred place on earth, we learn from the Lalita Vistara, a work which is supposed to date from the third century before Christ, and which I shall follow in the next few pages.[2]

[1] Years afterwards Buddha revisited his native city and had a most affecting interview with his wife, whose conjugal love, equal to any sacrifice, led her to become one of the first of the Buddhist nuns.

[2] "The highest authority on the life of Sâkya is the Lalita

In accordance with the requirements of Hindu religious opinion in such matters, Gautama now resolved to carry out a six years' penance or mortification of the flesh. Selecting a suitable place, he sat there cross-legged for the appointed period, exposed, through summer and winter, to sun, wind and rain, practising the severest penances and self-mortifications, in which fasting and suspension of the breath are especially mentioned, till he was reduced almost to the verge of death. A scarcely living skeleton,[1] naked and covered with dirt, the sage, who looked like a churchyard ghost, was, we are told in the Lalita Vistara, an object of contempt even to the ignorant villagers of Uruvilva, who came to gather leaves and sticks about the place in which he had established himself. But the gods were watching the ascetic with intense interest, and fearing he would die, his mother, now Maya-Devi, descended from heaven in great distress, attended by troupes of *Apsaras*. The hermit reassured her, however, and after covering him with flowers from the Elysian groves, she gracefully retired to the sound of divine music. During his long penance Gods, Nagas, Asouras, and the other superhuman beings, waited upon Gautama night and day, and offered sacrifices to him; while, on the other hand, the wicked demons lost no opportunity of whispering doubts and discouragements into his ear, and making tempting suggestions in regard to easier and pleasanter ways of attaining virtue and its rewards.

His painful austerities were at length successfully accomplished, but, reduced to a condition of great enfeeblement, he felt that he could not thus reach the goal of his endeavours. He resolved, therefore, to abandon all further self-mortifications, and did so, to the great

---

Vistara. Parts of it were compiled either in his lifetime or immediately after his death, and others within a century and a half of that event" (Dr. Mitra's "Buddh Gaya," p. 22). A French translation of the Lalita Vistara, published in Paris in 1848, by M. Foucaux, introduced this ancient work to the Western world.

[1] An interesting little piece of sculpture from the Yusufzai district, now in the British Museum (case No. 5), represents the emaciated and repulsive form of Gautama after his arduous penance of six years on the banks of the Narainjana.

astonishment and disgust of his five companions, who thereupon left him and went away.

It would, to say the least, be both tedious and unprofitable to reproduce, with all the miraculous and trivial details in which the Lalita Vistara abounds, the story of the subsequent events in the hermit's life at Gaya; so I shall, in the interests of the reader, condense the exuberant narrative into the briefest epitome possible.

Watched over by admiring gods, Gautama bathed himself in the river Narainjana, put on new clothes, and partook of food prepared for him by a village maiden from the milk of a thousand cows. Vigour and beauty returned to him, and he proceeded to the *tree of knowledge*. His course was a grand triumphal procession, in which Gods, Upsaras, Nagas, and other divine or semi-divine beings in thousands and millions took part. Flowers rained down from heaven, perfumed breezes sported over the favoured land; jewelled pavilions, costly banners, cool tanks of limpid water appeared along the way, while divine music filled the delighted air. Gautama, whose tread shook the startled world, took his seat on some tender grass under the Bo-tree, and commenced his meditations. A brilliant light issued from his body, and attracted a countless host of Buddhas and Bodhisattvas (Buddhas elect), who came to do him homage. When these had retired, Gautama shot forth from between his eyebrows a terrible flame, which warned Mara, the Evil One, of his approaching triumph. This challenge, for such it was intended to be, aroused the angry passions of the demon king, and he resolved to attack Gautama beneath the Bo-tree.

Legions of hideous demons, some headless, some with as many as a hundred thousand heads, capable of assuming at will monstrous, terrible, and disgusting shapes, hurried to the Bo-tree. Armed with all sorts of deadly weapons, their hands and feet entwined with venomous serpents, their ugly features still more deformed by passion, their eyes red and flaming, their misshapen mouths bristling with enormous teeth and spitting forth flames and venom, the host of Mara, howling savagely, amidst a terrible war of elements, surged around Gautama on that eventful night.[1] But the demons could not daunt or even disturb the sage, against whom their weapons were powerless; their very missiles discharged against him being changed to flowers. The Evil One, foiled and disappointed, essayed to compass Gautama's defeat by other means. Instead of the deformed and terrible monsters who had threatened his personal safety, there now appeared before him, near the Bo-tree, forms of voluptuous and entrancing beauty, female forms of different ages from girlhood to ripe maturity, who endeavoured to attract his attention by the witchery of their charms. Some exposed their rounded busts and shapely forms while pretending to adjust their garments, others coquettishly veiled their beauties under diaphanous draperies. Some artful ones tried the power of flattery. Some bolder than the rest drew attention to their own charms of person, and invited the sage to share with them the delights of love. Two and thirty modes of seduction were tried by these lovely syrens, but tried in vain. All their soft wooing, all their lascivious blandishments, all their winsome beauty and subtle arts of love, were powerless against Gautama, who had conquered and was superior to all sensuous passions, all carnal desires and weaknesses, and met their advances with a homily on the evils to which the passions give birth.

The author of the Lalita Vistara lingers over the details of the voluptuous scene, which affords ample opportunities for poetical and artistic treatment.

After the discomfiture of the fair temptresses, the demons made one more furious attack upon Gautama, and tried to overwhelm him with, amongst other things, red-hot globes of fire of the size of Mount Meru; but the sage had only to strike the ground with his hand to prostrate his enemies in helpless ruin.

A curious fresco painting from the caves of Ajanta, reproduced in Dr. Mitra's "Buddh Gaya," is supposed to represent Mara's assault on Gautama under the Bo-tree. In the centre of the picture is the colossal and

[1] The reader will hardly fail to recall to mind, and to contrast with this, Milton's description of the temptation in the wilderness.

conventional figure of Buddha in contemplation, seated cross-legged on a raised throne. The demons, armed with swords and other weapons, crowd about him with threatening gestures. Some of them, in a rather childish way, are making grimaces at him. One monster, with a stupid face, is pulling down his lower eyelids with his fingers in order to display the whites of his eyes; another is stretching his own mouth, as naughty boys sometimes do, with his two forefingers, and glaring at the sage with fiendish eyes. At each side of the throne, and leaning on it, stands an exuberantly developed, bejewelled woman, while four others, languishing and characterless beauties of the same type, occupy, in a listless and objectless manner, the foreground of the picture in front of and below the throne. Apparently the artist has endeavoured to combine in this one picture the twofold trial to which Gautama is said to have been exposed; but the grotesque arrangement of figures he has produced, though not wanting in some good touches, fails entirely to do justice to the poet's conception of either ordeal in the wilderness at Gaya.

From his conflicts with the powers of evil, Gautama eventually arose with the assurance of complete enlightenment and knowledge of the way of deliverance from the ills of existence. He was now a *Buddha*. All nature thrilled with intense rapture at the glad event, and to this day the large long-stalked leaves of the Peepul-trees everywhere quiver with excitement at the recollection of the scenes which were witnessed under the Bo-tree at Gaya. All former Buddhas rejoiced exceedingly, and hosts of heavenly beings hastened to pay their respects to the new Buddha. Without the aid of gods or men, Gautama had, by persistent effort through many lives, at last found the sure path for himself, and had reached the golden summits whence he could look down upon care and sorrow, upon birth and death. Emancipated, enlightened, he had now only to enter into his rest. The foiled demon-king ventured once more into the presence of the Buddha to suggest that his work was accomplished, and the long-sought goal—eternal rest—at hand. "No!" said the Enlightened One, "not until my followers understand the law and can teach it; not until Buddha, the law and the order, are established, shall I enter into my rest." With inordinate vanity the three daughters of Mara came forward, even at this eleventh hour, to tempt the Buddha with their mature loveliness, but, as they stood near the Bo-tree, they shrivelled up into aged decrepitude, from which state they were, however, released on humbly asking the Buddha's pardon.

But, after all, was it worth while to think of other and less fortunate beings? Would they understand the method of salvation? Would they, discarding all sensual pleasures and relinquishing all trust in asceticisms, be able to follow the eightfold path that leads to enlightenment and eternal rest? viz. 1. Right Belief. 2. Right Aims. 3. Right Speech. 4. Right Action. 5. Right Means of Livelihood. 6. Right Endeavour. 7. Right Mindfulness. 8. Right Meditation.[1] Such were the thoughts of the Buddha, and, according to the Lalita Vistara, it was nothing short of a direct, earnest, and humble appeal made by Brahma, Indra, and the other gods, that induced the Enlightened One to share his knowledge with the rest of the world.

The resolution thus adopted led to the formal preaching of the law at Benares, where, in the Migadāya wood, or "Deer Park," the eightfold way of deliverance was made known for the benefit of gods and men. "Five months after the crisis under the Bo-tree, and three months after Gautama's arrival at the Migadāya wood, he called together all his disciples, who are represented to have numbered already sixty persons, and sent them in different directions to preach and teach, Yasa only remaining at Benares, near his parents."[2] And after this, for the long period of five and forty years, did Buddha proclaim his doctrines to the world, performing no less than three thousand five hundred miracles in attestation of his power.

For those who care to look below the surface, the story of the great renunciation, of the temptation under the Tree of Knowledge at Gaya, and of the hesitation which

[1] Prof. T. W. Rhys Davids' "Buddhism," p. 47.
[2] Ibid. p. 55.

Buddha felt to proclaim his discovery to the world, overlaid though it be with a rank growth of sickly legend, has a permanent interest which time cannot destroy.

By a judicious, if necessarily arbitrary, system of elimination and pruning—a system, however, by no means to be depended upon for truthful results—the legend of the Buddha may be made to yield an attractive picture of an earnest human soul striving nobly, honestly, and fearlessly to understand and to explain the mystery of sorrow and happiness, of virtue and wickedness. The son of a princely, if not very powerful house, brought up in comfort and honour, of a speculative turn of mind, caring little for the martial pursuits of his peers, comes, through circumstances which it is needless to speculate about, to ask himself, as did the preacher of old, "What profit hath a man of all his labour which he taketh under the sun?"

An heir having been born to him, his duty to his family and society was fulfilled. He had attained the mature age of twenty-nine. It was time to retire from the world with its hollow vanities, its stale pleasures, and its unprofitable duties; it was time to join the society of holy hermits, who, in the solitude of the forest, were striving for peace of mind and for communion with the Deity. To the forest he goes, and after years of self-imposed penance, of study, of intercourse with dreamers and teachers, orthodox and heterodox, the noble devotee arrives at certain conclusions of his own in respect to religious doctrines and practices. After some natural hesitation as to the prudence or desirability of making his opinions known to an ignorant and sinful world, he decides to do so, and sets up as a regular teacher in the holy city of Benares.

As I recalled the old story in the shadow of the temple at Buddh Gaya, I felt it a privilege to stand on a spot connected with so many poetic and religious associations, so many episodes embalmed in verse, recorded in sculpture, and still living in the hearts of many nations. Near this memorable spot, the river may still be found as of yore—sometimes flowing, sometimes dry—a veritable emblem of the instability of things terrestrial; and the eternal, if not very imposing, hills are there also, still dreaming, perhaps, of the saintly hermits who once peopled their dark caverns. A substantial temple commemorates, rather inadequately, the great deliverance of gods and men; but no Buddhist pilgrim, no Buddhist monk, was to be found in the neighbourhood of Buddh Gaya when I visited it, and not a single worshipper within many and many a score of leagues of it.[1] The memory of other days lingers only in the *name*. The religion of Buddha, supplanted by Hinduism at Gaya about fifteen hundred years ago, has nearly forgotten its birthplace, while, under the unsparing criticism of modern European investigation, the personality of Buddha himself assumes the most uncertain outline in the dim background of Indian history. Not only has the Buddha's form become shadowy behind the mist of legends raised by his followers, but their very endeavour to glorify him has led some scholars to doubt whether the entire story about him is not, after all, only a solar allegory, as the learned M. Senart maintained.

Is the Buddhistic legend only a sun myth? was the unwelcome thought which flitted through my mind as I sat down on an old memorial stone to contemplate the temple as the sun (the real Buddha?) flooded the old building and its surroundings with a glory which ennobled and transfigured whatever it touched, even the restored edifice, hardly venerable now in its nineteenth-century gilt and plaster. The pleasant voices of three or four brown-limbed children, with large soft eyes, who had wonderingly followed me about, and were now timidly asking for "backsheesh," recalled me gently from the regions of solar allegory.

When imagination, literary ingenuity, and destructive

[1] Within recent years, since my visit to Gaya, the Buddhists of Ceylon, Burmah and even Japan, have been aroused to a sense of their almost sinful neglect of the birthplace of their religion, and under the auspices of the Maha Bodhi Society measures have been adopted to establish a Buddhist monastery on the sacred spot where Gautama obtained Buddhahood, and others at his birthplace, Kapelavastu, at Benares, where he first preached the word, and at Kusanagara, where he laid down the burden of existence But there are difficulties in the way, especially as regards the temple at Buddh Gaya, where the Hindu abbot has to be reckoned with.

criticism have done their utmost, there still remains the fact of the Buddhist religion, behind which a veritable Buddha too is faintly discernible, obscured, it is true, by such absurd legends as those, amongst a host of others, which record how, before his birth, the embryo Buddha preached to the angels who watched over him, and how in the sixth year of his Buddhahood he visited heaven to teach his dead mother the way of deliverance. But notwithstanding the legends, we may perhaps be able, under the guidance of modern research, to form a more or less accurate idea of the circumstances under which Buddhism arose, and of the earliest form of a religion which, like every other religion, has passed through different phases and undergone much modification and alteration.

Preparing to leave the ancient temple at Buddh Gaya about which I have been writing, I witnessed a scene which showed me how completely Hinduism had appropriated to its own use this holy place of the Buddhists, and how futile had been the teaching of Buddha to lift from off the shoulders of his countrymen the burden of the Brahmanical ritual. Near the venerable temple two men were performing the ceremony of the *shraad*. They had come from long distances, and were both elderly men. A boy Brahman officiated. These three sat down on the ground together; the boy repeated the prescribed formularies, and from time to time took lumps of wheat-flour mixed with water from a brass plate and placed them on the ground before him. The two men repeated the words of the Brahman youth, and put little pats of flour on the ground as he did, and their ancestors had gained one more step towards the attainment of happiness.

A last look at the old temple with its new face, and then homewards. My path lay by the tombs of the *Mahants*, who had appropriated to their own use this sacred spot at Buddh Gaya. If the Buddhists are right, those defunct Mahants must still have been near me, though somewhat transformed, for Buddhaghosha assures us that "whoever shall take for himself or for another any consecrated land, shall become a mite, or white ant,

4

upon that consecrated land for the whole of a hundred thousand cycles." Perhaps I inadvertently crushed some of them under foot, only to be re-born there and then.

SECTION II.—THE RISE AND DEVELOPMENT OF BUDDHISM

The commonly accepted idea which finds a place in nearly every text-book of general or Oriental history, and in special works on the history of religions, is that Buddhism was a revolt against the intolerable burden of the Brahmanic ritual, a reaction against the galling chains which the ceremonial law of the Brahmans—the most complicated system of sacrifices and ceremonies ever invented—had coiled round the life of the people of India, till all freedom of action was stifled, and men and women were mere slaves and puppets in the hands of the hereditary priests, who claimed the knowledge and arrogated the right of regulating the minutest details of public or private life. Buddhism is also usually represented as being pre-eminently a manly and vigorous protest against *caste*, as well as all other invidious distinctions between man and man. These views would not, we may presume, have been put forward and been favourably received by competent scholars had there not been some plausible grounds for their support. But with the growth of knowledge in respect to Buddhist literature, an excellent plea for a reconsideration of the older opinions regarding the origin and object of Buddhism has been made out by learned students of comparative theology, and particularly by Professor Oldenberg of Berlin, in his important work, "Buddha: his Life, his Doctrine, his Order."[1] According to this learned Professor, India in the time of Buddha was divided into many kingdoms, and that portion of the country which was the scene of Buddha's missionary activity, far from being under the grinding yoke of the Brahmans, was somewhat beyond the pale of Brahmanical influences; at any rate a good deal more free from such influences than the country

[1] Translated into English by Dr. William Hoey. Williams and Norgate, London.

which lay further westward. This Eastern, and perhaps heterodox, land became the theatre of the activities of rival religious teachers, who, it would appear, were, according to the fashion of the time, founders or important members of competing monastic orders. Amongst these leaders of men, who were not necessarily Brahmans, the noble Gautama attained a pre-eminent position; not to the exclusion of others, however, for a certain contemporary and rival of his, Nâtaputta, founded a sect (the Jàins) which exists in India even to this day; and one of Gautama's own followers, Dewadatta, broke with his master and founded an order of his own during Buddha's lifetime.

The community in which Buddha and his contemporaries laboured had already attained its maturity. It had grown familiar with discussions on all the important problems of existence; and it is evident from the extant literature that disputatious philosophers, conceited sophists, overbearing and vain-glorious dialecticians, not slow to slander one another or use opprobious epithets, were only too common in the time of Buddha.[1] The religious and philosophical opinions current in that land were not those which find favour with a fresh, vigorous, and progressive race, an historical people confident in themselves and in their protecting gods; but rather those which are natural to a worn-out society, only anxious for peace and rest. "The old childlike joy in life so manifest in the Vedas had died away."[2] The Aryans in their new home had pondered and disputed till they had philosophized away all that makes life beautiful, enjoyable, glorious; leaving only a residue of misery and death as the undesirable heritage of unhappy man. Whence this pessimism? Surely the endless monotonous plains, the brazen sky of summer, the soppy ground and steamy heat of the rains, the malaria-laden atmosphere of autumn, redeemed only by the briefest of mild winters, is sufficient to account, in a good measure, for the feeling. Where everything grows up rapidly and as rapidly

[1] See Dr. Fausböll's "Sutta Nipâta," pp. 164–174.

[2] Professor Rhys Davids in the "Encyclopædia Britannica," article 'Buddhism.'

decays, where men and women who reckon not many years of life have already, in the relaxing climate of Eastern India, passed their prime, have already outlived passions and ambitions, the desire for rest and retirement comes early. To live a quiet inactive life in a shady grove, honoured of men, and with little if anything to do, seems, under the circumstances, to be the most desirable existence possible, when once the too short days of youth and vigour are gone. All excitement, even intellectual excitement, becomes distasteful. Quiet contemplation and mystic reverie are alone tolerable. "There is," says the Dhammapada, "no happiness higher than rest."[1] But the climate, unfavourable though it be, does not account for all. Those other and important factors, the leaden weight of despotism, rigid caste distinctions, a vegetarian diet, and the circumscribed, uneventful life, must also have produced their full effect. The prevailing pessimism of which I write gives us the key to Buddhism, which is "to be regarded as pessimism pure and simple, and as the direct progenitor of the modern German systems."[2]

Notwithstanding the religious activity of a heretical character in Behar during the time of Buddha, there is a good deal of evidence to show that the Brahmans, far from being treated as enemies in the early Buddhistic literature, were always mentioned with the greatest respect; and as for caste, it does not appear that the Buddhists, in their day of power, ever attempted to abolish it. Caste exists with Buddhism in Ceylon, and indeed it is doubtful whether it was not introduced into the island by the Buddhists themselves.[3]

There was, as we shall presently see, no place in the system established by Buddha for any active opposition to caste, any open hostility to Brahmanism, or any revolt against despotism. There was no special thought of the rights of man, or of the brotherhood of men and nations. The object of Buddhism was to *escape from* the social and political world—not to improve it. Deliverance from

[1] Professor Max Müller's "Dhammapada," verse 202.
[2] Sully's "Pessimism," p. 38.
[3] Barth's "Religions of India," p. 125.

suffering and death—that was the keynote of Buddhism; that was all it aimed at. "As the vast ocean, O disciples, is impregnated with one taste, the taste of salt, so also, my disciples, this Law and Doctrine is impregnated with one taste, the taste of deliverance." [1]

Buddha was neither a social nor a political reformer! He professed only to point out the means of escape from the world of transmigrations.[2] On the other hand, we shall also see that his way of deliverance manifestly implied the insufficiency of the national gods, the futility of the ceremonial law, the inutility of sacrifices and austerities, and the uselessness of the Brahmanical priesthood. In so far, then, though without open warfare against or active condemnation of the existing *régime*, Buddhism undoubtedly introduced and popularized a *new* order of conceptions, and has probably on this account been sharply opposed to and contrasted with Hinduism by Oriental scholars.

However, or whenever, it may have originated, the doctrine of the transmigration of souls was at the time of Buddha an accepted doctrine of Brahmanism, and must detain us a moment if we are to form a just conception of Buddha's work and his place among religious teachers. Metempsychosis, or the doctrine that the soul passes through the bodies of various men in successive generations and even takes up its temporary abode in animals and plants, though it finds no place in the Rig Veda,[3] is a fundamental one in the Brahmanic religion, and, as Professor Knight observes, "is probably the most widely spread and permanently influential of all speculative theories as to the origin and destiny of the soul." [4] Pythagoras (530–500 B.C.), who is stated to have travelled in Egypt, appears to have introduced the

[1] Cullavagga, ix. 1, 4, quoted in Dr. Oldenberg's "Buddha," p. 205.

[2] The Hindus are also devoted to the same object. "The one prevailing idea with the Hindu," says an Indian writer, "is how to get rid of future births and obtain eternal beatitude."—T. Rama Krishna, B.A., "Life in an Indian Village," p. 201.

[3] Professor Max Müller's "Chips from a German Workshop," vol. i. p. 45.

[4] "Fortnightly Review," September 1878.

doctrine to the Greeks. Plato (429–347 B.C.), as every one knows, indulged in fanciful speculations about the human soul, arguing for its pre-existence on the basis of the curious doctrine of reminiscence. He also believed in the immortality of the soul, and held that its transmigration into successive bodies took place for its punishment or its purification.[1] And it is a very remarkable fact in the history of human opinions that there have been sects (*e. g.* the followers of Carpocrates) who have believed that successive re-births were necessary in order that souls should "pass through every form of action usually reputed sinful, in order to complete their defiance of the powers which rule the world."[2]

When and how the doctrine of reincarnation originated in India is not known. It has at any rate been an article of faith there for at least twenty-five centuries. If not derived directly from the indigenous populations amongst whom the Aryans settled, it seems probable that the intense deep-rooted pantheism of the Brahmans may have suggested the idea, as an inference from the belief in the unity of all life, human or other, and the indestructibility of life as such. The ethical justification of this doctrine is the apparent injustice of the distribution of riches and poverty, of happiness and misery, in this present life. The sufferings of the virtuous become intelligible if they are the punishment inflicted for evil done in a previous existence; so also the triumph and happiness of the wicked are reconcilable with the sense of abstract justice, if the life of the present time is only one phase of a series of successive existences. That in the opinion of the Oriental world the doctrine of metempsychosis could afford consolation and teach fortitude in trouble, we may judge from the story of Queen Samavati, who, when her palace was on fire and all hope of escape cut off, exhorted her attendants to bear in mind that "in the countless existences that have had no beginning it

[1] "Meno," pp. 260–273; "Phædo," pp. 418, 429, 430, 463; "Phædrus," pp. 582, 583, of Professor Jowett's translation of the "Dialogues," vol. i. 1871.

[2] Dean Mansel's "The Gnostic Heresies of the First and Second Centuries." London: John Murray, 1875.

would be impossible to reckon the number of times that they had perished by fire." [1]

Wherever the doctrine may have come from, or however it may have originated, its early acceptance in India is certain, and equally certain that while accepting it as the decree of a Fate superior to all gods, the Indian, in a sort of despair, cast about for some means of escape from its pitiless round of formation and dissolution. Life, in the opinion of the Indian sage, being not worth living, the idea of an endless succession of lives was simply intolerable, and the object of every religious teacher was to show a way out of this gloomy vortex of endless births and endless deaths.[2] Buddha accepted the doctrine of the transmigration of souls. He had himself—like every one else—passed through a long series of previous existences, and we are in possession of a big story-book containing accounts of some five hundred and fifty of his previous lives, a story-book so ancient that it is believed to be the oldest collection of folk-tales in the world. Old though it be, it has not yet lost its charm for the simple children of the East, who, in the lovely palm-groves of Ceylon and elsewhere, still listen to its recital with wonder and delight.

In respect to the Buddhist doctrine of metempsychosis, we are warned by competent investigators that, according to Buddha's teaching, it is not one and the same soul which inhabits in succession a series of different forms; but that, by the operation of a primordeal, inexorable, and, no doubt, inexplicable law, the action of one sentient being gives rise at its dissolution to the birth of another sentient being, whose state or condition is good or bad in accordance with the merits or demerits of the being, or long chain of sentient beings, whom it succeeds.

"Karma, from a Buddhist point of view, avoids the superstitious extreme, on the one hand, of those who believe in the separate existence of some entity called the soul; and the irreligious extreme, on the other, of those who do not believe in moral justice and retri-

---

[1] Captain Rogers' translation of Buddhaghosha's "Parables," p. 56.

[2] "Religious Thought and Life in India," by Sir Monier Williams, p. 41.

bution. Buddhism claims to have looked through the word soul for the fact it purports to cover; and to have found no fact at all, but only one or other of twenty different delusions which blind the eyes of men. Nevertheless, Buddhism is convinced that if a man reaps sorrow, disappointment, pain, he himself, and no other, must at some time have sown folly, error, sin; and if not in this life, then in some former birth. Where, then, in the latter case, is the identity between him who sows and him who reaps? *In that which alone remains* when a man dies, and the constituent parts of the sentient being are dissolved; in the result, namely, of his action, speech and thought, in his good or evil *Karma* (literally his 'doing') which does not die."[1]

Like the flame of a lamp, which is not the *same* flame at successive moments, but is, as it were, being uninterruptedly extinguished and re-kindled, so sentient existence flows on, never the same, yet always linked with preceding sentient existences. But "the number of these beings never varies save on those few occasions when one of them, either in earth or heaven, attains Nirvana."[2] Such were the subtle ideas of the Buddhist metaphysicians; which did not, however, trouble the common people, who naturally believed in the identity of the person or soul through successive lives.

According to the Buddhists, the eightfold path leading to enlightenment and deliverance is made up of right faith, right resolve, right speech, right action, right living, right effort, right thought, right self-concentration,[3] and involved, it will be observed, not only good conduct, but also intellectual excellence and self-restraint. Self-mortification, which holds the first place in the Hindu scheme of deliverance, and which, as we have seen in the preceding chapter about *Yogis* (pp. 18–24), promises such boundless power to the successful ascetic, is left out by Buddha, whose teaching in this respect diverges entirely from the orthodox school from which it sprang. "Not nakedness, not platted hair, not dirt, not fasting, or lying on the earth, not rubbing with dust, not sitting motionless, can purify a mortal who has not overcome desires."[4]

[1] Professor Rhys Davids' "Buddhism" (1907), p. 107.

[2] Professor Rhys Davids in the "Encyclopædia Britannica," article 'Buddhism.'

[3] Dr. Oldenberg's "Buddha," p. 128.

[4] Professor Max Müller's "Dhammapada," verse 141.

Then again the gods, whether Hindu or other, have no special place in the original Buddhistic system. The existence of gods and spirits is not denied—quite the reverse; but the gods, like men, are themselves subject to the evils of birth and death. They may in previous lives have been men, or animals, or may again in future lives pass through like forms, so it is useless to look to them for assistance. True, the gods enjoy a very much longer and happier existence than men do, but the world of the gods, like the other worlds, has its limit of duration and is reorganized at the end of each *Kalpa*. Under such a system of belief the gods dwindle away into insignificance, and with the degradation of the old gods their priests necessarily sink into the background. Indeed "God and the Universe trouble not the Buddhist; he knows only one question, How shall I in this world of suffering be delivered from suffering?" [1]

The morality of Buddhism is of the highest type. "It will not be deemed rash," says the Roman Catholic Bishop Bigandet, "to assert that most of the moral truths prescribed by the gospel are to be met with in the Buddhistic scriptures." It should be borne in mind, however, in this connection, that Buddha says coldly: "Let no man love anything; loss of the beloved is evil. Those who love nothing and hate nothing have no fetters. . . . From affection comes grief, from affection comes fear; he who is free from affection knows neither grief nor fear," [2] which may be wise counsel from Buddha's point of view, but is assuredly selfish, and differs unmistakably from that other injunction: "Love thy neighbour as thyself." But leaving comparisons aside, the accepted Buddhist doctrine of moral retribution must have had a wholesome effect upon the life of the follower of Gautama, who is warned that "not in the heavens, not in the midst of the sea, not if thou hidest thyself away in the clefts of the mountains, wilt thou find a place on earth where thou canst escape the fruit of thy evil actions." [3] On the other hand, good actions as certainly brought their reward

[1] Dr. Oldenberg's "Buddha," p. 130.
[2] Professor Max Müller's "Dhammapada," verses 211, 213.
[3] "Dhammapada," verse 127.

in the present or some future life; in this or some other world. But even good actions cannot relieve a man from the necessity of re-birth, though they might help him to the attainment of that frame of mind which leads to enlightenment and eventual emancipation from birth and death. Final and complete deliverance could be attained only through *Nirvana*, which (we here follow Professor Rhys Davids) is a sinless, calm state of mind; perfect peace, goodness, and wisdom; to be followed after the natural dissolution of the body by "utter death, with no new life to follow." Professor Max Müller, while admitting that, according to the Buddhist canon, "Nirvana, the highest aim, the *summum bonum* of Buddhism, is the absolute nothing," believed that the popular view of Nirvana represents the original teaching of Buddha, and that according to this popular view Nirvana is "the entrance of the soul into rest, a subduing of all wishes and desires, indifference to joy and pain, to good and evil, an absorption of the soul in itself and a freedom from the circle of existence from birth to death, and from death to a new birth."[1] But an existence without wishes and desires, without joy and pain, without even a preference for good or evil, if not annihilation is very near it indeed. Professor Oldenberg, on his part, endeavours to show that Buddha himself purposely and deliberately evaded this important question.

Whatever may have been the stern creed of the philosopher, the rank and file of Buddhists did not look forward to annihilation, even as a *final* state, to be reached by the soul "after having passed through the worlds of the gods and of the highest spirits,"[2] and it was, perhaps, rarely if ever seriously sought after even by the philosopher. The popular mind never did accept the philosophical negation, but imagined for itself pleasant heavens of enjoyment beyond the dark valley. And there were hells, too, for the wicked. "Some people are born again; evil-doers go to hell, righteous people go to heaven; those who are free from all worldly desires

[1] Introduction to Captain Rogers' translation of Buddhaghosha's "Parables," pp. xl., xlv. Trübner and Co., 1870.

[2] Professor Max Müller's "Essay on Buddhistic Nihilism."

enter Nirvana."[1] Virtue and good works here would entail, as a natural consequence, happiness and reward in the next existence: wickedness and wrong actions the reverse. This was enough, surely, for the ordinary man. He was by no means under the necessity of seeking after annihilation, and if it was really—as their philosophers perhaps held—the highest attainable good; why, let those who wanted it strive for it. The layman, at any rate, had no hope of attaining Nirvana and annihilation as the result of his labours and conduct in this life. It was the monk and the monk alone who, cut off from contact with the world and its temptations, could have any rational expectation of attaining the necessary freedom from desires of all kinds which preceded and led to Nirvana—renunciation of the world being indeed the first step towards freedom. Accordingly we find that Buddhism was essentially a monastic system, "a church of monks and nuns," with the absolutely necessary and very convenient addition of lay sympathizers, supporters, and followers, who, if cut off from the highest possible reward, had still much to look forward to. For, as Professor Oldenberg remarks: "The Buddhist believer who did not feel in himself the power to renounce the world, could console himself with coming ages; he could hope for this, that it might then be vouchsafed to him, as a disciple of Mettayya, or one of the countless Buddhas who shall come after him, to don the garb of a monk, and to taste the bliss of deliverance."[2] This, then, was the religion which Gautama went forth from Uruvela—now Buddh Gaya—to preach to men and gods.

From the very earliest times this was the most sacred spot in the Motherland of Buddhism. Here was the "Tree of Knowledge" which early became an object of deep veneration and a place of pilgrimage for monks and nuns, and the celebration of special festivals. Where the temple of Buddh Gaya has stood for thirteen centuries, there was, before its erection, a *Vehara* or monastery. So that on this spot, year after year, tonsured monks in orange-coloured rags, admitted from all

[1] Professor Max Müller's "Dhammapada," verse 126.

[2] Dr. Oldenberg's "Buddha," p. 387.

castes without distinction,[1] pledged to poverty and chastity and bound to abstain from willingly taking the life of any creature, have passed the rainy season in quiet meditation and solitary study, or perhaps not less frequently in quarrelling, evil-speaking, and cursing, for we learn from the story of Tissa-Thera and others that the monks were not above such weaknesses.[2] From this place they would go daily, almsbowl in hand, to the neighbouring villages, to beg the morsels for their daily meal of rice, bread, fish, or even meat;[3] and here, in accordance with the rules of the order, they would punctually meet twice a month, at night, for the performance of the most important duty of the public confessional. Nuns, too, probably availed themselves of the shelter afforded by the Vehara at Buddh Gaya, for women were admitted into the order, although always regarded as in subordination to the monks.

When the rainy season was over, the monks would begin their annual wanderings through the country, carrying with them the doctrines of their church. Doubtless it was these annual missionary wanderings which helped so much to spread the religion of Buddha amongst a people who, weary of Brahmanical tyranny and interference, must have sighed for a little freedom of thought and action.

The Buddhism which spread far and wide amongst the people could not, however, have been the philosophical creed which has as its highest aim *Nirvana and annihilation*, to be attained only after complete extinction of all desire for life, all preference for good or evil, all leaning towards right or wrong. Such a creed was undoubtedly calculated to produce only a narrow, selfish, and exceedingly limited sect. What the Buddhism was which made its way to popularity we may gather from

[1] This was not a Buddhist innovation. Admission to Hindu ascetic orders was also open to men of all castes, a fact which looks like a standing protest against the proud exclusiveness of the Brahman.

[2] Buddhaghosha's "Parables."

[3] The use of meat as food does not appear to have been prohibited, although the monks themselves were required not to kill any living thing. Buddha himself died after a hearty meal of young pork.

such a work as Buddhaghosha's "Parables," a collection of very ancient stories,[1] designed, it would seem, to illustrate how virtue, and especially liberality to monks, is rewarded; and how wickedness, but more particularly offences against the monks, is punished in succeeding existences. One gem there is in this collection, the story of the girl Kisâgotami and her dead child, in which the universality of death is touchingly and beautifully brought home to the understanding of the bereaved mother. The girl carrying her lifeless infant to the sage implores him to restore it to life. Touched with compassion, the sage instructs the distracted mother to go to every house in the village and collect some ashes from each of the dwellings where there had never been a death, and then return to him for help. With hope in her heart Kisâgotami proceeds to carry out these instructions; but, alas! nowhere can she find a cottage in which death has not been known at some time or other, and then she realizes too well that hers was but the common lot. But apart from such literary interest as they may possess, these so-called parables are almost all of them extravagant, stupid, and tiresome, full of marvels and puerilities. For example, in these tales the monks fly about and transport themselves from place to place in an incredibly short space of time. One monk forbids the sun to rise, and it obeys; another, to gratify a whim, peoples a monastery with a thousand phantom monks of his own creation, and so on. What these parables really do inculcate is liberality and kindness to monks.[2] Be liberal to the monks, and you will get an immediate and manifold reward, or perhaps as soon as you die you will be re-born the son of a great king, or other important personage. Do evil, and especially be niggardly towards the monks, and you must expect poverty and want in your next life, or you may

[1] "I do not think that scholars calling these parables the parables of Mahinda, if not of Buddha himself, and referring their date to the third century B.C., could expose themselves at present to any formidable criticism."—Professor Max Müller's Introduction to Captain Rogers' translation of Buddhaghosha's "Parables," p. xvii.

[2] Referring to Christian Europe, the late Mr. W. E. H. Lecky wrote: "It is no exaggeration to say that to give money to the priests was for several centuries the first article of the moral code."—"History of European Morals," vol. ii. pp. 228–229.

be condemned to boil for ages, like a grain of rice, in the great hellpot prepared for evil-doers. Such a system, leading inevitably to the pride, luxury, ignorance, and corruption of the monks, contained within itself the seeds of its own decay; and it is not surprising that when it degenerated—as it seems to have done quickly enough into devil-worship[1] and witchcraft, the powerful hereditary Brahmanical priesthood were able to exterminate Buddhism in India during the eighth and ninth centuries of our era. Of the history of this period we know nothing. History was, for many reasons, never cultivated in India; but if Dr. Mitra is right, we have, alas! instead of the history of the stirring events of a most important period, a monstrous and absurd allegory, referred to in a previous page, about a giant some hundreds of miles high.

In connection with the conflict between Brahmanism and Buddhism, it is worth noting that the Brahmans having extirpated Buddhism in India have adopted Buddha as the ninth of their ten principal *avataras*, or incarnations, of Vishnu for reasons which throw a curious light upon the methods and casuistry of the hereditary priesthood. From the Puranas it would appear that the real object of this incarnation was inimical to demons and wicked persons, who, having learnt that dominion over the world could be obtained by certain sacrifices and ceremonies inculcated in the Vedas, had, in the interests of the gods, to be dissuaded from practising rites so dangerous to the peace of heaven and earth. This difficult task was undertaken by the artful Vishnu, who in the person of Buddha represented the cruelty of animal sacrifices with such touching eloquence and deep feeling that the demons and others were induced to abandon such sacrifices, thereby losing their chances of universal dominion, and at the same time becoming guilty of mortal sin by their contempt of the teaching of the holy Vedas.[2] Thus did

[1] In Buddhaghosha's parables we are told that "all who make offerings to the guardian-Nats of trees will be rewarded" ("Parables," p. 139).

[2] See "The Ten Principal Avataras of the Hindus," by Dr. Sourendro Mohun Tagore, pp. 115–117. Calcutta, 1880.

It is worthy of note that this idea of circumventing the enemy

the wily Brahmans, following their usual tactics, adopt and bring into their own pantheon a once formidable rival, but altered out of all recognition to suit their own purposes.

If the foregoing very brief account of early Buddhism be a fairly correct one, the reader may well ask why there is any temple at all at Buddh Gaya. If the gods cannot help men, to whom has the temple been erected? Let us explore the fane itself for an answer. Entering the *cella* by the eastern and only door, we find a huge gilt figure of Buddha. There it is, seated cross-legged, with listless hands and impassive features, stiff, constrained, conventional, yet undeniably impressive; the embodiment, in concrete form, of the highest ideal of Indian religious aspiration; "the man who is free from credulity, but knows the uncreated, who has cut all ties, removed all temptations, renounced all desires." [1] There sits the Buddha of the East, a duly canonized saint of the Romish calendar, for, strange as it may seem, Buddha and St. Joshaphat are undoubtedly one and the same person.[2] Although not a god, it is not difficult to understand how the gratitude of men would lead them to raise temples in honour of the man who, higher than gods, taught them the path of deliverance, and indeed he has not only been "deified and worshipped, but represented by more images than any other being ever idolized in any part of the world." [3] But after all, in a religion which retained, however slightly, the spirit of what we understand to have been the primitive Buddhism, the temple would be an anomaly, and a well-informed

---

finds a strange parallel in the history of Christianity. Holding that Christ paid the ransom which rescued men from hell, Irenæus and Origen, Augustine and Gregory of Nyssa taught that the ransom "was paid to the *Devil*, who, by his successful offer of temptations, had become absolute proprietor of men, but who forfeited his right by being himself tempted to put to death the sinless Son of God, and, having fallen into this trap, was obliged to surrender his spoil." —"The Seat of Authority in Religion," by James Martineau, D.D., p. 135.

[1] "Dhammapada," chap. vi. p. 97.

[2] On this point the reader may consult Professor Max Müller's essay on the 'Migration of Fables' ("Selected Essays," vol. i. pp. 541–547).

[3] Sir Monier Williams' "Buddhism," p. 467.

writer tells us that in China, where Buddhism is the nominal religion of the majority of the people, the temple "is from time to time used as a theatre, a club, a caravanserai, or a market. It contains no other furniture than the altar and the stools on which rest the different forms of Buddha," which are readily removed and placed upon the ground without ceremony to suit the convenience of the traveller who may use the temple as a rest house.[1]

The life history of Buddha, and what he himself actually taught, some four-and-twenty centuries ago, must ever remain doubtful matters. In the absence of any reliable chronology to help us, and with a mass of legends at our disposal instead of history, we shall never be able to know, with any degree of accuracy, at what particular time special institutions, ceremonials, or creeds came into existence in the East; we shall never have any reasonable confidence in the dates assigned, by this or that scholar, to the ancient works on which we must fall back for our facts about the Eastern world; nor probably will scholars ever be able to tell us to what extent these works have undergone alteration and modification in comparatively modern times. Under such circumstances, the interesting controversy as to whether the undoubted resemblances between the Christian monastic and ritualistic system and that of the Buddhists of Ṭibet (Lāmaism, in fact) are due to the influence of Buddhism on Christianity, or the reverse, will probably remain unfruitful in its results.[2] Of this, however, we can assure ourselves, from many authoritative sources, that *primitive* Buddh-

[1] "China: Its Social, Political and Religious Life," by M. G. Eug. Simon, pp. 64–65. London, 1887.

[2] "Lāmaism, indeed, with its shaven priests, its bells, and rosaries, its images, and holy water, and gorgeous dresses; its service with double choirs, and processions, and creeds, and mystic rites, and incense, in which the laity are spectators only; its abbots and monks, and nuns of many grades; its worship of the double Virgin, and of the saints and angels; its fasts, confessions and purgatory; its images, its idols and its pictures; its huge monasteries and its gorgeous cathedrals, its powerful hierarchy, its cardinals, its Pope, bears outwardly at least a strong resemblance to Romanism, in spite of the essential difference of its teachings, and of its mode of thought."—Professor Rhys Davids' "Buddhism" (1907), p. 250.

ism was something very different from, something very superior to, contemporary Buddhism, of which, as might have been expected, there are many existing varieties, each, strange to say, with its own gods, and goddesses too, of quaint and grotesque shapes, each believing its absurd and fantastic legends, each with its superstitions, priesthoods and mummeries. In some cases, too, Buddhism, having succumbed to the insidious spell of the Sakta worship and the Tantric cult, is not free from the grossest obscenities of practice. In Tibet, China and Japan, in Nepal, Burmah and Ceylon, Buddhism in diverse forms still flourishes; but needless to say it is nowhere the cold philosophical creed of a purely monastic order, nor faithful to the doctrines ascribed to one Gautama in the fifth century before the advent of Christ.[1]

Even the stay-at-home Englishman has become familiar with the Buddhist idols in the museums, and their so-called prayer-wheels, hollow cylinders containing written prayers, which, set revolving by water power or other means, grind out the prayers of a household or a village. He will even find, in the national collections, the hideous masks used in Ceylon[2] and elsewhere by modern Buddhists in their devil-worship; and he can see supposed sacred relics of Buddha himself in the British Museum.[3] The worship of relics early obtained favour in the Buddhist Church, and has not lost its hold over the followers of Gautama, if I may judge from what I saw in 1874, when I had the good fortune to witness the procession of elephants carrying, by torchlight, the supposed tooth of Buddha through the streets of the beautiful mountain town of Kandy in Ceylon, with the usual accompaniment of drums and other equally noisy instruments of music. With respect to these worshippers of the tooth relic, the Bishop of Colombo remarked :—" In practice the Ceylon Buddhist, among the masses, is both better and worse than his creed.

[1] For a general view of contemporary Buddhism, Sir Monier Williams' " Buddhism " may be consulted.

[2] British Museum, case 19–26.

[3] Ibid. case 155.

Better, because instead of a distant Nirvana, or a series of births, he has before him the next birth only, which he thinks will be in heaven if he is good, and in hell if he is bad; because he calls on God in times of distress, and has a sort of faith in the One Creator, whom his priests would teach him to deny. Worse, because his real refuge is neither Buddha, nor his books, nor his order, but devils and devil-priests, and charms and astrology, and every form of grovelling superstition." [1]

How remote these people are, in both theory and practice, from the original teaching of Buddha is manifest enough, but in the great awakening of the Far East, which is a notable feature of our time, efforts towards the realization of the primitive cult and its underlying philosophy will certainly not be wanting, and we learn, with mild interest, that already Buddhist missionaries are on their way to Europe to teach the self-opinionated Westerns the eight-fold path that leads to eternal rest.

[1] Article on 'Buddhism' in "Nineteenth Century" for July 1888.

CHAPTER III

A STRANGE CULT; THE WORSHIP OF ZÂHIR-PIR

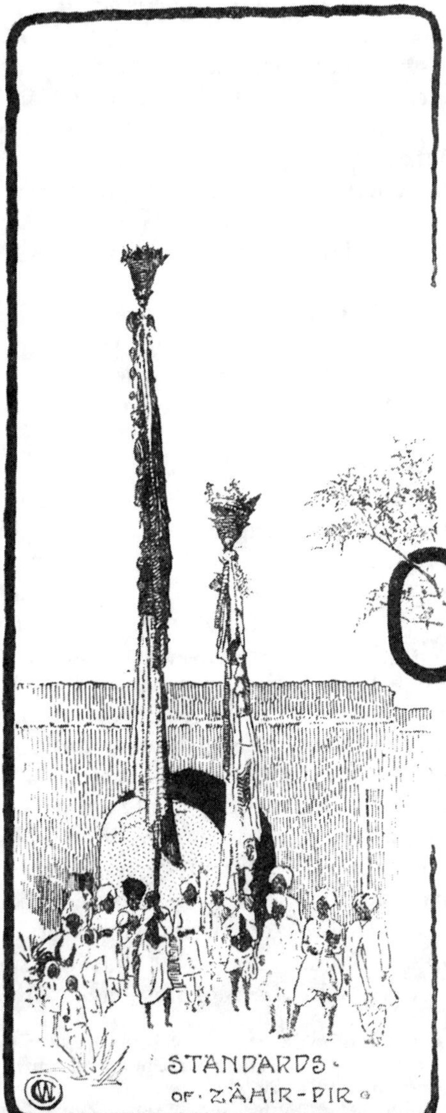

"The Lalbagis once a year erect a long pole covered with flags, coloured cloth, and other things, including cocoa-nuts, in honour of Pir Zahir, or Lal Guru, as he is likewise called; to which they render worship as to a god. In this they are like the low Muhammadans, who worship a similarly decorated pole erected to Gazi-Mian, a pir or saint."
—SHERRING'S "Hindu Tribes and Castes as represented at Benares."

ON the fertile religious soil of India, there flourish, in rank luxuriance, many strange forms of worship, one of which forms the subject of this chapter.

The quotation at the head of the page alludes, very briefly, to the religious observances I am about to describe; but, like too many such condensed descriptions, it is not quite accurate, for, as far as I have been able to learn, the pole is nowhere *worshipped as a god.*

At Bâgar, in the district of Bikanir, is the tomb of a *Pir* or saint, well known from the Himalayas to the Narbada, of whom the following marvellous and unmeaning story is told.[1]

A Raja of Bâgar-des had two wives (twin sisters resembling one another very closely), Bâchal and Kâchal by name. Both were childless, and both anxious to become mothers. Bâchal, perhaps even more than her sister, longed for the honour of maternity. In order to obtain her object, Bâchal served Guru Goracknâth, a celebrated yogi, in a menial capacity for some twelve years. The all-powerful yogi, who lived in the Raja's garden at Bâgar, pleased with her assiduous attentions to him, promised that on a certain date he would grant her request. In the meanwhile, the Raja's sister was doing her utmost to get her royal brother to repudiate Bâchal, who, she said, had degraded herself by performing menial offices even for a yogi, and ought to be sent back to her own people. Unaware of the intrigues in the palace, Bâchal was looking forward with eager hope to the fulfilment of the yogi's promise, which she had foolishly (as after events proved) made known to her twin sister Kâchal. On the appointed day Kâchal rose very early, and, trusting to the close resemblance she bore her twin sister, presented herself before the yogi, boldly asking him to redeem his promise. The holy man, unconscious of the deception that was being practised upon him, put two grains of wheat into her hand with instructions to eat them, upon doing which her desire would be accomplished. Thus reaping where she had not sown, the unscrupulous and unsisterly Kâchal hurried away home. A little later Bâchal came and prostrated herself before Guru Goracknâth, claiming the promised reward of her long and faithful ministrations. The saint was puzzled and, after what had occurred in the morning, not a little

[1] The legend as I give it in this paper differs in some, though not very essential, points from that contained in General Cunningham's Archæological Report for 1878–79, vol. xiv. The General does not deal with the religious ceremonies and observances I have described. For another variant of the legend of Zâhir-Pir, see the "Popular Religion and Folk-lore of Northern India," by Mr. W. Crook, vol. i. p. 211.

incensed at Bâchal's request; but when he understood the real state of the case, said that though he had already given two sons to Kâchal, he would not suffer the woman who had served him with so much devotion for years to go away unrewarded. To this end he handed her an apple, of which she was to eat three-fourths and give the remainder to her favourite mare. While these events were transpiring, the Raja's sister had succeeded in inducing him to put Bâchal away, and the unfortunate princess was accordingly packed off to her ancestral home. In due course Kâchal became the mother of twin sons, and the event was celebrated with great rejoicings. Bâchal's time was also drawing nigh, but she was now in her father's house. At this stage certain marvellous events occurred. Bâchal's unborn child, addressing its mother, advised her to go back to her husband's home, as it would not be creditable for him to be born away from the paternal roof. The mother objected that her father would never hear of her returning to a husband who had repudiated her, and that if she insisted upon going she would have to walk the whole way, as she would, on no account, be helped by her own people in carrying out such a project. The child then told its mother to have a tree that stood before their house felled, and a cart made out of the wood. As for oxen to draw it, he informed his mother that if she sent a servant into the neighbouring forest, he would there find a pair, named Sona and Mona, ready for use. The mother pointed out that the only carpenter available was blind, but the child got over that difficulty by telling her to instruct the carpenter in question to press his hands over his eyes and his sight would be restored. Everything turned out exactly as the child had predicted. The cart was duly made, the oxen found and yoked to it, and the journey towards Bâgar commenced. Freighted with such an important burden, the cart, as it passed along, seemed to shake the earth to its very foundations. The king of the *serpents* was in his subterranean kingdom, and sent some huge snakes to destroy the audacious mortals who dared to invade his repose. His commands were so far carried out, that the driver of the cart and the two oxen were killed; but

Bâchal escaped on foot, and returned to her father's house in deep distress. She upbraided the child who had caused all this trouble, but he maintained that neither the oxen nor the driver were dead, and desired her to send men to inquire about them. True enough, they were found restored to life, and, after a little delay, the journey was resumed. The Raja of Bâgar-des received his wife back again, and the marvellous child was ushered into the world with the customary rejoicings. Shortly after his birth he was, in accordance with universal custom in India, laid in the sun, in order to be purified by the rays of that god. He was left alone for a few minutes, and when his attendants returned they found him playing with a deadly cobra. They looked on in mute terror, which turned to horror and amazement when they saw him put the cobra's head into his own mouth and suck it.[1] The infant, *mirabile dictu*, suffered no harm, and this incident, I was gravely assured, gave rise to his popular name of Zâhir-Pir (or poison saint).[2] When he arrived at man's estate he succeeded his father on the *masnad* (throne). Of course a wife was found for him, and while he was away from home on a visit to his bride's father, his half-brothers (the twin sons of Kâchal) plotted to seize the throne with the assistance of the Emperor of Delhi. The young prince had only just reached home with his bride, when he was obliged to defend himself against a force raised at Delhi and headed by his brothers. In hot haste he collected such of his men as were at hand, and mounting his steed Leilah, a foal of the mare that had been favoured with a bit of the yogi's apple, he set out to meet his adversaries. When about to start for the battle-field, his mother laid

[1] The idea of the superiority of a saintly child to the terrible destructive power of serpents is an old one, and occurs in the mythology of many nations. "Thus it is said that Ali, when an infant, was left alone in Mecca, the inhabitants, including his parents, having fled at the approach of a huge dragon. The infant rent it asunder by the jaws" (Conway's "Demonology," vol. ii. p. 12).

[2] General Cunningham says that this saint "received his title of Zâhir-Pir, or the 'manifested saint,' because he appeared to his wife after death" ("Archæological Report," vol. xiv. p. 84).

her solemn injunctions upon him to spare the lives of his brothers.

In the heat of the contest that ensued, Zâhir-Pir was miraculously protected from harm. The birds hovered over him to shield him from the sun, they received on their own wings the bullets that would have struck him. His mare Leilah performed wonders. She literally flew about, and in one of her wild swoops the Pir's sword struck off the heads of both his brothers at one stroke, and, in some inexplicable manner, they rolled into his lap. He gathered up his clothes round his waist with the two heads, and rode on. The chiefs thus disposed of, the battle was over. His enemies melted from the field, and Zâhir-Pir returned home. At the gate he was met by his mother, whose first question was about the fate of Kâchal's sons. Instead of replying, the exhausted soldier asked for water; but without giving him what he wanted she again pressed him for news of his brothers. Irritated at her solicitude regarding the fate of his treacherous foes, the victor told her that he had brought some cocoa-nuts for her, and, so saying, rolled out upon the floor the bloody heads which he had carried in his girdle. The old Ráni started back with horror from these gory trophies, and in her indignation vowed that she would see her son's face no more.

Up to this time the prince had been a Hindu. He now turned Muhammadan, and went off alone on a pilgrimage to Mecca. His mother thought he was dead, and his young bride mourned his loss, but he came back safe and well, and secretly made himself known to his wife, whom he found means of visiting clandestinely. An evident change in the bearing and manners of the supposed widow, her cheerfulness and gaiety, so out of harmony with her condition, aroused the suspicions of the mother-in-law. The old Ráni reproached her daughter-in-law with forgetting her duty as a widow, and even accused her of unfaithfulness to her dead husband. Stung by the keen edge of the old lady's tongue, the princess determined to clear her character. She invited her mother-in-law to conceal herself in her bedroom at night. The prince came as usual. The mother recognized her son. All her maternal affection went out towards him, and, unmindful of her vow, she rushed forward to embrace him; but the prince, who had been deeply mortified by his mother's conduct and her vow, fled away hastily and never returned again. His mother had him searched for high and low, far and near, but without avail. At length it was discovered that he had found a quiet refuge in the bosom of mother Earth, into which he had gently descended, steed and all, leaving only the head of his spear and the pennon attached to it to mark the spot of his engulfment. On this now sacred spot his mother erected a mausoleum, which is the centre of attraction to his followers.

Somehow this Pir has been specially selected as the patron saint of the Lalbagis, a section of the *Mehter* or sweeper caste, who, in affliction or trouble, vow to make certain offerings at his tomb, or in his name, in the hope, or on condition, that he will help them in their distress. But the tomb is remote from the great centres of population and wealth. Lalbagis, like other people, need some more present object to quicken their devotion and open their purse-strings than a distant grave. This the custodians of the tomb thoroughly understand, so they periodically send out missionaries to remind the Lalbagis of the necessity of contributing towards the maintenance of the tomb and its guardians, if they desire to enjoy a continuance of the blessings secured to them through the favour of the saint.

The missionaries, who are Muhammadans, go over the country promising the protection and good offices of the Pir to those who will become his followers. Offerings of some sort are, of course, expected; empty-hand worshippers are of little account. Men who in infancy were specially dedicated by their parents, with suitable ceremonies and offerings, to the saint of Bâgar, enjoy certain privileges on the occasions selected for publicly honouring their patron. As might have been expected, children devoted to the special service of the Pir are generally sickly ones, for whom his fostering care is deemed necessary.

In their periodical wanderings, the missionaries of the Zâhir-Pir grant, for a stipulated consideration, permission to a few *Mehters* in each district to raise the standard of the saint for a fixed number of days, and to carry it about in procession. These privileged men are known as *Bhaggats*. I believe it is generally understood that they have visited the saint's tomb in person and been authorized on the spot "to raise his standard," as the phrase is. A pilgrimage to Bâgar is quite a solemn affair. One of my servants, employed as a sweeper, performed the journey to the saint's tomb in order to obtain the coveted rank of Bhaggat. While he was away his family, particularly, of course, the women-folk, had to keep very straight indeed, as any slip or laxity on their part would assuredly bring serious trouble upon the pilgrim. They had to pay their adorations three times a day to the standard; and the man's wife, good little woman, used to have *mashks* (leather bags) of water poured on the ground near it, in order to keep the road to Bâgar cool for her husband.

To the credit of the family, especially the women-folk, the pilgrim returned safe and well, arrayed, like a Sádhu, in orange-coloured garments and with a huge *chimta* (tongs) in his hand. When his arrival at the railway station was announced, his friends and relations went forth to meet him and conduct him home. They made offerings of sweetmeats to him, and bowed down in respectful salutations to the man, now a saintly Bhaggat, who had, it seems, been at one time admitted into the Christian fold and, as I knew, claimed on occasion to be an *Esahi*.

According to popular belief, the standard, at any rate a portion of it, is received direct from the custodians of the Pir's tomb, upon which it has been duly laid, thus acquiring a portion of the sacredness of the holy spot from which it comes. The custodians of the tomb at Bâgar exercise a sufficient control over the Bhaggats, and insist upon the observance by them of the customary practices. A case of irregularity happened at Lahore in 1885. A Bhaggat, in order to steal a march upon the others, set up his standard before the usual time, and began to perambulate the city for contributions. He met with tolerable success; but on the representation of the other Bhaggats he was fined and severely reprimanded by the missionaries from Bâgar, who moreover allowed the other Bhaggats to extract from him his irregularly-gotten gains.

The standard consists of a long bamboo tricked out with scraps of gay-coloured cloth, having at the top of it a sort of huge brush, covered on the outside with peacocks' feathers. Along the length of the pole are suspended bunches of cocoa-nuts, with fans and *morchals* (fly-whisks). This is the appearance it has to an uninitiated onlooker. Indeed, I was for a long time under the impression that the pole, with the tuft of feathers at the top, was nothing but a huge broom, the most important implement of the Mehter's (sweeper's) trade. But I was utterly wrong. To the initiated this huge broom adorned with flags, fitted to a gigantic handle, and carried by a man, is transfigured into *a bridegroom dressed out in his wedding garments, and seated on horseback.* In fact, it represents Zâhir-Pir himself on the memorable occasion of his return home with his bride, the occasion on which he slew his half-brothers and incurred the displeasure of his mother. The cocoa-nuts, I presume, have some connection with the Pir's grim jest about the heads of the sons of Kâchal, but why there should be more than two suspended to the pole I failed to find out. In such cases consistency can hardly be expected, and should not, perhaps, be looked for. Already, it would appear, the symbolical character of the cocoa-nuts is forgotten, and it is an object of pride to the Bhaggat to outdo his rivals in the number of nuts suspended from his pole. The fans and morchals are probably attached as emblems of royal, or at any rate of exalted, rank.

The dressing-up of the pole, or standard as they call it, is quite an elaborate affair, and is carried out to the accompaniment of the drum and vocal music. The tall bamboo is first anointed with mustard oil, next coloured with a yellow ochre, and then washed with milk sponged over it with a handful of *doob* grass. After these anointings and ablutions the *sirmohr*, or head-dress, is tied on.

Such a head-dress is only worn by bridegrooms on their wedding day. Two large triangular pieces of cloth, one blue, the other red, are next attached to the pole, and the costume of the bridegroom is completed by the addition of a couple of fans, one or two morchals, and a large number of cocoa-nuts wrapped in cloth and tied about the place where his neck might have been and quite to the bottom of the pole. Thus completed the standard is of considerable weight.

The festival in honour of Zâhir-Pir takes place about the month of July or August every year. A great number of people assemble to see the standard raised, and follow it to the accompaniment of a noisy band of drummers and fifers. Disciples specially dedicated to the saint enjoy the privilege on such occasions of acting as his *horses.* They carry the standard by turns, supported in a sort of strong leather cup sewn on to a stout belt of the same material fastened *round the waist.* By this arrangement the hands are free to steady the pole and keep it erect. As each man (or "horse") receives the sacred burden, he salutes it with joined palms and a look of rapt adoration, the genuine character of which there is no reason to doubt. The privilege of carrying the standard is a much coveted one. Each "horse," as he staggers about under the sacred burden, shouts out, "I am his horse," while the followers cry, "Victory to Zâhir-Pir." To carry the fiction of their equine nature still further, the "horses" are actually made to eat some *gram* (a pulse on which horses are fed in India) and a few blades of green grass.

Wrought upon by the drumming and shouting, the "horses" imitate the pawing of a spirited steed, and prance about as much as the weight of the pole and their own strength will permit; but should they begin to caper too much, the Bhaggat smacks his whip, made of iron chains mounted on an iron handle. Should their capering be due to their being possessed by some demon unfriendly to the Pir, the Bhaggat soon whips the unwelcome intruder out of his subject; but it is well known that if the capering of the "horse" be due merely to the influence of the sacred afflatus of the "Pir Sahib," why then the whip of iron chains falls quite harmlessly upon the back of the lively steed, and there is more glory to Zâhir-Pir. To steady the pole and obviate any chance of its falling, a catastrophe which might be followed by very grave consequences, it is usual, though not absolutely necessary, to have three or four long stay-ropes attached high up. The ends of these are held by appointed persons, whose duty it is to watch the pole and keep it as vertical as possible. Should the pole, however, owing to the curvetting or awkwardness of the "horse," lean over too much to one side, a shout is immediately raised of "*Kurryhee! Kurryhee!*" which means *dish*, *dish*. The "horse" is immediately relieved of his sacred burden, his belt is formally taken away, and he is deprived of his privileges until he atones for his carelessness by treating his caste-mates to a *dish* of sweetmeats.

All who follow the procession are expected to have had a bath and to have put on clean clothes. They are required to attend barefooted and to dispense with the luxury of an umbrella. During the festival they are also to abstain from both *beef* and *pork*. I was told of the case of a woman who ate beef in defiance of these rules, and lost her life by an attack of cholera. Beyond following the standard and shouting "Zâhir-Pir Ke Jye," or victory to Zâhir-Pir, the adoration consists, practically, in a humble obeisance to the decorated pole on the part of each person, and the presentation of some gift, however trifling, to what we may call the lessees of the standard.

Women, always in an inferior position in the East, are on no account to touch the sacred pole. If they have offerings to make they hand them to the Bhaggat, who graciously accepts the gifts and then, after applying a bundle of peacocks' feathers to the pole, touches the female worshippers with it in token of the Pir's goodwill and protection.

After being carried about for hours with deafening shouts and more deafening drumming, the standard is taken to a river, whither the other standards from the same town are also carried on the same day. The bearer steps into the stream and, raising some of the water in his hand, pays his respects to the river. A day or two later the standard is carried round on a begging expedition, which, in the particular case I took note of, was hardly successful, seeing that the net result of the whole day's work was only one rupee and four annas. The standard is also taken on an appointed day to the house of any one who is willing to give a feast, or a present, in fulfilment of some vow or other.

On a bright moonlight night all the standards are set up in some populous centre, and a *mela* or fair is held there. Stalls for the sale of sweetmeats and tea, etc., are arranged upon the spot, and merry-go-rounds are erected for the amusement of the young. Fun and frolic reign supreme, and the fair is kept up to a late hour. The hoarded or borrowed pice (more frequently the latter) are freely produced, and go to swell the gains of the enterprising dealers in the saint's good offices. On the following day all the standards are carried to some appointed meeting-place with any amount of tom-toming, singing, and noise. The cocoa-nuts are now removed from the sacred pole, and some of them are given as prizes to the successful competitors in foot-races or other sports, open to all comers. The remainder of the cocoa-nuts are distributed in little pieces to the saint's followers, by whom they are much prized as charms. In this distribution the "horses" get the largest share, and sometimes they even receive a small proportion of the Bhaggats' profits. It is easy to see how the honoured position accorded to the "horses" at these religious gatherings becomes an object of desire; and how parents, to secure the envied precedence for their sons on such public occasions, are willing to pay the price demanded by the dispensers of such favours. My inquiries satisfied me that, apart from any theoretical considerations, it was a subject of pride to a Mehter's family to have one member at least enrolled as one of the Pir's "horses."

The practical working of this system and the nature of the worship may be illustrated by the following facts. On one occasion of the annual celebration a quarrel arose as to who should carry the standard. One young man got possession of it, and was acting "horse," when he received a blow on the face which caused the standard to sway and nearly fall to the ground. The blow which caused this was clearly an act of sacrilege. It was a blow given to a young man while acting in the capacity of "*ghora*," or horse, to the "Pir Sahib," and could only be expiated by a heavy fine and a general feast to the caste-fellows. There and then the excited crowd excommunicated the bold and impious man whose hand had struck the offensive blow, and it was months, nay years, before he was quite reinstated in social position amongst his brethren; not, indeed, until the emissaries from Bâgar had themselves condoned his rash act for a certain number of rupees and a promise of better behaviour in the future. On another occasion a young fellow entrusted with the standard allowed his attention to wander towards the women, and the pole became unsteady. A zealous, but too rash attendant, *not himself a ghora*, carried away by his indignant feelings, ventured to strike the pole-bearer, and for this irregularity his hand became partially paralyzed, and only recovered its full power after years of propitiation had appeased the outraged saint. As for the too eager admirer of the fair sex, he became very ill and lost his life shortly after.

To give something of a serious, solemn character to the elevation of the Pir's standard, all the "horses" are required to undergo a sort of purificatory penance for a month previous to the ceremony. They are required to abstain from all indulgences, and to sleep not on a bed of any kind, but on the bare floor, alone, and quite apart from all other members of the family. When in attendance on the standard, they are expected to keep their minds free from carnal thoughts and desires. I heard of the case of one man who met with a severe fall while attending the procession. The nature of the accident was much exaggerated, and was attributed to the Pir's anger at some unbecoming thoughts having entered into the mind of the sufferer. And within my own knowledge a case of severe illness was put down confidently to an infringement of the strict rules for the conduct of a pure life enjoined on these occasions. The Pir, unfortunately, cannot or will not give a favourable answer to every prayer. A little infant was dying in my compound of what seemed to me to be want of nourishment. The father begged a rupee and received it. I naturally concluded he would buy milk and such-like suitable food for the little starveling; but after the child's death, which took place within a day or two, I found out that the rupee had been put into a small bag and tied round the child's neck, with the vow that if Zâhir-Pir would preserve the little one's life, the rupee would be expended in the purchase of a kid to be sacrificed in his honour.

The curious cult of which I have just given an outline sketch is not undeserving of study. The Mehters are an inferior caste, subdivided into seven sub-castes, one of these (the Shaik) professing the Muhammadan religion. The other six sub-castes, including the Lalbagi, although reverencing the Brahmans and holding strictly enough to caste observances, do not, as far as I have been able to ascertain, consider themselves Hindus. Whether the Mehters are descendants of Hindu outcasts, or of aborigines who have adopted the caste system, I cannot say. At the present day their occupation is for the most part that of sweepers and scavengers. The Lalbagis then, be it remembered, are rejected of Hinduism. They do not even call themselves Hindus, although often classed as such by Europeans. They are certainly not Mussulmans. But, like a race of outcasts, they haunt the outer courts of the temples of both religions to pick up such crumbs of comfort as they may be permitted to appropriate. They believe in the Brahman; they consult him on most occasions of life and he takes their money. The Muhammadan Faquir is equally an object of veneration to them, and many an offering do they make on the graves of Syads. Although neither Hindus nor Muslims, they take part in many festivals peculiar to the two creeds, and have succeeded in finding for themselves a patron saint who combines in himself the double advantage of having belonged at different times to both religions, having been, as stated before, born a Hindu and dying a good Muslim.

The pole itself would seem to be essentially a compromise. A visible symbol was demanded, as the object of worship; indeed more than that, an anthropomorphic symbol. But the stern and sweeping condemnation of idolatry in the Koran could not be disregarded by the Muhammadan custodians of the tomb. Out of these conflicting elements has come the decorated pole which I have described—a mere standard of the saint to those who desire to so regard it; but to the imaginative Lalbagi, a veritable representation of his patron at the most critical and interesting moment of his life.

When this cult arose, and how it arose, I have not been able to ascertain. For the patron saint no greater antiquity is at present claimed than the age of Akbar, A.D. 1556–1605.

What a certain popular school of mythologists could make out of the stories which have clustered about the name of Zâhir-Pir, I would not venture to say. Perhaps they could prove that the whole is a solar allegory; a myth of the dawn, or something of that sort. The Pir's voice before birth is perhaps the fresh breeze which precedes the rising sun. His conquest of the serpents, a victory over clouds and darkness. His wonderful horse is obviously one of the coursers of the sun. The journey *westward* to Mecca is the great luminary on his *westward* march, his temporary concealment is an eclipse, and his final disappearance beneath the earth only a sunset; while the spear-head left above the ground is surely a last lingering ray of the vanished sun striking across the sky and visible to men after the bright orb itself has sunk to rest. Comparative mythologists have not to be told, for the point is too obvious, that in this way the life of almost any famous man may be resolved into a solar myth. There are first the symptoms of his advent, then his early struggles, followed by the dangers and conflicts of manhood. To this succeeds his meridian splendour, then his gradual decay, and his disappearance into the bosom of mother earth. Finally comes his spiritual rebirth. Mr. Tylor has shown admirably, and most ingeniously, how even a nursery rhyme, like "Four and twenty blackbirds baked in a pie," may be explained as a solar myth. But we have so many old stories explained as solar myths or myths of the dawn or fire, that one can hardly resist the temptation of speculating regarding the fate of such a legend as that of Zâhir-Pir in the hands of certain professed comparative mythologists. We are told that

> "The story of Herakles' life and labours is a pure but most elaborate sun-myth. From his birth, where he strangles the serpents in his cradle—the serpents of darkness, like the python which Apollo slew—through his *Herculean* labours to his death, we watch the labours of the sun through the mists and clouds of heaven to its ruddy setting; and these stories are so like to others which are told of the northern Herakles, Thorr, that we cannot refuse to believe that they were known in the main in days before there were either Greek-speaking Greeks or Teutons." [1]

Again, the well-known story of William Tell, which proved to have really no foundation in history, is, it appears, nothing but a solar myth :

> "William Tell, whether of Cloudland or Altdorf, is the last reflection of the beneficent divinity of daytime and summer, constrained for a while to obey the caprice of the powers of cold and darkness, as Apollo served Laomedon, and Herakles did the bidding of Eurystheus. His solar character is well preserved, even in the sequel of the Swiss legend, in which he appears no less skilful as a steersman than as an archer, and in which, after traversing, like Dagon, the tempestuous sea of night, he leaps at daybreak in regained freedom upon the land, and strikes down the oppressor who has held him in bondage." [2]

The story of the wanderings of Ulysses, and a hundred other stories equally well known, are, we learn from the mythologists, sun myths and nothing more. The histories of Buddha and Jesus of Nazareth have been denied all historical foundation, and been explained away as solar allegories, according to the approved principles of interpretation adopted by an influential school of mythologists.

To my mind it seems probable (I write with great deference to the opinions of learned mythologists) that at least a large number of the so-called *solar myths* have originated in the circumstances of the life of some very substantial human being distinguished above his fellows in his day and generation, and that his form seen through

[1] Kearny's "The Dawn of History," p. 136.

[2] "Myths and Myth-makers," by John Fiske, M.A., LL.B., p. 24.

the mists of time has loomed larger and larger upon the mental vision of his followers or descendants, who by a very natural process have come to compare him to the most glorious object in nature, the sun, and perhaps have given him some name derived from the great luminary, or even identified him with it. The process has not been one of personifying the sun and inventing a history with apparently human actors built upon the daily or annual course of the sun in the heavens with its attendant incidents, but something very different, viz. the exaggerated comparison of a remarkable human life lived upon this earth of ours, to the progress of the bright orb which in every clime is the most striking object in nature. As to Zâhir-Pir, I think we need not resolve him into an unsubstantial solar myth; but may without much scruple admit that the original of the extravagant legend given in the preceding pages did really walk the earth in human form, and was bruied at Bâgar in the desert of Bikanir —although it would be very unwise to follow the Euhemeristic method of simply stripping off all improbabilities in the legend and accepting the remainder as genuine history.

ENTRANCE · TO · THE · GOLDEN · TEMPLE

CHAPTER IV

THE GOLDEN TEMPLE OF THE SIKHS

SECTION I.—A VISIT ON THE OCCASION OF THE DIWALI FESTIVAL

THE fertile religious soil of India has been productive of many interesting creeds, amongst which that known as *Sikhism* (the religion of the *Sikhs*) certainly holds a very important and in many respects unique position. Its beginnings are coeval with the Reformation in Europe; it has passed through many and strikingly different stages, and has experienced many vicissitudes of fortune. The word *Sikh*—now so familiar to the British public—means a *disciple*, and is the distinguishing name of the followers of a non-idolatrous religion or sect which first came into existence in the Punjab in the early part of the sixteenth century. Founded originally by Baba Nanak (A.D. 1469–1539), a Hindu of the Bedi Khatri caste, Sikhism, though enduring from time to time much persecution at the hands of the Muhammadan rulers of the country (not solely on account of its religious professions), grew and developed gradually under the leadership of nine spiritual successors of the founder of the sect; these nine, with Baba Nanak himself, being the *ten Gurus* or prophets of the Sikhs. In connection with the lives of the gurus many miraculous legends of an extravagant character have been recorded, and are devoutly believed by the Sikhs generally, though some of the better-educated members of the sect seem disposed to regard them as purely mythical. However, the story of the gurus is not entirely legendary, but enshrines many striking and romantic situations, many extremely pathetic and tragic incidents which have an undoubtedly historical basis, and are often in the thoughts and on the lips of their faithful followers.

Baba Nanak's religious teaching, which was of a dreamy, philosophical character, differs remarkably from that of the modern Sikhs, who follow the precepts of Govind Singh (A.D. 1675–1708), the tenth and last of the *gurus;* for, under the pressure of political circumstances, Govind converted the Sikhs into a militant sect aggressively hostile to Muhammadanism.

The most sacred book of the Sikhs, the authoritative scriptures of the sect, known as the *Adi-Granth*, is a large volume of mystical rhapsodies, often beautiful but more often incomprehensible, compiled, from the writings of Nanak and other mystics, by the *fifth* guru, Arjan (A.D. 1581–1606).

As to the tenets of Sikhism it may be sufficient to note here that this creed upholds the Hindu belief in reincarnations, with the important modification that by whole-hearted, unquestioning devotion to the guru the disciple may escape the otherwise inevitably long (almost interminable) succession of re-births *under the law of Karma*, and may thus attain salvation immediately after his present life.

According to the latest census (1901) the Sikhs num-

From a painting by an Indian artist

GURU NANAK, WITH HIS FAITHFUL ATTENDANTS MARDANA AND BALA

To face page 84

bered 2,195,339 persons, over 95 per cent. of the entire body being residents of the Punjab. They are a professedly warlike community, and for a brief period attained predominance in the Punjab during the troubled times which attended the decline and fall of the Mogul Empire in India. About the middle of the last century, 1845–49, the Sikhs came into collision with the East India Company and made a gallant, if unsuccessful, resistance to the British arms in many a well-fought field.

Of all the sacred places of the Sikhs the Golden Temple, known amongst the people as the *Darbár Sahib*, is the most important. To be seen to advantage, this temple should be visited on the occasion of the *Diwali* festival, when the fane and its surroundings are brilliantly illuminated with thousands upon thousands of those little terracotta lamps, known in India as *cheraghs*.

The Diwali festival takes place annually, on the darkest day of the year, according to Hindu reckoning; and on this day I paid a visit to the temple, accompanied by my wife and children.

Passing through the very narrow and crowded streets of the city, we suddenly entered a large open space, bounded by stately buildings, and there before us lay a fine sheet of water, from the centre of which rose like a fairy island the beautiful Sikh temple with its marble walls and gilded cupolas. A broad walk, for the greater portion paved with marble, runs along the four sides of the spacious tank in which it stands. A wide causeway of cut stone, also paved with marble, joins the north side of the temple to the land. The lower portion of the building is decorated with the handsome inlaid work so common in India. The dome and cupolas, and the major part of the upper portion of the building, are covered over with sheet copper, richly gilded; hence the name "Golden Temple" usually applied to it by Europeans. Viewed from the terrace on the east side of the artificial lake, or, better still, from an elevated position like the lofty tower known as the Baba Atal, the temple with its surroundings forms a picture both unique and beautiful. According to Professor Sir Monier Williams, it may be said to rank next to the Taj at Agra as one of the most striking sights in

India;[1] while Dr. Fergusson considered this temple as "splendid an example of its class (of nineteenth-century temples) as can be found in India;"[2] though he did not commend either its outline or its details. The building, which combines in itself characteristics of both Hindu and Muhammadan styles of architecture, is not imposing in its dimensions; the dome, too, is low and squat; but the material of the structure is marble, the finish elaborate, and, taken as a whole and in connection with its surroundings, the Golden Temple is a decidedly attractive and pleasing object.

When our little party arrived at the temple, about an hour before sunset, the scene was extremely picturesque and animated. A stream of human beings was setting steadily towards the central building, and the crowd was every minute getting more and more dense. Looking down from the platform at the base of the new clock-tower, there appeared a troubled sea of white and coloured turbans, filling the entire approach to the temple. We told some policemen, who were there on duty, that we wished to go inside the building. At first they raised difficulties about it, saying that the crowd between us and the Darbár Sahib was too great to admit of our passing forward. Seeing, however, that we had a strong mind to try, they undertook to conduct us to the sanctuary. But certain preliminaries had first to be gone through. We were asked to sit down on a bench and exchange our boots for moccasins made of cloth, as it was not admissible to tread the hallowed precincts of the Darbár Sahib shod with leather. This necessary concession to Sikh customs having been satisfactorily carried out, two tall policemen undertook to clear the way for us—no easy matter at first sight, for we had to get through a closely packed and struggling mass of human beings, which occupied the entire space between us and the door of the shrine. But the policemen, representatives of the irresistible power of the *Sarkar*, brought us safely, and in a very few minutes, to the desired goal. With loud shouts, vigorous pushes to right and left, and, it must be confessed, free

[1] "Religious Thought and Life in India," p. 175.
[2] "History of Indian and Eastern Architecture," p. 469.

Photo by Lala Jadu Kishan

THE GOLDEN TEMPLE AT AMRITSAR

To face page 86

use of their official batons on the turbaned heads of their unoffending countrymen, the policemen cleared the way for us, without, as far as I could observe, creating the smallest outward sign of irritation in the men so unceremoniously handled. Possibly the stolid countenances of the Sikhs masked the resentment which such treatment would only too naturally awaken. I tried, but unsuccessfully, to restrain the superabundant energy of our guides and protectors. They were apparently acting according to their ordinary procedure, and smilingly protested that no harm was being done.

When we reached the door of the shrine, it was thronged by a crowd of eager visitors. On the pavement, damp and dirty from the feet of the multitudes that had already been there, devout pilgrims were prostrating themselves with touching humility; whilst others were silently, and very undemonstratively, struggling to enter the holy place, in order to present the offerings, rich or trifling, which they had brought in their hands.

We entered the inner room or sanctuary, a vaulted chamber of very moderate dimensions, with a richly ornamented ceiling. In the centre of it was a heavy canopy or baldaquin of cloth of gold, supported on four silver posts. Under this was the sacred book of the Sikhs, the *Adi-Granth*, covered over with costly brocade, and before the volume, facing the main entrance, sat a *Granthi*, one of the principal priests of the temple. Round about were several *Pujaris* or lesser priests. On one side squatted three or four musicians, who, while we stood there, were playing on stringed instruments (*sitars* and *sárángis*), with the accompaniment of the *tabla* or drum, the well-known air of "Taza ba Taza," the ever-popular song of Hafiz, breathing of love and wine.

There was no idol nor graven image in the shrine. The only object of veneration was *the Book*. We stood for a few minutes to watch the scene. Thousands had come from distant places to pay their respects and perform their devotions at the temple on this important occasion. They struggled, a few at a time, into the chamber where the sacred volume lay, and made their offerings of money, sweets or flowers; receiving back from the hands of the priest some trifle—perhaps a crushed and broken flower taken from the heaps before him.

Observing our presence in the temple, one of the priests came forward and began directing our attention to various points of interest in the architecture of the place. He also handed us a couple of lumps of sugar-candy, and some flowers. I ventured at first to decline these presents; but he pressed them upon us so courteously that we were obliged to accept them. A visit to the upper floor of the building and to the roof well repaid us for the slight trouble of ascending a well-built staircase. The prospect from the windows was strikingly beautiful and interesting. The bright *water of immortality* (for such it is to the Sikhs) reflecting the image of the Golden Temple, with the surrounding structures, and disturbed only by a few devout bathers near the shrine, lent a peculiar charm to the view, and tempted us to linger undisturbed for many minutes in the quiet upper storeys of the building. On one side, towards the causeway, the *Akal Bunga*, the stately palace of the *Akalis*, with its gilded dome and towering flagstaffs, made a fine object; on another, the palace of a Sikh Sirdar with its lofty minarets attracted the eye; and a little way off the gigantic tower, surmounted by a gilt cupola, which covers the remains of *Baba Atal*, gave additional beauty to an unusually striking panorama.

With the site of the temple, and more particularly with the lake, are connected legends, which date back to prehistoric times, and others which enshrine the story of miraculous events of not more than three or four centuries ago; while historical recollections of bloody martyrdoms and proud triumphs are associated with various spots in the immediate neighbourhood of this stately shrine. The sacred pool itself which lay below us, excavated by Guru Ram Das in 1574, has known many vicissitudes. More than once has it been filled up by the Muhammadans, and in 1762 it was desecrated by Ahmed Shah, who caused slaughtered cows to be thrown into the holy water. But this sacrilege was amply avenged in later years, when "numerous mosques were demolished, and Afghans in chains were made to wash the foundations with the blood of hogs."[1] The temple which now stands in the centre of the quadrangular tank owes its gilding to the piety or superstition of Mahárája Ranjít Singh (A.D. 1780–1839), who, in his day of power, despoiled many of the finest Muhammadan tombs in Lahore and its neighbourhood, to embellish the chief temple of the sect to which he belonged; an act of vandalism not yet forgotten by the Punjab Muslims, to whom the Darbár Sahib is a standing eyesore to this day.

While we were at the temple, preparations for the illumination were being vigorously pushed on. The *cheraghs* were being arranged as closely as possible, along all the principal lines of the architecture. On the roof itself, these little lamps were screened on the outer side by a row of thin glass flasks containing water, variously coloured to produce the effect of polychromatic lights, and well indeed, as we afterwards saw, was the desired result secured by this very simple device.

The return through the closely packed crowd was only a repetition of our progress to the temple, and was accomplished without any *contretemps*. Near the clock-tower we found that the authorities (municipal or other) had placed several rows of seats for European spectators of the illumination. Here we settled ourselves down to watch the gradual lighting up of the temple and its surroundings. In an open space just behind us, a band of musicians—the town-band, I suppose—were treating us to popular English airs. As the dusk of evening approached, the appearance in quick succession, on different parts of the temple, around the boundaries of the tank and on the adjacent buildings, of bright points of fire, each point faithfully reproduced in the bosom of the tranquil lake, told us that the cheraghs were being deftly lighted by many practised hands. Silently and rapidly line after line of fire flashed into existence, revealing to our admiring eyes the gemmed outlines of a veritable fairy city. When the buildings had all been lighted up, we were treated to a brilliant display of fireworks on three sides of the tank, the effect of the whole, as a display of light and colour, being most striking and

[1] Cunningham's "History of the Sikhs," p. 103.

admirable. But, for my part, I would willingly have dispensed with both the English band and the pyrotechnics, for they seemed to me out of keeping with the place and the occasion.

One consequence of the fireworks was to set in wild confused flight over our heads a host of pigeons, birds held sacred in so many religious cities, and not less sacred at Amritsar, where it would be dangerous for any one to kill a pigeon near the Golden Temple.

Unfortunately illuminations and fireworks are not free from smoke. We were soon glad to leave the heavy air in the neighbourhood of the temple, and take our way back through the now brilliantly lighted streets of Amritsar. The Diwali festival, in honour of which the temple and the city were illuminated, is known in Bengal as the Kali Poojah, and in that province is attended with the sacrifice of countless victims, particularly sheep, goats, and buffaloes.[1] In the North-Western Provinces of India and in the Punjab, the Diwali day is that on which the Hindu tradesmen open their account-books for the new year and indulge largely in gambling as an omen of the luck they are to have during the ensuing twelve months. *Lakshmi*, the goddess of fortune, is on this night worshipped in the form of a current gold or silver coin. The dwelling-houses are all thoroughly cleaned and set in order, if only on this one occasion in the year, to be fit places for the reception of the goddess; while the illumination is to keep devils from entering the houses under cover of the darkness.[2] Some say that in rural Punjab the lamps are chiefly lighted in honour of the spirits of departed ancestors.[3]

Be the object or origin of the festival what it may, every town in Northern India glitters on Diwali night with thousands upon thousands of twinkling lights, while the Hindu inhabitants perform such rites as they deem likely to bring them good fortune. The Sikhs, although seceders from orthodox Hinduism, are unwilling to lose their chance of the good fortune that Lakshmi may be

[1] Shib Chunder Bose's "The Hindoos as They Are," p. 138 *et seq.*
[2] Ibid. p. 140.
[3] Mr. (afterwards Sir) Denzil Ibbetson in the "Civil and Military Gazette," March 1884.

disposed to give her votaries, so they too illuminate their temple in her honour, and with no niggardly hand.

On Diwali night the Indian bazaars, swept, garnished, and brilliantly illuminated, are crowded with people. The prominent feature of the occasion is the abundance of toys: toys in sugar, in clay, in paper. The toy shops and sweetmeat shops are full to overflowing with houses, towers, and boats; with men, elephants, and horses; with oxen, fishes, and birds. Indeed the variety of shapes in sugar and in baked clay, gorgeously painted and tinselled over, which compete for public favour, must be quite bewildering to the little ones who, dressed in their holiday finery, crowd round the stalls. Amidst the toys there are many representations of the gods of Hindustan; but nothing having the slightest claim to artistic merit is to be seen anywhere. Some interesting objects may, however, reward the quest of the curious in such matters. For example, an Indian form of the scientific toy with concealed syphon—known as the *Cup of Tantalus*—may be bought at some of the shops. It is a small basin of burnt clay, in the centre of which is the figure of a man carrying on his shoulders the god Krishna. When water is poured into the cup, it rises to the feet of Krishna and then flows away—commemorating an event in the history of that favourite Hindu deity, who, being carried across the Jumna, was saluted by the river, which rose up in adoration to touch his divine feet and then respectfully retired.

All along the crowded streets, men carrying Chinese lanterns, suspended from light bamboos, tempt the children to spend their money, while others exhibit a large cylindrical paper lantern over the sides of which a number of shadow-figures pass noiselessly in succession. The lantern has within it a light frame set with paper figures, which is made to revolve round the central lamp, hence the shadows. It was a lantern of this kind, long familiar to the East, which suggested that well-known quatrain in Fitzgerald's version of "Omar Khayyam":

> "We are no other than a moving row
> Of Magic Shadow-shapes that come and go
> Round with the Sun-illumined Lantern held
> In Midnight by the Master of the Show."

After an interval of sixteen years I attended, with pleasurable anticipations, another Diwali illumination of the Darbár Sahib; but somehow the display did not strike me as being as effective as on the occasion of my previous visit. Very probably the change was in myself —I cannot tell. Certainly, however, there were other more manifest changes both amongst the spectators and the illumination itself, which deserve at least a passing notice. One of these was the presence of certain Indian barristers in European evening dress, with the prescribed swallow-tailed coat, a lavish expanse of shirt-front, white tie, and neat button-hole. Another, an English lady, leaning confidingly on the arm of her Indian husband, promenading on the terrace above the lake; and yet another novelty, the garish electric light, installed on the temple itself amidst the modest, old-world cheraghs, looking like an ill-mannered, obtrusive upstart completely out of its proper element. Sixteen years had brought these changes, and, for the moment, they seemed to be discords, though some might see in them healthy signs of both social and material *progress*.

Section II.—A Leisurely Visit on an Ordinary Day

As I wished to see the Darbár Sahib on an ordinary occasion, free from the bustle and confusion of a grand festival, I paid it another visit early one September morning. The causeway was occupied by a crowd of visitors going to and returning from the shrine.

The temple itself is open on all four sides, a fact which has been interpreted to indicate " that God may be worshipped from every side," while at the same time " people of every creed can enter and hear the praises of God that are always sung there." [1] On the side farthest away from the causeway a flight of steps, known as Harkipouri, leads into the tank. To bathe and drink water at these steps is a meritorious act. Here caste distinctions are supposed to disappear in partaking of the water of

[1] "A Brief History of the Hari Mandar" (Golden Temple, Armitsar), by Gurmukh Singh, Chandhar, Professor Oriental College, Lahore, p. 5.

immortality; here too important oaths are often solemnly, if secretly, ratified. When I entered the sanctuary itself a *Granthi* and several attendants were seated near the Adi-Granth, which, covered over with a handsome cloth, lay on a small stand, a few inches above the floor. It was the object of special adoration, and was being fanned the whole time, as Hindu idols and great chiefs always are on ceremonial or state occasions. So sacred is the Granth held by the Sikhs, that the rich and ignorant amongst them consider it meritorious even to have it read *for* them, from beginning to end, and delegate the duty to a priest, who duly performs it for a trifling consideration—four or five rupees and a suit of clothes. Sometimes this ceremony, known as *pât*, is performed for the benefit of a dead person at the expense of his surviving relatives. Near the Granth in the Golden Temple, four or five musicians were playing on their instruments, and occasionally a song or hymn was set up, filling the vaulted chamber with a loud but not unpleasant sound. The numerous worshippers, mostly women of the middle class, many of them Hindus not properly belonging to the Sikh sect, performed their devotions by peregrinating the corridor which surrounds the central chamber three, five, or seven times, and then laying some small offering before the *book*. This circumambulation, known as *pradakshina*, is a common feature of Hindu worship throughout India. As on the occasion of my previous visit the chief priest's duty seemed limited to receiving the offerings and making a trifling return in the shape of a flower or two.[1]

I was assured that the service which I have described was carried on without intermission from early morning till late at night (3 A.M. to 11 P.M.) by relays of priests and attendants, there being no less than twenty-four parties of vocalists and musicians to sing hymns uninterruptedly during the twenty hours devoted to the daily service in the temple. I had, however, seen a much

[1] The oblations, when they are not of small value, are given in fulfilment of some vow or other. I was shown in the temple grounds a richly caparisoned horse which had been presented by a Sikh Raja, and which was to be maintained at his expense for one year and then sold for the benefit of the temple.

more interesting religious service in another Sikh place of worship—the *baba ka baree* in Sealkote—where I found a mixed congregation of Sikhs and Hindus listening most attentively to the reading and exposition of the Granth. I learned, on inquiry, that in an upper room of the Golden Temple the sacred book was similarly expounded every day, and this I found to be correct.

Within the fane I was struck with the decorum and the air of superiority discernible in all the proceedings, as compared with what one sees in any orthodox Hindu temple. The Sikhs, as a rule, dress well and take a pride in their personal appearance, cultivate handsome beards and wear well-tied turbans on their heads. Consequently they possess a far more dignified presence than the so much *un*-clothed Brahmans and visitors one sees in Hindu shrines. Here in the Darbár Sahib priests, singers, instrumentalists and the audience too, though in a lesser degree, were decorously, cleanly and neatly dressed, and it would be superfluous to dilate upon the marked difference which good clothes make not only in the *appearance* but the *bearing* of men and women in any private or public assembly.

Hardly less interesting than the Darbár Sahib are its surroundings; for on the four sides of the tank are various places and objects which cannot fail to attract the visitor's attention. Chief amongst these is a building known as Akal Bunga,[1] which stands facing the principal entrance, by the causeway, to the temple. Within this edifice I was shown the chamber in which the Adi-Granth of the temple is placed for safe custody for four hours at night, and whence it is carried each day before dawn, with great state and ceremony, to the shrine. Here is the throne of the sixth *guru* of the sect (Har Govind, A.D. 1606–1638); here, amongst other weapons, are his two swords, symbolizing spiritual and temporal sovereignty; here, also, is the chief baptistery of the Sikhs.

The ceremony of Sikh baptism, or receiving the *pahul*,

[1] "Bunga means a place of rest, from the Persian bunga, a tent, a dwelling. Akal Bunga means place of rest or dwelling dedicated to the deathless being."—"A Brief History of the Hari Mandar," by Gurmukh Singh, Chandhar.

is very simple. A little water drawn from the sacred tank is placed in a small vessel and sweetened with sugar. Five men sit round it, reciting prescribed prayers and stirring the water with a dagger or miniature sword. When the prayers have all been duly said, a little of the now-consecrated water is sprinkled over the neophyte's head and eyes, and he is then required to drink the remainder; after which he eats *Karah-parshal*[1] with, I presume, the five Sikhs who have taken part in the initiatory rite. As might have been expected, the Sikhs claim that receiving the *pahul* is a ceremony of vital importance, having a mysterious regenerating effect upon the initiated, inducing a daring courage in the most timid hearts. At the Akal Bunga I learned that at the initiation of every man, whatever be his nationality, he is required to say he was born at Patna (which was the birthplace of Guru Govind Singh), that he is a resident of Aliwalia (where Govind Singh's home was), and the son of Govind Singh (the tenth and last *guru* of the Sikhs); it being intended that by these transparent and pointless misstatements should be indicated that all Sikhs have a common nationality and a common spiritual father.

In front of the Akal Bunga is an open space used for various purposes. Here on the Dasera festival goats are slaughtered,[2] and here I myself witnessed, from the top of the fine gateway leading to the causeway, a rough-and-tumble, but on the whole good-humoured, scrimmage amidst pools of red-coloured water during the lively days of the annual Holi festival.

Leaving the Akal Bunga and walking on to the open space just referred to, I observed that seated on the marble slabs a Brahman was reading out of and interpreting one of the Hindu shastras, to a small knot of women and children. Walking round the margin of the tank, within the sacred precincts which I was not permitted to tread with shoes on my feet, I found artisans manu-

[1] "A kind of pudding made of flour, butter and sugar," etc.—"A Short History of the Hari Mandar," compiled by B. S. S. Akalia, son of B. Teja Singh, Multáni, Akal Bunga Sahib. Published by B. Buta Singh, Amritsar, 1898.

[2] Gurmukh Singh's "A Brief History of the Hari Mandar," footnote, p. 9.

facturing and selling neat little wooden combs. Others were displaying for sale various articles made of iron, particularly the ornaments worn by Sikhs as distinguishing badges of the sect. Others, again, were laying down marble flags on the broad roadway beside the tank, visible signs, I presume, of the pious generosity of the followers of Guru Nanak and Govind Singh. Here a physician, with the least possible quantity of clothing on his person, was applying a plaster to the head of a squalling infant; there several persons were circumambulating a sacred plum-tree planted by some holy personage; while one or two yogis, rubbed over with ashes, sat, seemingly rapt in contemplation, on the cold pavement. In one place a woman, seated behind a covered volume, was conversing with some members of her own sex. In another a *Granthi*, with a similar covered-up book before him, was carrying on a confidential conversation with a middle-aged man, probably a shopkeeper. As I passed I caught the words, "It can be managed," uttered confidently by the possessor of the sacred book. On inquiring about these irregular teachers, male and female, clinging, as it were, to the outskirts of the temple, I learned that they were despicable wretches who, under the garb of religion, lent themselves to the furtherance of the most immoral practices. Seated tranquilly behind the sacred volume of their faith, they arrange illicit meetings, for which I was told the purlieus of the temple afford only too great facilities.[1] Although local circumstances may, in the case of the Golden Temple, favour the exercise of their calling by these shameless wretches, who make a disgraceful profit out of the frailties of others, the class to which they belong probably owes its origin and prosperity to the restrictions imposed upon social intercourse between the sexes in India.

[1] In a memorial, dated December 22, 1906, addressed to the Lieutenant-Governor of the Punjab by a Sikh society, regarding the mismanagement of the Darbár Sahib, I find the following:

"There are frequent references in the vernacular press to the demoralizing atmosphere of the Bungas, and many are openly classed with houses of ill-fame. Persons of low moral character also frequent the precincts of the Darbár Sahib in large numbers during all hours of the day, and render it unsafe for ladies to go their rounds unattended."—"The Tribune," February 28, 1907.

SECTION III.—A CIRCUMAMBULATION OF THE TANK, AND VISITS TO GURU BAGH AND BABA ATAL

My two visits already described had by no means exhausted the interest of the Darbâr Sahib and its surroundings, that was quite clear to me; so, when the opportunity offered, I gave myself the pleasure of a quiet stroll round the tank, following, in fact, what is regarded as the "greater ambulatory," the lesser one being within the fane itself where the sacred Granth is adored. I was accompanied by some young Sikh gentlemen, whose special and local knowledge helped to enlighten my ignorance and make the promenade both agreeable and profitable. With them I sauntered along the four sides of the noble expanse of water, many passing incidents and objects of interest claiming my attention. Very soon I realized that heterogeneousness was a marked characteristic of the environs of the Golden Temple, and I drew forth a note-book to set down details too numerous and disconnected to be trusted to the memory. From these jottings-by-the-way I select the following, as they provide particulars enough to enable the reader to form his own mind-picture of the environs of the famous temple.

Proceeding along the north side of the pool we encountered at one place a Brahman worshipping tiny images of Ganesh and Krishna; at another a representative of the same hereditary priesthood engaged in adoration of the sun. Noteworthy facts which gave me something to think about. A little further on we passed a school of small children receiving instruction in the rudiments of knowledge under a beautiful peepul-tree. At the north-east corner of the tank in the umbrageous shelter of a fine banyan-tree, we came upon a temple of Siva represented, as usual, by a lingam, which in this instance was about four inches high with a brass bell over it; the whole standing upon a substantial brick and marble platform at the foot of the spreading tree. Here my companions pointed out to me the backs of certain *akharas* (Sikh monasteries), which I had visited on another day in their company.

Advancing along the eastern side of the tank we arrived

at a spot known as *dukh bhanjance* (pain destroyer), where the most notable miracle of healing associated with the water of immortality[1] took place. Near this spot a lecturer was expatiating to a small knot of listeners upon the duties of life, quoting, while I stood there, the Christian scriptures in support of his teaching. Within a short distance we passed a little temple sacred to *Devi*, with the accompaniment of Granth Sahibs and a brass plate with a picture in relief of the famous miracle to which allusion has just been made. Next came a *ghat* and then a Gurdwara of Guru Arjan, and after that a little kiosk with a gilt dome in perfect condition, but with a reed hut alongside. Again we encountered Brahmans engaged in worship, *separately*, of course. One had before him a saligram[2] and a *picture* of the temple of Badrinarain; while the other was adoring a saligram and a *tulasi* (holy basil) plant. The latter worshipper appeared quite at home in the precincts of the Sikh temple, for he blew sundry loud blasts by means of a *conch*, from which he managed to produce some three or four distinct notes.

Walking along the southern side of the tank we arrived at Shahíd Bunga—a place of martyrdom, and the Sikhs have many such to point to—with its flagstaff surmounted by a spear-head and carrying a yellow flag. The Bunga commemorates the death of Shahíd Dip Singh, and within was a picture of the martyr armed with sword and pistol, for the Sikh martyr did not die tamely, but fighting for his faith and its sacred shrine against the Muhammadans. Near by a Sikh artisan was busy making the iron emblems—miniature swords, quoits, and other articles—affected by his co-religionists, and within a few yards of him some eight men in a row were busy reading Granth Sahibs, perhaps vicariously, for men and women who could pay to have it done for the benefit of themselves or their ancestors.

At the south-west corner a number of craftsmen were hard at work making box-wood combs with envi-

[1] *Vide* "The Brahmans, Theists and Muslims of India," pp. 262–3.

[2] A species of ammonite held sacred by Vaishnavas.

Photo by Lala Jadu Kishan

THE GATEWAY OF THE GOLDEN TEMPLE, AMRITSAR

(Showing the inscriptions referred to in the text)

To face page 99

able skill and wonderful celerity—others were selling photographs.

On the west side was established, with the object of acquiring merit, a *chabîl* to supply visitors with drinking water, and beyond this spot were pandits and more pandits, and at the north-west corner a lame *Sádhu.*

But the most interesting object on the western side was an inscription in two languages upon plates fixed one on either side of the handsome gateway, which stands at the head of the causeway leading to the temple. The inscription in English, which is on the left-hand side of the entrance, is as follows :[1]

> "It should be generally known that a wonderful event took place lately in the Golden Temple. This building was erected by the great Guru Ram Dass King of Kings and incarnation of Ram who gives blessings and receives worship from all creatures. The following is an account of what occurred on the 30th of April 1877 at 4.30 a.m. about 400 persons according to ancient custom were praying in this Sri Durbar Sahib and listening to psalms whose music was almost drowned by the roar of thunder Suddenly a flash of lightning fell from heaven and entered the holy place by the northern door close to the singers and musicians a ball of fire of about two seers in weight burst in the temple shining with dazzling and terrible brightness. Then immediately after shining before the holy book it returned to the sky through the southern entrance and although it fell with such awful violence and so loud a report yet there was no injury caused to the durbar Sahib or to human life. Therefore all who were assembled joined in ascribing this miracle to Ram Dass who dedicated this temple to Hari. We think it is also a sign of the great prosperity of the British rule also we are thankful to the Empress of India we pray to the creator of all things for a daily increase in their happy influence and for the destruction of

[1] Copied from a photograph which I procured from Amritsar in November 1907.

all the enemies of her Imperial Majesty. The government inspector waited on the Comr. and informed him of this remarkable event. The following gentlemen viz the Commissioner Rajah Surat Singh Sardar General Gulab Singh Bhagowalia Sardar Mangal Singh Ramgharia and all the worshippers agreed :—That money being collected by friends of the Golden Temple half should be given towards the support of the sacred edifice and half to pay for a dinner to the poor Sufficient money was gathered to pay for seven readings of the Granth Sahib and to feed some thousands of poor people who all expressed their gratitude. This notice is also intended as a memorial of the superintendence of Sardar Mangal Singh over the Sri Darbar Sahib of Hari and as a remembrance of the miracle of Guru Ram Dass and the prosperity of our rulers which we pray may last to the end of time B.K."

The *globular* lightning referred to, which is a very rare phenomenon, naturally produced a deep impression upon those who witnessed it. How they came to estimate its weight at two seers (four pounds) is an insoluble mystery. However, the affirmation that Guru Ram Dass was an incarnation of the Supreme Being is certainly significant, and the rest of the inscription is at least deserving of note.

By the time I had read the inscription evening was approaching, and having completed the circuit of the pool, I paused to survey the whole scene, which, with the westering sun lighting up the temple and its gilded domes, the tranquil water and the picturesque surroundings, was one worth a long journey to see. There is nothing quite like it anywhere else, but I could not help wishing that the incongruous modern clock-tower could be blotted out of the view.

A stroll through the Guru's Gardens close by and a visit to the tomb of Baba Atal adjoining it were proposed and carried out. In the gardens I saw several *Sádhus* (Hindu ascetics)—of whom I would gladly have had photographs —fellows with matted hair and rubbed over with fine

Photo by W. Campbell Oman

UDASI SÁDHU

(The entrance to his *home* [a hole in the ground] is seen on the left. The inset-photograph at the right-hand upper corner shows the Sádhu looking out upon the world)

To face page 100

ashes; but even these men, influenced probably by their environment, seemed to have taken unusual pains with their simple toilet and in the arrangement of their garments, such as they were. Some *Akalis* were also in the gardens, bristling with weapons, but somehow they did not look imposing, only ridiculous.

There were a good many people, mostly women, already in Baba Atal's shrine when I went in. Many women were gently pressing the marble pillars of the enclosure round about the tomb. Some women seated were gently beating the marble slabs between the pillars with their closed fists in the fashion so agreeable to the luxurious Indian, being a sort of massage universally practised and much appreciated in India. This peculiar exhibition of feminine tenderness led me to inquire into the history of Baba Atal, and I learned that he was the youngest son of Har Govind the sixth guru of the Sikhs. One of his playmates, it seems, died somewhat suddenly, I suppose, and he, the guru's son, in his extreme grief, performed the miracle of bringing his dead companion back to life. His father was very angry when he heard what had occurred, but little Baba, only seven years of age, said, in extenuation of his presumptuous act, that he had given his own life for that of his friend, and saying this fell down and passed away. The seven storeys of the tower, which is the tomb of Baba Atal, are said to commemorate the age of this unselfish child.

The miraculous power of Baba Atal is still an article of faith with the Sikhs and attracts them to his tomb, which is to them a veritable temple where the saintly child is invoked for the removal of troubles or the fulfilment of desires.

From what I had seen in the various visits described in the preceding pages, it was an obvious deduction that if Brahmanism and the Hindu gods had been excluded from the *sanctum sanctorum* of the temple, they were more than tolerated in its environs.

For years past the question, "Are the Sikhs Hindus?" has been raised from time to time, and discussed in public prints, not without acrimony. By a certain "advanced" party the question has been answered emphatically in the negative; but the old Sikhs, including some of the ruling Sikh chiefs, have expressed the opposite view, and the conflict of opinions has been productive of what might almost be regarded as a schism in the sect. Of course the question is primarily one for the Sikhs themselves, and not for outsiders; though the Indian Government, with a view to creating a valuable recruiting ground for its army, has, through its military officers and otherwise, done what was possible to foster the growth of Sikhism as a *distinct cult*. The idea underlying this policy is apparently that Sikhism, divorced from ordinary Hinduism and stimulated by its own martial traditions and its militant creed, would provide a special, distinct and numerous class of professional fighting men available for the Indian army. That this State encouragement, or stimulation, has not been without results, would appear from the increase in the number of Sikhs *as recorded in the latest census returns*.[1] In the interests of army recruiting, the policy adopted by the Indian authorities will doubtless prove advantageous, until, perhaps, the fateful day comes when Guru Govind Singh's parasitic peepul-tree (have others ever heard of it, or is it only mythical?) shall have completely destroyed its host at Sohawah Sahib in Bikanir. *Then*, if I have not been misinformed, a new chapter of history is to be unfolded. Time will show.

Meanwhile I may note that as recently as 1905 the "advanced" party seems to have had sufficient influence to have Hindu idols removed from the *parkarma* or larger ambulatory referred to on a previous page. Nevertheless, only last year (1907) an apparently well-informed writer

[1] Referring to this point, Mr. M. MacAuliffe, I.C.S., M.R.A.S., made the following remarks in a lecture which he delivered in July 1903 at Simla, on "The Sikh Religion and its Advantages to the State." "I have seen it stated that the last census shows an increase of the Sikh population. The increase is only in the figures, not in the population. At former enumerations village Sikhs, in their ignorance, generally recorded themselves as Hindus, though in the column for sect they often described themselves as Sikhs, but they were frequently totalled up as Hindus, as indeed they virtually were. With the experience gained by time a sharp line of demarcation has now been drawn between Sikhs and Hindus, but in reality there has been a great decrease in the Sikh population."

in the " Civil and Military Gazette " of Lahore, lamented the fact that the distinctive differences between Sikhism and Hinduism were melting away, a conclusion at which I had myself arrived some years ago. To me, a mere outsider, it appears that, at the present time, Sikhism, *as a distinct religion*, possesses little vitality, and that it will, in all probability, be reunited in a generation or two to the Hinduism from which it sprang, and with which it has so much in common. To pave the way for this reunion, the Brahmans, on their part, would, I dare say, willingly recognize Baba Nanak and Govind Singh (the founder and the reorganizer of Sikhism) and the other eight gurus also, as incarnations of some god or other, and find good scriptural authority for the worship of the *Granth*, which, it would appear, is already an object of adoration to many Hindus; while the many Sikhs, who still respect and even appeal to the old divinities of India, would not, in all likelihood, object to the formal admission of their *Gurus* and their *Book* into the Hindu Pantheon.

CHAPTER V

THE CENOTAPH OF MAHARAJA RANJIT SINGH AND THE BARBAROUS RITE OF SATI

WHAT may be called the period of the Sikh theocracy—when, as stated in a previous page, the ten inspired gurus or prophets successively directed the affairs of the community—was succeeded by a time during which the warlike followers of Guru Govind Singh, the last of the gurus, taking advantage of the unsettled and unprotected condition of the country, incident to the breaking up of the Great Mogul Empire, formed themselves into marauding bands, looting wherever opportunity offered, and retaining whatever they could. It was their day of revenge for past persecution; and villages in flames, with attendant horrors, bore painful witness to their religious zeal; but more particularly to their avarice and lust and to their detestation of the Muslims. Disorder reigned supreme, but the work of plunder and spoliation by the Sikhs was not unopposed by the Muhammadan and Hindu population of the lands they harried; and so it came about that self-interest drove the sporadic bands of lawless plunderers to place themselves under the ægis of the more adventurous and successful leaders of the sect who, with their trusty swords, were carving out fortunes for themselves and their retainers. Out of the prevailing conditions arose in due course various confederacies with barons at their heads, possessed in some cases of great power and prestige, and who by annexing cities and lands and appropriating the imperial revenues, became important and more or less independent territorial magnates. These confederacies, at least the strongest ones amongst them, were known as *misls*, and to the bold head of the Sukarchakia *misl*, Sardár Mahán Singh, was born in 1780 a son, Ranjít Singh, who by his indomitable courage and untiring persistence, by his remarkable astuteness and utter unscrupulousness, by his ruthlessness and the basest treachery, raised himself to a dominant position in the Punjab north of the Sutlej, and also in some of the neighbouring states, Jummu and Kashmir, for example. Over the wide territories which his genius for command had welded into one kingdom and his unbending will had kept in orderly subjection, Ranjít Singh ruled as Mahárája until his death in June 1839. But when this "lion of the Punjab," as he was called, passed away, his kingdom soon fell to pieces, and within only ten years of his demise it was conquered by British troops and incorporated in the possessions of the East India Company.

Without the walls of the city of Lahore, on the border of a vast *maidan* or open plain, and flanked by monuments of historical interest, stands the *Samadh* of Ranjít Singh, a photograph of which, with the mosque of Aurangzeb in the background, is reproduced opposite this page. The photograph, which was taken from an elevated standpoint within the Fort, shows sufficiently the main features of the structure with the central building surmounted by ornamental kiosks and a dome which, though attractive in appearance, is still in striking contrast with the noble simplicity of the marble domes of the stately mosque to the left in the picture. The place itself can boast of no antiquity. It is barely more than half a century old,[1] but yet old enough to carry one back to a state of society very different from the present, and to inhuman customs which have been suppressed by the firm hand of a civilized and civilizing Government. On one side of it is the little garden known as the Hazooree Bagh, the work of Ranjít himself, and on the other side stands the shrine of the Sikh Guru, Arjan Mal. Facing the cenotaph is the entrance to the fort and palace of the Mogul Emperors, now guarded by British soldiers.

Viewed from the open space between it and the Fort, the building presents a long double-storeyed façade which nearly conceals the cenotaph itself from sight. From a distance the mausoleum, with its domed roof and gilt finials, though not an imposing object, presents to the eye of the spectator a by no means unpleasing illustration of the mixed Hindu and Muhammadan style of architecture. A small central portal fitted with a carved wooden door gives entrance to the Samadh. Images of Hindu deities cut in red sandstone ornament the doorway.

The mausoleum, or rather cenotaph, has been erected in honour of a man conspicuous in his day and generation, and both on this account and because of certain interesting details connected with its history and architecture, is not undeserving of attention.

Passing through the small entrance doorway, I entered a long low room or vestibule. It contained a native string-bottomed cot, a rickety old table, a small pile of firewood, and a tin mug, evidently the property of one of the custodians of the place, who would see nothing inappropriate in letting these homely articles of domestic

[1] Mrs. Hervey saw it in an unfinished state in November 1850 ("Adventures of a Lady in Tartary, Thibet, China, and Kashmer," vol. i.).

Photo by Lala Jadu Kishan

THE CENOTAPH OF MAHÁRÁJA RANJIT SINGH, WITH THE MOSQUE OF AURANGZEB IN THE BACKGROUND

To face page 10

use lie about the very entrance to the Samadh of his venerated chief. Within this room is a staircase, by which I ascended to a large terrace on a level with the upper floor of the frontage.

Before entering the Samadh, I noticed an apartment in which the Ashtpujee Debi was enshrined in state. The Brahmans in attendance were very civil, but objected to admit me into the sacred chamber with boots on. I removed mine. Within the chapel there was nothing of any special interest. I was told that the *hom* is burnt twice a year on the uncovered space before the door of the Debi's chapel, and the exact spot, blackened by fire, was pointed out to me.

In reply to my inquiries the attendants asserted that the Ashtpujee Debi was the goddess who had given into the hands of Guru Govind Singh the sword of which he taught his people to make such good use, and hence the special place of honour assigned to her in the Samadh.

The central portion of the terrace already referred to is occupied by the lofty tomb, if it can be called so, of the Sikh king, and the posterior part of it by a separate building of very subordinate character, which covers the ashes of Ranjít's son Kharak Singh, and his grandson Nao Nihál Singh. The elder of these princes, there is good reason to believe, was slowly and deliberately poisoned; while the younger one, by a convenient accident, was crushed to death, by the falling of a portion of an archway on the very day on which the body of his father, Kharak Singh, was committed to the flames.

The building is a specimen of the mixed Hindu and Muhammadan style of architecture which came generally into fashion in Northern India after the time of the Emperor Akbar.[1] It consists of a lofty central chamber surmounted by a dome, with galleries all round. The ceiling is elaborately decorated with convex mirrors arranged in patterns bedded in stucco. In the middle of the central chamber is a marble canopy or baldachin about ten feet high, raised on pillars over a platform of marble. Beneath lie, perhaps, some of the ashes of the chief and

[1] Fergusson's "Handbook of Architecture," pp. 116–117.

of several others besides. Upon a small carpet on one side rests a copy of the "Granth Sahib," with a velvet coverlet over it. The side walls of the arches in the gallery are decorated with fresco paintings representing scenes from Hindu mythology taken chiefly from those inexhaustible sources of Hindu legendary lore, the Mahabharata and Ramayana. But the marble platform under the canopy is the most noteworthy object here. It is surmounted by a large lotus of the conventional pattern, also in marble, having grouped round it thirteen similar but smaller ones of the same material. Of these the big central ornament commemorates the departed king; four of the smaller ones as many wives who performed the rite of *sati* with their dead lord. Seven others mark the devotion of seven female slaves who also perished with the body of Ranjít Singh; the remaining two marble lotuses stand for a pair of pigeons, who, it is said, voluntarily fluttered down to die in the flames of the funeral pyre of the unscrupulous profligate but successful chief.

Several persons, hereditary custodians of the tomb and hangers-on generally, followed me about from idle curiosity or the hope of *backsheesh*. Conversing with these, and carefully avoiding the expression of any opinion of my own, I found that they were unanimous in praise of sati, and disapproved of the suppression of that rite by the British Government. It might have been a half-hearted regret on their part, and a mere captious disapproval of the interference of an alien government, but the feeling, as far as it went, appeared to me to be quite genuine.[1]

One of the custodians of the place explained to me that when a woman performed the rite of sati with the corpse of her husband, her act was so meritorious that it ensured for herself and her dead lord a place in heaven for as

[1] "The old crime of Sati, whereby Hindu widows were burned alive on the funeral pyres of their husbands, has ceased long ago throughout the British territories. The ideas from which it sprang have no longer any hold upon the minds of the highly-educated classes. Possibly the practice would revive among the less-educated classes if the British prohibition were withdrawn. The monuments always erected on the spots where the dread rite has been observed are regarded with popular veneration."—Sir R. Temple's "India in 1880," p. 196.

many years as there were hairs on her body. And I subsequently learned that the Brahmans, in order to give a precise idea of the period in question, reckon the hairs on the human body at some thirty-five millions.[1] Considered from this point of view, of what æons of bliss has not the Act for the suppression of sati deprived the much-married Hindu! When I spoke of the sufferings of the unfortunate women, I was assured that from the moment they ascended the pyre they were insensible to all pain, and only rejoiced at their fate amidst the flames that consumed them. As a matter of fact, they were often drugged with opium and bhang.[2]

The reality of sati was never so forcibly brought before my mind as when standing by these memorials of painful suffering. Sati, even to the Anglo-Indian, seems a far-off dimly historical thing like the gladiatorial contests in the Flavian Amphitheatre, but these eloquent stone records of only the last generation bring it nearer to one—obtrude it, as it were, into the very present. Standing here, one can picture the terrible scene as it occurred on thousands of occasions. One can see the bustling eager crowd, the excitement and the hubbub of what was really a holiday. One can hear the remark: "So and so is to be burnt to-day, and his wives will be burnt with him. Let us hasten to the scene, let us secure good places!" One can see the funeral pile erected upon an open space, and the victim, adorned as for a great festival, led three times round the pyre by the officiating Brahmans, in presence of the assembled multitude. One can see the dead man's son apply, with filial piety, the torch to the dry wood, and the devoted woman ascend the already kindled pile.[3] One can see the smoke and blaze, and hear, above the shouts of the

[1] Colebrooke's "Essays," vol. i. p. 135.

[2] "Travels in Kashmir," by G. T. Vigne, vol. i. pp. 82–86, may be consulted for some interesting details regarding satis witnessed by the author.

[3] "With this benediction, and uttering the mystic Namo Namah, she (the widow) ascends the flaming pile" (Colebrooke's "Essays," vol. i. p. 135). It would appear, however, that the widow was often placed upon the pyre and even bound down upon it with cords, or regularly and completely thatched in, before the torch was applied to the wood.

excited crowd, the agonized shrieks of the suffering woman in the grasp of the consuming flames. But, indeed, we are not left entirely to imagination, for European travellers, ancient and modern, have witnessed such scenes of horror and have described them. Bernier[1] tells of women whom he had seen forced into the fire by the Brahmans with long sticks, and of others, sometimes mere children, whom he had seen tied down hand and foot upon the pyre.

On the other hand there cannot be any doubt that in many countries, women have often voluntarily perished after the death of their husbands, animated by heroic devotion,[2] pride of race, or religious excitement. But in India the strongest motive would undoubtedly be horror of the Hindu widow's miserable, degraded, and abject position.

"One morning on dismissing the regiment from parade," writes Sir George Lawrence, "the havildar major (native adjutant) requested my permission to attend a 'tomasha' (an extraordinary sight). On inquiry it turned out that a suttee was about to take place in the neighbourhood of the cantonment of Neemuch, and I resolved to witness it myself. On reaching the spot I found a large crowd collected around a funeral pyre, on which a poor victim about to immolate herself was seated. Seeing a number of my own troopers in the crowd, I asked them if they would stand by me if I attempted to rescue the woman from her dreadful fate, and finding that they were quite willing, I approached the pyne near enough to address her, saying I was ready to save her life if she desired it. She expressed her gratitude, but refused, saying she was willing to die. Immediately afterwards the flames enveloped her, and in a few seconds she was burnt to ashes. Her calm intrepidity was most

[1] "Voyages," vol. ii. pp. 117–119.

[2] "Garcilasso says that a dead Ynca's wives volunteered to be killed, and their number was often such that the officers were obliged to interfere, saying that enough had gone at present; and according to Cieza, some of the women, in order that their faithful service might be held in more esteem, finding that there was delay in completing the tomb, would hang themselves up by their own hair, and so kill themselves."—Herbert Spencer's "Principles of Sociology," vol. i. p. 205.

astonishing, especially as she had not even the excitement of her husband's body to be consumed with her, only a portion of his clothes, as he himself had died far from his home." [1]

The great missionary Carey describes a sati which he witnessed in 1799. The victim ascended the pile "and danced on it with her hands extended as if in the utmost tranquillity of spirit," in order to show her contempt of death. When she lay down on the wood, she was secured in the usual way with bamboo poles laid across and fastened down, and was then consumed amidst the deafening shouts of the bystanders.[2]

The story of one romantic rescue from the pyre, and the sequel, can bear repetition. It is related of Job Charnock, the East India Company's agent in Bengal, and founder of Calcutta, that he

> "went one time with his ordinary guard of soldiers to see a young widow act that tragical catastrophe, but he was so smitten with the widow's beauty that he sent his guards to take her by force from her executioners, and conducted her to his own lodgings. They lived lovingly many years and had several children. At length she died, after he had settled in Calcutta, but instead of converting her to Christianity she made him a proselyte to Paganism; and the only part of Christianity that was remarkable in him, was burying her decently. He built a tomb over her, where all his life, after her death, he kept the anniversary day of her death by sacrificing a cock on her tomb, after the Pagan manner; this was and is the common report, and I have been credibly informed, both by Christians and Pagans, who lived at Calcutta under his agency, that the story was really true matter of fact." [3]

In regard to the sati of the wives of Ranjít Singh we have ample details. After the Ranís—unveiled to the public eye for the first time in their lives, and on foot, but accompanied by their attendants—had distributed their jewels amongst certain of the bystanders, the funeral procession was arranged, and proceeded slowly towards the pyre already erected for the dreadful ceremony. Heading the procession came the corpse of the deceased Mahárája, borne on a bier made in the form

[1] "Forty-three Years in India," by Sir George Lawrence, pp. 3–4.

[2] "Life of William Carey," by Dr. George Smith, pp. 107–109.

[3] Captain Hamilton, quoted in Wheeler's "Early Records of British-India," pp. 189–190.

of a ship, with sails and flags of cloth of gold, and the costly shawls of Kashmir. Next came the Ranís, habited in simple silk attire, without any ornaments about their persons, no longer on foot, but carried in open palanquins, offering to the onlookers an example of quiet dignity and heroic self-sacrifice. Immediately behind the princesses walked seven barefooted slave-girls, some of them not more than fourteen or fifteen years of age, whom superstition, and perhaps unlawful threats, had driven to sacrifice their young lives in the cruel flames, to add to the pomp of the deceased king's funeral. Arrived at the pyre, the Mahárája's bier was divested of its costly ornaments, which were then given away. The drums kept up a low solemn rumbling. The funeral ceremonies for the dead were performed by Brahmans, as well as by Sikh Gurus, while the Muhammadans, not to be behind the others in testifying their respect for the departed Mahárája, broke in frequently with "Ya-Allah." When the appropriate rites, which occupied nearly an hour, were completed, the corpse was respectfully deposited, by the grandees of the court, on the top of the funeral pile, built of dry wood strewn over with cotton seeds. The Ranís, one by one, taking precedence according to rank, ascended the ladder to the top of the pile, and seated themselves at the head of the corpse. The slave-girls then mounted and took up their position at the feet of the royal body. As they sat there awaiting their now inevitable doom, "a strong thick mat of reeds" was brought and put over them, and probably secured. They had looked their last on earth! To add to the combustibility of the mat it was saturated with oil. All the needful preparations being now completed, the sardárs and attendants descended from the pile, which was then lighted at the four corners. In a few minutes eleven human victims perished in the smoke and flames; but the pyre took two days to be entirely consumed.[1] From its ashes a few human bones and relics were carefully and privately gathered. These, after being placed in separate mortuary urns, were conveyed in great

[1] That sati was not exactly a compulsory ceremony is evident from the fact that some forty of the Ranís of Ranjít Singh survived him, of whom three were living in 1882.

state to the banks of the Ganges and committed to the waters of the sacred river. The remains of Ranjít Singh and the four Ranís were carried away from Lahore in five palanquins, with all the pomp and attention the deceased were accustomed to in their lifetime. The palanquin which contained the ashes of the Mahárája had its screens drawn back, while the others were closely curtained as though their modest occupants still shunned the public gaze. Tents of Kashmir shawls, having poles overlaid with silver and gold, were provided for the march, and these, with innumerable costly presents, were given away to the attendant Brahmans at the place where the remains of the chief and his consorts were finally entrusted to the sacred river.[1] Regarding such remains of the slave-girls as the fire may have left, the chronicler says nothing, so we may presume that they were neglected as unworthy of any special attention. On the spot where the sati was performed, now stands the Samadh of Mahárája Ranjít Singh.

For a people who believe in the transmigration of souls, and who practise cremation of the dead, monuments such as this can have but little significance; and indeed in their erection the Hindus merely followed the fashion of the Muhammadans, whose imposing and costly tombs formed so important a feature in the architectural works of the Muslim conquerors of India.[2]

From the turbulent annals of Sikhism I borrow one other painful and tragic episode in connection with sati, as it throws light on some points of interest which have not been touched upon in the previous pages. I give the story as it was related to me by an educated Sikh gentleman with whom I was well acquainted, and I may add that it is an historical fact and well known.

[1] The above details have been taken from the narrative of an eye-witness, Dr. J. M. Honigberger, who was "Physician to the Court of Lahore." See his "Thirty-three Years in the East." H. Bailliere, 219, Regent Street, London, 1852.

[2] Referring to Hindu *tombs* Colonel Sheman remarked that the object of such *tombs* "is ostensibly to keep the ground on which the bodies have been burnt from being defiled; and generally Hindoos have been content to raise small open terraces of brick and stucco work over the spot, with some image or emblem of the god upon it."—"Rambles and Recollections," vol. ii. chap. viii.

Sardár Jawahir Singh,[1] being suspected of treachery to the *Khalsa* or the *elect* (*i. e.* the Sikh brotherhood taken as a whole), was murdered by the Sikh soldiery, and as a sequel to this bloody deed his four widows were constrained, against their wishes and in spite of their entreaties, to become satis upon his funeral pyre, which was prepared on the maidan outside the Lahore Fort. In family conclave it had been decreed that these four innocent women should, in the presence of the assembled multitude, be burnt to ashes with the corpse of their husband, the fiction being, of course, maintained that the act was a *voluntary* one on their part.

On these solemn occasions the satis, conveniently presumed to be voluntary victims, are objects of especial veneration to the Hindus; and, when persons of rank, distribute amongst the bystanders, in their progress to the place of cremation, money as well as ornaments in token of their final farewell of this world and its vanities, while the admiring crowd respectfully crave their blessing. Jawahir Singh's four unhappy widows, advancing reluctantly towards the fatal pyre, were carrying out this usual procedure, attended by a guard of soldiers charged to protect them from the rabble and to ensure their duly reaching the place of sacrifice. But such uncontrollable rapacity had the demoralizing effects of constant looting produced in the hearts of the Sikh soldiery that the guards told off for the protection of the unfortunate women fell —both officers and men—to snatching the money and jewels from their nerveless hands. Nor were they content with that, for when the victims were on the point of ascending the funeral pile, the inhuman soldiery actually perpetrated the pitiless barbarity of *plucking* off the women's earrings and noserings, regardless of the pain they inflicted upon these helpless creatures in the bitterest moments of their supreme trouble. It was a disgraceful, a brutal scene; followed by another of striking and dramatic character.

Upon the fatal pile, and about to perish by fire, the

[1] Sardar Jawahir Singh was brother to Raní Jindan, the reputed mother of Mahárája Dhulíp Singh, who was for many years a well-known figure in English society.

women were, in the eyes of the multitude, transformed into true sibyls endowed with prophetic vision and capable of reliable vaticinations. Urged to disclose the future for the benefit of the people, the injured and indignant women, clothed in the dignity of conscious innocence, cursed the Khalsa from the bitterness of their hearts, and proclaimed aloud that their day of power was fast drawing to its close, and that within a twelvemonth the *raj* would pass into the hands of the *Angraz* (English), and so it came to pass!

The sati I have described was carried out on September 22, 1845; on December 14 of the same year the Sikhs crossed the Sutlej and attacked the British, and by February 20, 1846, Lahore was occupied by Sir Hugh Gough, and the strength of the Khalsa broken, though the final annexation of the Punjab did not take place till March 1849.

The rite of sati was once practised in nearly every part of India on the authority of certain texts and injunctions in the sacred books of the Hindus, from the Rig Veda downwards.[1] Some authorities, however, maintain that the Vedas do not sanction the rite of widow-burning, but rather the reverse. Indeed, the late Professor Max Müller affirmed that the particular text of the Rig Veda usually cited in support of sati was deliberately falsified by the unscrupulous Brahmans.[2]

At what precise period the rite of sati became general in India, history does not inform us. We know it was practised to some extent at the time of Alexander's invasion of India in the fourth century before the Christian era, and it is alluded to in the Ramayana and Mahabharata.[3] The causes which probably helped to encourage and perpetuate this cruel custom are well and briefly stated by Sir A. C. Lyall in the following words:

"Perhaps the best example of a selfish device obtaining vogue under the cloak of a necessary rite is afforded by the famous practice of a widow becoming *Sati*, or burning herself alive with her dead husband, which is undoubtedly, as Sir H. Maine has pointed out,

---

1 Coleridge's "Essays," vol. i. p. 135.

2 Professor Max Müller's "Selected Essays," vol. i. pp. 333–336.

3 Dr. Rajendra Lala Mitra's "Indo-Aryans," vol. ii. p. 137.

connected with the desire to get rid of her right, if she is childless, to a tenancy for life upon her husband's lands. It is also connected, among the great families, as may be easily observed still in certain parts of India, with the wish of an heir to free himself by this simple plan from many inconveniences and encumbrances entailed upon him by the bequest of a number of stepmothers, who cannot marry again."[1]

Polygamy may also, as Dr. Marshman believed, have contributed in another way to encourage sati, through the jealousy of the old husbands of young wives, who, clinging to their exclusive possession even in death, would leave instructions with their heirs to use every possible means to accomplish the desired sacrifice.[2] But the origin of the custom must be looked for deeper and further back. From the very earliest ages down to our own times it has been the practice amongst many barbarous peoples, who believe in the existence of the soul after death, to kill the wives and favourite slaves of a king, chief, or other person on the occasion of his funeral obsequies, in order that they might attend the deceased and minister to his wants in the shadow-land beyond the grave. The practice is still in full force and carried to terrible excess amongst many African tribes. It was at one time very widely spread, but came in many countries to be gradually replaced by ceremonies derived from the original observances, but not involving loss of life. For instance, the widow would be laid upon the pyre, but removed before the flames actually reached her; or images representing wives and slaves would be consumed with the corpse. There would appear to be some ground for concluding that in the Vedic age in India the practice of widow-burning had gone somewhat out of fashion, though, perhaps, never quite given up, and that modified ceremonies like those to which reference has just been made were coming into favour. The subsequent revival, under Brahmanical influences, of widow-burning, and its continuance to our own day, may be largely due to the causes pointed out by Sir Henry Maine. Of course, the degradation of the widow who chose to survive her husband would

[1] "Asiatic Studies," by Sir Alfred Lyall, p. 56.

[2] Bishop Heber's narrative of a journey through the Upper Provinces of India, 1824–25.

be a necessary complement to sati. Make the position of the widow intolerable, and sati would be chosen by every high-spirited woman as the lesser of two evils. To the affectionate wife and to the timid soul, the priest offered reunion with the dead and long ages of happiness in the celestial mansions, thereby throwing the halo of religious sanctions over a horrid and revolting custom. Indeed, sati would seem to be a survival of a very ancient rite, fostered and maintained for selfish ends. Unfortunately, the women of India have not only suffered in person by the cruel rite of sati, but have had a slur—no doubt an unmerited one—cast upon them by historians seeking to account for the origin of the hideous custom. Strabo [1] tells us, and several travellers have repeated the same story,[2] that sati was introduced by law in order to put a stop to the widespread crime of husband-poisoning, to which Indian wives who fell in love with young men were said to be particularly given.

I am not aware that, with the exception of Ram Mohun Roy, who was largely a product of European influences, any one of the many religious reformers who have appeared from time to time in India, loudly preaching theological doctrines more or less heterodox, made any effort whatever to suppress, or even to discourage, the inhuman rite of sati. It is true the author of the Dabistan (A.D. 1615–70) observes that:

> "The enlightened doctors say that by a woman's becoming suttee is meant that on her husband's decease she should consume in the fire along with him all her desires, and thus die before the period assigned by nature; as in metaphysical language woman signifies 'passion'; or in other words she is to cast all her passions into the fire; but not throw herself into it along with the deceased, which is far from being praiseworthy."[3]

Probably Muslim influences and feelings opposed to sati were finding expression in the doctrines thus referred to by Moshan Fani; but it remained for foreign rulers,

[1] Strabo, bk. xv. chap. 30. The great geographer himself doubts the existence of the law, and, necessarily, of the reason assigned for its enactment.

[2] For instances, see Dr. Norman Chever's "Indian Medical Jurisprudence," p. 104.

[3] "Dabistan," translated by Shea and Troyer, vol. ii. p. 77.

unhampered by unhealthy Brahmanical traditions, to discountenance and eventually abolish the barbarous practice. The Emperor Akbar, we learn from Abu-l-Fazl, appointed inspectors to prevent women being forcibly burnt with their dead husbands, and on one occasion he mounted his horse and rode at full speed to prevent, in person, an unwilling woman being sacrificed on the pyre to the unnatural bigotry of her son.[1] But whatever the Mogul rulers may have done towards mitigating the horrible custom, the credit of abolishing it belongs to the British.

In 1824–25, Bishop Heber, travelling through the Upper Provinces of India, learnt from Dr. Marshman that satis had latterly become more frequent in Bengal, and that the famous missionary attributed this unhappy fact to the increasing luxury of the upper and middle classes, and their expensive imitation of European habits, which often so narrowed their means as to make them anxious to be freed from the necessity of supporting their widowed relations. If the presence of the European in India tended, however indirectly, to increase the sacrifice of Hindu widows, it is satisfactory to know that, within five years of the Bishop's tour, vigorous preventive measures were adopted by Lord William Bentinck, who, as Governor-General of India, passed a law in 1829 under which any one who abetted the act of sati would be considered guilty of culpable homicide. The effect of this regulation has been the almost complete suppression of sati throughout the British possessions in India, though it still prevails in the Independent Hill States on the borders of British territory, and occurs occasionally in the countries ruled by feudatory princes. In 1883 a sati was performed at Utarna, in Rajputana, within five miles of a British cantonment, but the abettors of the crime were severely punished by the Jeypore Durbar, probably at the instance of the Governor-General's agent.

Quite recently, too, that is in 1904, 1905 and 1906, a few widow-burnings have, in spite of the law, been carried out in British territory under the influence of a Hindu revival. Yet we may be permitted to hope that a few generations

[1] 'Akbar-nama of Abu-l-Fazl,' Elliot's "Muhammadan Historians of India," edited by Dowson, vol. vi. pp. 68–69.

hence, the crime which had been countenanced and encouraged in India for more than twenty centuries will be extinct, and become as revolting to the feelings of the people as to those of their foreign rulers, affording an illustration of the mode in which legislation may contribute to form the manners, the morals, and the character of a people.

CHAPTER VI

BRAHMOS OF THE PUNJAB

SECTION I.—SIXTEENTH ANNIVERSARY OF THE LAHORE BRAHMO SAMAJ

ALTHOUGH by no means unaware of the existence of the new sect of theists known as Brahmas, or Brahmos, nor unacquainted with their interesting history and generally-accepted doctrines,[1] I had not visited any of their places of worship when the following public notice attracted my attention :

"The sixteenth anniversary of the Punjab Brahmo Samaj will be celebrated on Sunday, the 9th of November, 1879, at the Brahma Mandir, Anarkali, Lahore. The public are cordially invited to attend on the occasion."

Taking advantage of the Society's invitation to the public generally, I went to their place of worship in time for the morning service.

I found the mandir situated in a poor quarter of the town, and devoid of any architectural pretensions whatever; a mere hall about fifty feet long, by eighteen or twenty feet wide, with a verandah in front, partly converted into a little vestry, where Brahmo publications were exposed for sale; and two narrow verandahs on the right and left sides, running along the entire length of the building, which, to suit the climate, was provided with ample means of ventilation.

On the occasion of the anniversary celebration, regarding which I am writing, there were no pictures, statues, or such objects, in the hall. They would have been out of place in the temple of this purely theistic and

[1] Of these I have given an account in my book, "The Brahmans, Theists and Muslims of India." T. Fisher Unwin. 1907.

iconoclastic sect. The occasion was, however, a special one, and some attempt at decoration seemed not only permissible, but called for. Flowers and leaves were innocent enough to be admitted into the precincts of the austere theistic hall, and were used, though not profusely, in giving something of a festive character to the blank walls of the plain brick building. Between the doorways, on small wooden brackets, were placed glass vases with flowers in them; the doors were ornamented with strings of leaves and flowers. Within the hall, on one side of the entrance doorway, stood an American clock, and on the other a charity-box, labelled in English and, lower down, in Urdu characters.

The floor was carpeted with cotton carpets, known in India as *daris*. White floor-cloths (not quite clean) were laid for the people to squat upon. A portion of the extreme end of the hall—perhaps a fourth or fifth of the entire room—had been partitioned off by a temporary screen for the accommodation of such women and children as might care to attend. From this extemporized gynecium they could hear, and perhaps see, all that was going on, without being exposed to the rude gaze of the male worshippers. Yet, when the service was proceeding, some little children, and a few girls of about ten or eleven years of age, well dressed and well bejewelled, more irrepressible or more curious than the rest, came tripping, with tinkling anklets, into the verandah, to have a few furtive looks through the open doors at what was going on within the hall. With the exception of myself all present were natives.

A little in advance of the temporary screen of the gynecium the Brahmo missionary from Bengal took up his position. There was no pulpit or raised platform of any kind for the preacher. The Eastern does not like to stand, and our Brahmo missionary from Bengal was no exception to the general rule, for he sat squat on the floor, the place immediately in front of him being walled in by flower-pots and strewn with flowers. Here he prayed and preached and sang in turns, seated the whole while, and with his eyes shut. The hymns for the day were taken from a small vernacular hymn-book of only a few printed pages. The choir-singers and musicians were the same three Muhammadans I had seen at the Arya Samaj, described in the next chapter. Several persons present joined in the hymns, swaying their bodies about gently to the measure. There were prayers, long ones too, in which the congregation took part in a devout manner.

In his prayers the Brahmo missionary asked that Brahma would cause the Hindus, Muhammadans, and Christians to turn to him and become Brahmos. I could not help thinking that much of the forms of the prayers, or rather the style of the expressions used, were copied, consciously or unconsciously, from the Prayer-book of the Church of England.

During his lecture the missionary, to give point to his speech, quoted an episode from the Ramayana about "Seta Dabi" and "Hanooman Sahib," in which the poet says that the monkey-god destroyed a certain city because he could not find the name of God there. At one stage of the proceedings, while a hymn was being sung, two or three men got up and went about placing garlands of flowers round the necks of the people present.

As far as I could judge, the congregation was drawn from the ranks of the well-to-do middle class of the native society of Lahore. The upper classes sent no representatives, nor did the labourers and artisans. Several Bengalis were present. The entire congregation, excluding the women and children behind the curtain, did not, on the sixteenth anniversary of the Punjab Brahmo Samaj, exceed fifty souls, and of these several had been present at, and taken part in, the Arya celebration described in the following chapter—a fact which, I take it, is a fair indication of the absence at that time of narrow sectarian feeling in both movements. At the door I purchased some Brahmo publications, and then left the hall, carrying away with me the impression that the Brahmo theistic church, which originated in Bengal, had certainly not met with much success in the Punjab.

SECTION II.—RENUNCIATION BY A BRAHMO OF HIS SECULAR LIFE

On a subsequent occasion I was present at an interesting ceremony which took place in the Lahore Brahmo mandir. Public notice of the event was given in the following terms :

" We have been requested to inform the public that Pandit ——, who is a minister of the Punjab Brahmo Samaj, has resolved to enter the Sanyasa Ashrama, *i. e.* to renounce his secular life, on the 20th instant, it being the 32nd anniversary of his birthday. The ceremony of his initiation into the new sphere of life will be performed in the hall of the Brahmo Mandir on that day, at 6.30 p.m. The public are cordially invited to witness the ceremony."

The public, at any rate the native public (for Europeans in India care for none of these things), accepted the invitation as cordially as it was given, and in hundreds thronged the Brahmo mandir long before the appointed hour. Through the courtesy of a member of the Samaj a chair was placed for me quite close to the raised platform, surrounded with plants and flowers, on which the officiating minister was to take his seat for the purpose of conducting the ceremony of initiation. The man who had determined to renounce his secular life was a married man with three children, and held a good appointment on a salary of a hundred and fifty rupees a month. He had deliberately resigned his post in order to lead a religious life, and the probable fate of his wife and family was a matter of speculation to many present that evening.

The proceedings, which were throughout conducted with great solemnity, were carried out in accordance with a programme of the evening's work, copies of which were distributed amongst the audience.

The candidate, with head and face shaved quite smooth, appeared before the audience, well-clad in garments dyed of the orange-yellow colour affected by ascetics in India. The officiating minister, a native gentleman of good standing, engaged for the most part in the secular work of vernacular education, wore his ordinary dress, but had, in honour of the occasion, thrown an orange-coloured sheet over his shoulders. After the preliminary divine service, the minister gave the candidate a new name, by which he was to be known henceforth, and read out various precepts, culled from the Hindu Shastras, in regard to a virtuous life. He whispered into the ear of the new ascetic the "sacred watchword," and then addressed him at great length upon the responsibilities which his new life imposed upon him.

But the most interesting portion of the evening's proceedings was the new sanyasi's own address, fluently delivered in Urdu, interspersed with a very few expressive English words and phrases. In this speech he explained to the assembly that the step he had just taken was not a hasty one, conceived and carried out on the spur of the moment, but had been the subject of anxious thought and long deliberation. Years previously he had proposed to abandon the world for the life of a sanyasi, but had been dissuaded from doing so by a most worthy man, himself a sanyasi, who strongly advised him not to act precipitately, but to wait till he felt strong enough to make so great a sacrifice. The time for action had at length come. In anxious and earnest prayer and communion with the All-father had been passed the night preceding the day on which the final step had been taken. Many conflicting feelings had contended for mastery in the speaker's breast. Sore had been the temptation of the world's emoluments and pleasures. Suggestions of the comfort, enjoyment and consideration to be derived from his regular and not inconsiderable earnings stole into his mind, in seductive whispers, but the thought of what Gautama, the Buddha, had voluntarily renounced—his princely rank, his lovely wife, his child but a day old—brought forcibly before the troubled mind of the doubter that, in his case, the sacrifice would, by comparison, be inconsiderable indeed. That reflection had determined his present action, and as for the future it was in God's hands. But though now a sanyasi and a beggar in the sight of men, he had no intention of abandoning his faithful wife and his little children; and it would be his care to provide for them in the years that were to come. This last statement was received with prolonged applause by the audience. Turning away from the assembled crowd and facing a screened doorway behind which his wife had, it appears, been placed, he addressed her in pathetic words broken with sobs, and so worked upon the feelings of his auditors that many in the hall that night were deeply affected even to tears.

The step taken by the pandit was of course freely criticized by the orthodox party and by non-Brahmos generally. It was asked, tauntingly, and perhaps not unreasonably, what Brahmos, who professed to have risen superior to all the puerile rites and ceremonies of ancient Hinduism, had to do with the yellow dress of the sanyasi? And the idea of a *grahasthi* (worldly) Babu initiating a man into an ascetic order, and conferring upon him the title of *Swami*, was held up to ridicule by the opponents of Brahmoism.

SECTION III.—A BRAHMA OR BRAHMO WEDDING

On the 3rd of January, 1884, I received the following invitation, beautifully printed in gold letters on a pink glazed card :

" *God's mercy alone availeth.*

" LALLA * * * *

presents his compliments to J. C. Oman, Esq., Professor of N. Science, and solicits the favour of his kind attendance at the Anarkali Brahmo Mandir on 5th January, 1884, at 6.30 p.m., to witness the nuptials of his daughter * * * with Lalla * * *

" N.B.—Kindly present this card at the door of the mandir."

At a quarter after six, on the appointed day, I was at the closed door of the mandir, and found it besieged by a crowd eager to get admittance. The Brahmo mandir I have already described, and will only add that, on this occasion, it was illuminated with *cheraghs* in the usual Indian manner. I took my stand outside amongst some native friends and waited. The door was at length opened partially, and then commenced a long struggle between the masters of ceremonies and the visitors. Probably some of those so anxious to assist at the ceremony had come uninvited and were denied admittance; be this as it may, the door was at very short intervals closed forcibly on all, whether invited guests or otherwise. Meanwhile, a band of native musicians, armed with instruments of European make, amongst which the shrill bagpipes were unmistakable, filled the air with what was looked upon as English music, "Auld Lang Syne," and "Home, Sweet Home," being at least recognizable in the medley to which we were treated. I pressed forward and stood as close as I could get to the entrance, when a native gentleman beckoned me to follow him, and introduced me into the mandir by a side door. On entering I had the pleasure of meeting and exchanging greetings with the president of the Society and the pandit—now *Swami*—who, as already described, had assumed the garb of an ascetic, and was going to act as priest for the solemnization of the marriage.

I was courteously accommodated with a chair quite close to the raised platform, where the nuptial ceremony was to be performed. When the hall was well filled, and the crowd induced to sit down on the floor as well as they could—a business of no little difficulty, and occupying more than an hour—the Swami took his seat on the daïs covered with red cloth, which had been erected against the side wall of the hall, between two doors. At the four corners of the daïs plantain trees had been put up, and the entire hall was decorated with strings of flowers.

After a preliminary hymn had been sung by certain hired musicians, the bridegroom, arrayed in scarlet clothes, entered, or rather slid noiselessly in, at one of the doors just beside the daïs, and sat down on the right hand of the Swami, while the bride's father, followed by the bride, entered by the other door, and, as unobtrusively as possible, took their places on the left hand of the minister, the father being somewhat in advance and the bride modestly in the background. At the entry of the wedding-party some rose-water was sprinkled about over the assembled guests as they sat huddled together on the floor.

How did the bride look? How was she dressed? How did she behave on this interesting occasion? I regret to have to confess that to these important questions I can give only very unsatisfactory replies. The bride was dressed entirely, from head to foot, in red. The *chádar*, or sheet, which covered her head was drawn completely over her face, so that her countenance was invisible to us all, and her voice, in responding to the minister's interrogations, was quite inaudible, even where I sat. The bridegroom, a good-looking young fellow of about twenty, seemed to be sufficiently self-possessed, and did his part creditably.

The marriage ceremony was very simple. It consisted in the formal declaration by the father, in words dictated by the minister, that he was freely bestowing the hand of his daughter on the bridegroom. The bridegroom was asked whether he would take the young woman to be his wife, and, of course, answered in the affirmative. The bride was similarly questioned with respect to the young man, and gave a suitable response. The minister then addressed the young couple on the duties and responsibilities of married life, and made each one repeat after him a formula, much resembling that in the Prayer-book of the Church of England (and probably adopted from it), which begins with the words, "I, *M.*, take thee, *N.*, to be my wedded wife," etc., etc.

When these formal and necessary declarations had been made and obligations accepted, the minister joined the hands of the bride and bridegroom and tied them together with a string of flowers. At this point the musicians set up an appropriate hymn, and, while the music continued, the wedded pair sat silently joined together by the floral chain.

The minister then addressed the married couple and the audience. He dwelt upon the many disadvantages and evils of child-marriage, and commended, in glowing terms, the courage of the bride's father, who, in defiance of custom and public opinion had, from a sense of duty, educated his girl with the care only given in ordinary cases to the education of a boy, and had not sought a husband for her till she had attained the mature age of *fifteen*, and was sufficiently instructed to take upon herself the responsibilities of married life. The minister condemned very forcibly the existing Hindu system of child-marriage, which led inevitably to the shipwreck of so many lives, and he exhorted his hearers to come forward manfully and assist, by example, the reform to which so many were ready to give their approval, but which so few were prepared to carry out in practice. The Swami spoke eloquently in respect to English home-life, as he had heard it described by Indians who had lived in England, and told his hearers that it was far more important for the people of India to learn from the Englishman how to make a quiet, happy home, than to acquire from him skill in any number of mechanical arts or industries, important as these may be to the welfare of the country.

The Swami's speech concluded the proceedings, and the meeting broke up with a distribution of garlands, and amidst showers of flowers.

A few years subsequent to the events just narrated the Swami referred to, Shiv Narayan Agnihotri, lost, for certain reasons, the goodwill of his *confrères* in the Brahmo Samaj, and, upon the advice of friends, tendered his resignation as a member of that Samaj. To his surprise and disappointment his resignation was accepted, and the Swami, a man of forceful character, thereupon set up, in 1888, a new religious sect, or society, under the name of *Dewa Samaj*, of which, perhaps, more may yet be heard, as it seems to have been manifesting signs of vitality as recently as 1905.

CHAPTER VII

THE ARYA SAMAJ AND ITS FOUNDER

SECTION I.—INTRODUCTORY

THE presence, as rulers, of the Muhammadans in India ever since the beginning of the eleventh century has had an influence upon the religious development of the Hindus, which the historical student can hardly help noting, as successive Hindu reformers appear—at long intervals it is true—on the stage of Indian history, bearing aloft the standard of revolt against the national polytheism and the rigid distinctions of caste. The direct influence of Islam on the teaching of many Indian reformers is unquestionable, and that particular form of the Muhammadan religion known as Sufiism—which, in all probability, owes its origin to a Hindu source (the Vedanta philosophy)—was welcomed home, as it were, by certain Hindus with a warmth which a purely exotic system of ideas would not have called forth.

One important religious reformation, Sikhism, alluded to in an earlier part of this volume, was undoubtedly due to the stimulating presence of Islam and the natural leaning of the Indian mind to the doctrines held by the Sufis. The theistic reforms now agitating India are, however, of a somewhat different character from those which preceded them, and bear the unmistakable stamp of Christian influence and of English political and social ideas and principles.

There have been two distinct developments of the modern theistic movement in India, known respectively as the Brahmo or Brahma Samaj and the Arya Samaj. The former sect, though consisting of a mere handful of men and women, has a reputation in Europe, because the leaders of the sect have been men who deliberately kept themselves as prominently as possible before the English world, visited England, won the personal regard of many Europeans both at home and in India, and unintentionally raised false hopes of their conversion to the religion of Christ. Indeed it is not too much to say that the appreciative welcome given to Brahmoism by many pious Europeans was due to a belief that Brahmoism was the first step towards a great turning of the people of India to the Christian faith.[1]

The Arya Samaj which forms the subject of this paper, though by no means less interesting than the Brahmo Samaj, is younger, and is certainly less known outside India.

Section II.—The Life and Teaching of Dayanand Saraswati Swami

Of the life of Dayanand Saraswati Swami, the founder and acknowledged head of the Arya Samaj, many interesting facts are known, and will repay study. In the latter part of 1879 Dayanand commenced the publication of his autobiography in the pages of the "Theosophist,"[2] and from this source as well as from "The Life and Teaching of Swami Dayanand Saraswati," by Bawa Chhajju Singh,[3] most of the particulars respecting his personal history here given have been drawn.

Son of a Guzerati Brahman, Dayanand's original name was Mool Shankar. According to his own narrative, he had been carefully instructed in the Vedas, which means that he had been made to commit a great portion of them to memory, and had been initiated at an early age into the rites and mysteries of the Saiva sect to which his family belonged; but while still a mere boy his mind had revolted against the practices of idolatry. He could not bring himself to acknowledge that the image of Siva seated on his bull, the helpless idol which, as he had himself observed in the watches of the night, allowed the

[1] I have treated of this subject, in some detail, in another book, "The Brahmans, Theists and Muslims of India," in a chapter entitled 'Theism in Bengal.'

[2] October 1879, December 1879, November 1880.

[3] Addison Press, Lahore. 1903.

SWAMI DAYANAND, FOUNDER OF THE ARYA SAMAJ

To face page 130

mice to run over it with impunity, ought to be worshipped as the Omnipotent Deity. To quote the autobiography :

> "Is it possible, I asked myself, that this semblance of man, the idol of a *personal* god, that I see bestriding his bull before me, and who, according to all religious accounts, walks about, eats, sleeps, and drinks, can hold a trident in his hand, beat upon his dumroo (drum), and pronounce curses upon men, is it possible that he can be the Mahadeva, the Great Deity?"

The sudden death of a sister produced a great impression on the naturally religious temperament of the young man. He resolved to give up the world and to devote himself entirely to a religious life. To marriage he had an extreme aversion, but his parents, believing that domestic life would tend to wean the young enthusiast from his religious mania, were all the more anxious to give him a wife, and made arrangements accordingly. Dayanand, however, now twenty-one years of age, ran away from home to avoid matrimony, and set out upon his wanderings with the object of pursuing, without let or hindrance, the study of metaphysics, a branch of knowledge which he hoped to acquire from the learned and devout pandits, sanyasis, and yogis, to be found in different parts of India.

After leaving home he got himself admitted into the ascetic order of Brahmachari, or religious students, and was wandering about in the habit of that order, and under a new name, when his father, a respectable man in easy circumstances, who had been constantly in search of his runaway son, at length traced him successfully and came up with him. The Swami relates most naïvely, and with apparent unconsciousness of the ugliness of falsehood and duplicity, that on the sudden and unwelcome appearance of his irate father, he at once assured the old man, falling at his feet in the most abject manner to appease his wrath, that in leaving his parents he had acted upon bad advice, that, like a true prodigal son, he was on the point of returning home, that his father's arrival at this critical moment was most providential, and that he would willingly accompany his parent back to his native village. The father, however, did not trust his pious son's protestations. He placed Dayanand under surveillance, but the young man managed to elude the vigilance of his guards and effected his escape, to pursue, without further interference from his parents (for they appear to have quite lost all trace of him), his wandering life of adventure in quest of knowledge.

Amidst pathless jungles, in busy cities, and amongst the snows of the Himalayas, did Dayanand travel for years with supreme indifference to bodily hardships; conversing and disputing with learned pandits and holy ascetics, ever in earnest search of "the *secret* knowledge, the Vidya, or true erudition of a genuine Yogi: the Mooktee, which is reached only by the purity of one's soul and *certain attainments*, unattainable without it. Meanwhile, the performance of all the duties of man towards his fellow-men, and the elevation of humanity thereby." Such is the statement of the object of his life which the Swami gave to the inquiring head of a prosperous monastery; but it would be very interesting to learn what Dayanand's idea of duty to his fellow-men really was, and whether his social and moral code recognized the obligations of strict honesty in word and deed. "It is the duty of every son to serve his parents with all possible devotion while they are still living"—a precept laid down by Dayanand himself [1]—is in curious contrast with his own conduct towards his parents, and only shows how little theoretical ideas of right and wrong govern men's actions.

While visiting the sacred places on the banks of the Narbada, as a religious student, the young Guzerati Brahman zealously sought admission to the sect of the Sanyasis; his chief reason, at that time, being that he was required by the rules which regulate the lives of Brahmacharis to prepare and cook his own food, which tasks made an undue demand upon the time he wished to devote to his studies. He was still under the age when men are ordinarily admitted to the privileges and duties of important ascetic sects; but favourably impressed by the student's diligence and character, and unable to resist his importunities, his then *guru*, one Purnanand, a learned sanyasi, initiated him into the sect in his twenty-

[1] "Theosophist," vol. i. p. 151.

fourth year. On that occasion the initiate received the name of Dayanand, by which he was known ever after.

Once, in his wanderings, Dayanand made the acquaintance of some Raj pandits of great learning, and was invited to dinner by one of them. He went, but what was his horror to find a large company assembled round a meat dinner, apparently including beef (for he refers to these pandits as "beef-eating"). Dayanand turned away in disgust from the repast, and hurried from the spot.

However, from these beef-eating pandits Dayanand borrowed a copy of the Tantras. "No sooner had he opened one of these than he was astonished at the nature of its contents. They were so obscene, so utterly subversive of the moral and social relations which have ever existed between one member and another of a family, and between one member and another of society at large, that no one, not absolutely and hopelessly depraved and debased, could help recoiling at the bare contemplation of what they taught." [1]

In his pursuit of the so-called science of Yog, the enthusiastic ascetic had been studying certain works which treated of the nervous system. He had not succeeded in grasping the descriptions and explanations he had read and pondered over, and began to doubt their correctness. While in this frame of mind, he happened to see a corpse floating down the river, and resolved, there and then, to bring to the test of actual comparison with nature the anatomical science of his books. He entered the river, dragged the corpse out of the water, and "with a large knife" commenced a dissection, which resulted in his satisfying himself that the books were totally and entirely incorrect, whereupon he tore them into pieces, and flung them into the river along with the mutilated corpse. Dayanand does not state what particular points of human anatomy he wished to clear up, and, when one calls to mind the refined methods of modern research, there is something droll about his proceeding to carry out his anatomical investigations "with a large knife." But even such a rude instrument would

[1] Bawa Chhajju Singh, "The Life and Teachings of Swami Dayanand Saraswati," p. 38.

be quite aid enough to demonstrate the untruth of much that is affirmed regarding the structure of the human body in Hindu books on anatomy. For instance, it is asserted in such works, and currently believed by the pandits, that six organs, known as *chakras* or wheels, somewhat resembling the lotus are to be found in the human body, placed one above the other, and joined together by three connecting vessels. These *chakras* have different colours, and from four to sixteen petals. But wild as are these statements they are sober when compared with the still more imaginative declaration that the human body contains a tortoise, a serpent, a goose, and fire. Whatever may have been the origin of these fanciful statements, a native writer in "The Calcutta Review," [1] assured us that they are accepted as verities by the Brahmans and, of course, by orthodox Hindus in general. Such being the teachings of Hindu anatomical science, we need be at no loss to understand how readily the Swami could, with the aid of his large knife, satisfy himself that they were utterly false and nothing but impudent fabrications, if, indeed, they were ever intended to be taken literally. At the same time, the fact that Dayanand could handle a corpse, and actually dissect it, proves to what a degree he had emancipated himself from the ordinary, but deep-rooted prejudices of Hinduism. The grand figure of the Guzerati Brahman,[2] angrily and contemptuously consigning to the flowing river the so-called *science* of his ancestors will make an excellent subject for the Hindu painter when, at some future time, art in India, rising above the very narrow conventionalities which have characterized it so long, shall attain a true conception of its scope and limits.

During his wandering life Dayanand, according to his own confession, acquired the habit of using *bhang* to such an extent as to be at times under its intoxicating influence. While in this condition the houseless ascetic sought

[1] Article: 'Physical Errors of Hinduism,' by Baboo Bipin Behari Shome, "Calcutta Review," June 1849.

[2] The Christian missionaries have discovered that "The founder of the Arya sect, the late Dayanand Saraswati, was out of caste altogether, being the son of a Brahman father and a low-caste mother." Rev. Dr. John Morrison's "New Ideas in India," p. 30.

shelter one rainy night in the verandah of a temple of the bull-god Nandi. For him the huge idol which stood there had no sanctity, as he had long enjoyed the full assurance that he himself was Brahma—"a portion of Brahm; Jiv (soul) and Brahm, the deity, being one." So, finding the hollow interior of the god a convenient resting-place, he crept into it, and fell asleep. In the morning a woman came to the idol with her simple offerings of sugar and curds, and, mistaking the Swami for an incarnation of the god himself, begged him to accept her gifts. Dayanand, being hungry, was nothing loath to oblige her, and disposed of the curds and sugar without, as he says, attempting to disabuse her of her false impression with regard to his divinity. He adds, thankfully, that the curds presented by the woman, being sour, served to cure him of the effects of the *bhang*,[1] which he had been indulging in. For how much of his ecstatic visions and self-hallucinations the yogi is indebted to *bhang* it would be profitless to speculate, but that powerful narcotic contributes largely towards the creation of his wild fancies no reasonable person need doubt.

As we have already seen, Dayanand, a diligent student of Sanskrit lore, had been admitted at a comparatively early age into the sect of the Sanyasis; but he was himself very sensible of his own deficiencies, and desired most earnestly to continue his studies further. In the course of certain wanderings the fame of the great teacher, Swami Virjanand of Mathura, reached Dayanand, and he resolved to seek this learned man and place himself under his tuition. In fulfilment of this resolution he journeyed to Mathura, which town he reached on November 14, 1860. Dayanand's reception by Swami Virjanand, and his final dismissal on the completion of his studies, are so characteristic of certain phases of Indian life that I cannot refrain from describing them here in the appreciative if sometimes quaint phraseology of his Hindu biographer.

"The accounts he had heard of Virjanand's learning proved only too correct, and he immediately sallied forth in quest of his dwelling, which he was not long in finding. For there was scarcely any one in Mathura who was unacquainted with the name of the

[1] "Theosophist," vol. ii. p. 47.

Dandi Swami, who had not heard of his vast learning, and who did not know that the stern old sanyasi always lived with his doors shut. Dayanand knocked at the door, and the question came in sharp tones from within, 'who is there?'

"'A sanyasi, Dayanand by name,' was the reply.

"'Do you know anything of Sanskrit grammar?'

"'Yes, I have studied Saraswata, etc.'

"At this reply the door opened and Dayanand went in. Virjanand examined Dayanand, and, on the termination of the examination, told him that there was a vast difference between the true Aryan literature and the books composed by common mortals, and as for himself, he had absolutely no respect for the latter and never taught them. Dayanand could not disabuse his mind of the idea he had clung to for years in a moment, but the arguments of the Swami prevailed, and he eventually consented to have nothing to do with the works which had not the stamp of true science and true wisdom on them. He even went so far as to present the Jamuna with his old stock, so that Virjanand might be pleased to admit him as a pupil. But, though all this was satisfactory enough, the fact could not be lost sight of that Dayanand was a sanyasi, and Virjanand could not see how a sanyasi could afford to carry on his studies with him. 'I am not in the habit of teaching sanyasis,' said he; 'but if I take *you* in as a pupil, how will you manage to live?' Dayanand replied that he would find himself food somehow or other, no matter if it was the coarsest possible; all he cared for was knowledge, and that, he hoped, Virjanand would not refuse him. Finding him persistent in his entreaties, Virjanand at last granted Dayanand's prayer; and having raised a subscription of thirty-one rupees got him a copy of the Mahabhashya to commence his studies with.

"Shortly after Dayanand had come and taken up his abode at Mathura, a severe famine spread in the land, and even the well-to-do became sparing of their gifts to the suppliants. * * Dayanand behaved manfully in this period of trial, living on roasted gram, or on dry bread made of the same article, from day to day. These came to him from the house of Durga Khatri, Dakawála. * *

"In course of time, a certain pandit, Amar Lal, a man of philanthropic impulse and of unbounded charities, struck with the virtues of Dayanand, took upon himself to supply him with food and with books. He made a point of taking him daily home, and of seeing him take his meals in his presence. * * Another person, to whom Dayanand was indebted for pecuniary help, was one Hardev, who used to give him two rupees monthly for 'milk.'

"A money-changer, named Govardhan Das, also assisted him according to his mite, defraying his expenses on oil, which came up to four annas a month."[1]

Notwithstanding extreme poverty and discomfort, Dayanand pursued his studies most diligently for two and a half years with his famous guru, a very irascible man, for whom the devoted student cheerfully performed the most menial offices. When at length Dayanand felt that his education was completed, he approached his guru

[1] Bawa Chhajju Singh: "The Life and Teachings of Swami Dayanand Saraswati," pp. 72–74.

and, in accordance with immemorial custom, laid a pound of cloves before him and asked his permission to depart.

"Virjanand gave him his blessing, and called upon him to produce, after the fashion of the students of yore, suitable *dakshina* (present), marking the termination of his course of education. Dayanand answered that he had nothing that he could venture to offer to his most revered *guru*. 'Do you think I would ask you for anything you have not got?' was the rejoinder. Being *silenced* by the loving rebuke, Dayanand *said*:[1] 'Most holy sir, I am ready to lay at your feet whatever you think I have really got in my possession.' 'Dear son, you have got it, and that is *true knowledge*. If you would pay me my *dakshina*, give this knowledge to thy mother-land. The Vedas have long ceased to be taught in Bhartvarsha, go and teach them; teach the true Shastras, and dispel, by their light, the darkness which the false creeds have given birth to."[2]

Dayanand's life is, in some respects, a good example of that led by thousands of men in India, who for various and very opposite reasons adopt the wandering habits of one or other of the ascetic orders. Supported by the voluntary liberality of the people, these restless spirits travel immense distances over the country, carrying with them, to the remotest corners of the land, the ideas fermenting in the minds of the more vigorous leaders of Hindu theological speculation. The adventures incident to their vagabond life, unaccompanied as it is by either special danger or peculiar hardship, have charms sufficient to allure a very considerable number of idle men to take up the calling of yogi or sanyasi. But the more earnest souls amongst them are often driven to despair by discovering the immorality, greed, selfishness, shallowness, and presumption of teachers of great reputation to whose feet they have come for knowledge. Disillusioned, they fall back upon that grand resource of the Hindu for solving the mysteries of the universe—*silent and solitary contemplation*. They retire to some lone place to think out the dark problem of existence, and, if their lives are spared for a few years, acquire, in proportion to their eccentricity and repulsiveness, the reputation of immense sanctity and superhuman wisdom.

[1] Rather odd! a creditable *hibernicism* on the part of Bawa Chhajju Singh.

[2] Bawa Chhajju Singh: "The Life and Teachings of Swami Dayanand Saraswati," pp. 76–77.

Dayanand, however, was made of different stuff, although like the great majority of his countrymen he was a firm believer in the importance of *yog*, of which I have given some account elsewhere,[1] and actually practised *yog* for a season in the desert of Chandi. Endowed with a robust frame and commanding stature, a self-reliant nature, a masterful temper, much knowledge of Hindu literature, and great eloquence, the Guzerati Brahman came forward after his long and arduous apprenticeship as an aggressive reformer. Eager to establish the correctness of his own views he was ever ready to meet, in open discussion, Hindu pandits, Christian missionaries, or Muhammadan moulvis, and, if his admiring followers are to be believed, quite as willing to convince an adversary with a stick as with a syllogism.

Professing pure monotheism, while admitting a plenary belief in the doctrines of metempsychosis and *Karma*, Dayanand embarked upon a strenuous campaign against idol-worship and the Hinduism which is based upon the Puranas. More particuiarly, being a Saiva or worshipper of Siva, did his anger blaze forth against the Bhagavat Gita, which he regarded as "an execrable production and an outrage upon the glory of the Supreme who alone should be worshipped and adored."

The Swami's violent attacks upon contemporary Hinduism provoked the bitter resentment of the Brahmans and of many prominent sectarians, and it is said that several attempts were made upon his life by his enraged antagonists. In respect to this matter his biographer says:

"Swami's lectures on 'idol-worship' becoming intolerable, a priest, with his heart filled with hatred, but yet suppressing his real feelings with a powerful effort, came up to him with a smile and presented him with a betel-leaf. The unsuspecting Swami took the leaf, but before he had eaten it many minutes, the poison swallowed with it began to show its effects. Realizing his danger, he sought the bank of the Ganges without delay, and descending into the water set about doing the *Neoli-Karm*, or swallowing large quantities of water and passing out the same, according to a *prescribed method*, from the intestines, so as to carry away gradually all hurtful matter from the stomach. The process was successful, and the Swami's life was saved. But according to the

[1] See chapter i., also "The Mystics, Ascetics and Saints of India," chapter viii., section iii.

fashion of great men, and in keeping with the traditions of the order to which he belonged, the Swami did not so much as administer a reproof to the murderous Brahman. Others, however, were not so forgiving. When Sayyad Mohammad, the Tahsildar of Anupshahar, heard of the Brahman's doing, he was very angry, and had the scoundrel sent to prison in a case pending in his court against him, though lighter punishment could have fairly satisfied the ends of justice. The Swami had great regard for the Tahsildar, but when the latter came to see him, after the Brahman had been incarcerated, and told him how the fellow had been dealt with, the Swami felt annoyed and would not talk with the official. On the Tahsildar's inquiring what he had done to displease the Swami, the answer was given in these words : 'I have come into the world to release people from captivity and not to see them sent to prison. If the Brahman would be base, why then let him have his way; why should I be false to my own self?' It is said that the Brahman was shortly acquitted in an appeal."[1]

What a remote and alien world of ideas does this singular narrative reveal! The poisoned *pán* smilingly offered to and eaten by the unsuspecting Swami, the removal of the dangerous drug from the victim's stomach by a very curious though "prescribed method," the refusal of the sanyasi to prefer a formal complaint against his would-be murderer, the friendly Tahsildar's peculiar notion of *administering justice* in such circumstances, and the subsequent reversal of his improper sentence by a higher court, the last event being, as we are left to infer, connected in some occult way with Swami-ji's magnanimity.

Dangers and opposition, however, did not daunt the reformer; they only served to stimulate his efforts for the conversion of his countrymen to the very pronounced opinions he had himself formed. During this strenuous period of his life Dayanand visited many cities of Northern and Western India, maintaining in public *shastraths* (religious discussions) his contention that the Vedas inculcated monotheism and did not countenance idolatry. More than that he upheld in public disputations with Christian clerics, Muhammadan moulvis and Jain monks the superiority of the *Vedic faith* to all other existing religions. From the records of these controversies we gather that, according to Dayanand's view, the eternal Supreme Being, who is not an impersonal God, created

[1] Bawa Chhajju Singh, "The Life and Teachings of Swami Dayanand Saraswati," pp. 111–112.

the world from *Prakriti*, the equally eternal and indistructible, primeval root-substance; that the creation of something out of nothing is impossible and unthinkable; but that the Infinite God causes *Prakriti*, the primordial atomic material principle, to assume various combinations which constitute the phenomenal and ever-changing world.

Regarding the human soul the Swami held that consciousness is its chief characteristic, while desire and other affections are also essential to it. Formless and indestructible, it was never born and will never die.

As to *incarnations* Dayanand denied that either Christ or Krishna, or any other man, ever was or ever could be *an incarnation of the Deity*, "who was all-pervading, infinite, omnipotent, free from the bondage of corporeity of every conceivable kind." He freely criticized the Bible and the Koran in his public controversies with followers of Jesus and Muhammad, and protested against the Christian and Muslim conceptions of God.

In opposition to the Christian missionaries who affirmed "that Divine forgiveness of sin was possible under certain circumstances, for instance, when a man came to have faith in Jesus Christ," Dayanand "maintained that forgiveness of sin was impossible, for to hold the contrary view was virtually to declare that God was the *encourager* of sin in the world. But, indeed, God was no such thing. Being absolutely just, He never forgave sins. On the contrary, He meted out punishments and rewards for all actions in all their fulness."

Not on open controversy alone did the reformer rely for the propagation of his ideas. He saw the value of having numerous missionaries to preach the *Vedic faith*, and he strongly advocated the establishment of schools and colleges in which his reformed Hinduism might be the basis of religious instruction.

As a Brahman Dayanand vigorously approved and supported *gauraksha*—protection of the cow.

In April 1877 Dayanand visited Lahore, and on the 26th of the following June the Lahore Arya Samaj was established. Connected with the Swami's sojourn in the capital of the Punjab, his biographer narrates that the reformer declared emphatically that it was not proper for women to take part in the meetings of the opposite sex, and that only worthless men permit their women to go anywhere and everywhere. He is also credited with the outspoken expression of an opinion about the present-day degeneration of Englishmen in India.

> "I have been," the Swami is reported to have said to an English clergyman who came to visit him, "I have been an early riser from my childhood. In the beginning I saw that Englishmen would get up early in the morning, and taking their children with them would go out for a walk. The excess of wealth, however, has made them indolent since. They are seen stretched on their beds in their bungalows till the sun is up, and I cannot but perceive that, like the old Aryas, the days of your fall are also coming."[1]

Without too much straining after the discovery of the more hidden causes of current happenings, we may perhaps be justified in recognizing in this significant condemnation and equally significant prediction, uttered by or attributed to Dayanand, an encouragement of the later political activities of the sect which he founded; particularly as the reformer was intent upon the *regeneration of Aryavarta*, and had the words patriotism and nationality constantly upon his lips. As early in the history of the Arya Samaj of Lahore as 1882, I find that the programme of the anniversary celebration contains the following item:

> "A lecture in Vernacular, by Bhai J * * * S * * *, secretary Arya Samaj, Lahore, on 'Nationality,'"

and the subject has, I know, been always much in the thoughts of the samajists.

During 1879 Dayanand met, first at Saharanpore and afterwards at Meerut, Colonel Olcott and Madame Blavatsky, founders of the world-known Theosophical Society, and it is stated that at the latter place, on May 4, Colonel Olcott in a public address said that he and Madame "had come to India accepting the Swami as their *guru* and guide." The history of the relations between the Theosophical Society and the Arya Samaj, though somewhat interesting, need not be considered here; it may be stated, however, that by the end of 1880

[1] Bawa Chhajju Singh, "The Life and Teachings of Swami Dayanand Saraswati," p. 348.

a complete disagreement was found to exist between Swami-ji and his American "disciples" in respect to their views about the existence of God, Colonel Olcott and Madame Blavatsky having openly avowed that they had *no faith in God.* A rupture between the Arya Samaj and the Theosophical Society became inevitable, angry passions were aroused, both sides indulged in accusations and recriminations. Swami Dayanand denounced his quondam American *disciples* in no measured terms as dangerous atheists, and taking the world into his confidence gave various instances of the duplicity of the Colonel and his companion in their dealings with himself and the Arya Samaj.

In the twenty years of his life which he had devoted to missionary wanderings the Swami visited the cities of many Hindu Rajas, and was treated by them with a respectful homage without parallel under similar or conceivable circumstances anywhere in Western lands at the present time. On his part Dayanand, if we may trust his biographer, although many times indebted to the great personages for substantial monetary help towards the objects he had at heart, never allowed either the courtesy or the liberality of his benefactors to influence him in the slightest degree in his self-imposed duty of denouncing false doctrine, censuring evil deeds, and rebuking immoral living, even when his stern reproofs had to be administered to persons in very exalted positions. And it was this fearless outspokenness of his which, in the belief of his followers, brought the Swami to an untimely end.

The Vedic reformer died at Ajmere on the 30th of October, 1883, at the age of fifty-nine, having, according to the accounts of his followers, been poisoned with arsenic by some of the many enemies whom his religious zeal had raised up against him. His end is said to have been edifying. His last word, we are told, was, "Shanti" (God's will be done). Of course the great event had its portentous accompaniments. That was inevitable. The sun grew pale when it knew that Swami-ji was wanted back in the celestial mansions, and shed tears which made themselves manifest in that remarkable fore- and after-glow in the morning and evening sky, which, at that time, attracted attention all the world over. The Earth, as soon as she became aware that Dayanand must return home, heaved a deep sigh, which rent her bosom, and resulted in the terrible and destructive outburst of Krakatoa, together with an earthquake in Greece. And when the fatal moment arrived, Aryavarta trembled to the very Himalayas, while a brilliant meteor flashed across the sky towards the northern pole.[1]

Here we have some natural phenomena, which actually occurred, ingeniously connected with the death of the Hindu reformer. And let European science offer what explanation it may regarding the phenomena referred to; let it eventually demonstrate the remarkable fore- and after-glow in the skies to be due to aqueous vapour, cosmic dust, or volcanic ashes, as the case may be, the more ignorant followers of Dayanand will, in all probability, ever connect the phenomena in question with the death of their venerated leader. As time goes by the death-scene will, in all likelihood, become, by an addition here and another there, more and more striking and impressive, until, at last, future generations will be asked to believe that the soul of the Indian prophet returned to God amidst the most awful convulsions of nature.

For years previous to his death the learned Swami was engaged upon a most interesting and important task—a translation into Hindi of both the *Rig* and *Yajur* Vedas.[2] This interpretation of the oldest of Sanskrit books, although not accepted by the orthodox Hindus, would, no doubt, repay translation into English.

What Dayanand has done in his Hindi commentaries on the Vedas is to give a *rationalistic* interpretation of these ancient writings. On the assumption that the Vedas are a direct revelation from the Supreme Being, it follows that they must be correct, and, therefore, cannot

[1] For the above particulars I am indebted to "The Regenerator of Aryavarta," vol. i. No. 45. (Published at Lahore.)

[2] "Veda-Bhashya, by Swami Dayanand Saraswati. A correct translation of Rig and Yagur Vedas as taught by Rishis in Anti-Mahabharat period, both in Sanskrit and Hindi." Vedic Press, Allahabad.

possibly conflict with God's other revelation to man, viz. the truths of science, physical and natural. Nothing, therefore, is necessary, but to put a rationalistic interpretation on the obscure and doubtful passages, and to find a new meaning for such statements or injunctions as seem to conflict with well-established facts and principles. With this method of exegesis and its unhappy results Europe has long been familiar, and the Hindu reformer does not seem to have been more fortunate in its application than Western theologians.

"To him not only was everything contained in the Vedas perfect truth, but he went a step further, and by the most incredible interpretations succeeded in persuading himself and others that everything worth knowing, even the most recent inventions of modern science, were alluded to in the Vedas. Steam-engines, railways, and steam-boats, all were shown to have been known, at least in their germs, to the poets of the Vedas, for Veda, he argued, means divine knowledge, and how could anything have been hid from that?"[1]

At one of the anniversary meetings of the Society, a member gravely stated that the Vedas mentioned *pure* fire, and as *pure* fire was nothing but electricity, it was evident the Indians of the Vedic period were acquainted with electricity. A leading member of the sect, who had studied science in the Government college, *discovered* in two Vedic texts, made up of *only eighteen words in all*, that oxygen and hydrogen with their characteristic properties were known to the writers of the *Rig Veda*, who were also acquainted with the composition of water, the constitution of the atmosphere, and had anticipated the modern kinetic theory of gases.

Under the guidance of Dayanand, the Aryas, as far as I can ascertain, profess to find pure monotheistic doctrines in the Vedas, and boldly assert that the different nature-gods of the Vedic Aryans, Agni, Vayu, Indra, are but one and the same god. Now the invocations in the *Rig Veda* are addressed to the dawn, to fire, to winds and storms, to Indra the sender of rain, and so on, but there appears to have been no order of precedence in this hierarchy of celestials, for the language of the hymns attributes supreme power to the god who may be

[1] Prof. Max Müller, "Biographical Essays—Dayananda Saraswati," p. 170.

the special subject of invocation and from whom benefits are being craved. As Professor Max Müller observed :

> " When these individual gods are invoked they are not conceived as limited by the power of others as superior or inferior in rank. Each god is to the mind of the suppliant as all the gods. He is felt at the time as a real divinity, as supreme and absolute in spite of the necessary limitation which, to our mind, a plurality of gods must entail on every single god. All the rest disappear from the vision of the poet and he only who is to fulfil their desires stands in full light before the eyes of the worshippers." [1]

Beneath these inconsistencies in the Vedic hymns the modern " Aryas " find a pure *monotheism*, where we would be more inclined to discover *pantheism* if anything. But the incongruities noticed above, if not due merely to exaggeration and flattery, may have arisen from the several gods invoked in the Vedic hymns having been peculiar and special *tribal* gods, before the hymns were brought together to form a *national* collection. In contrast with the denial on the part of the modern " Aryas " that the Vedas, when correctly interpreted, lend any countenance to pantheistic theories, is the fact that the founder of the sect himself believed in *yoga-vidya*, which surely cannot be reconciled with monotheism as ordinarily understood.

Not only monotheism and modern science did Dayanand discover in the Vedas, he also found in the Rig Veda the doctrine : " that the wife of a childless man while that man is yet alive may betake herself to some other married man in order to have a child by him." [2] The Rev. W. T. Williams, from whose pamphlet entitled " Exposure of Dayanand Saraswati and his Followers " this passage is quoted, states very positively that the doctrine in question, as enunciated by the founder of the Arya Samaj, is based on a deliberately false interpretation of a Vedic Text. However that may be, this custom, *Niyoga*, which is in keeping with certain primitive ideas, has been known in India since very early times, and instances of the practice are to be found recorded in that ancient epic, the Mahabharata.

[1] " Hibbert Lectures," 1878, p. 285.

[2] The raising of children to a *dead* man, known as Levirate amongst the Jews, is, of course, familiar to all readers of the Bible. *Vide* Deut. xxv. 5–10, and Gen. xxxviii.

This unsavoury subject cannot, unfortunately, be passed over if we are to have a correct idea of the tenets (and may be the practices) of a sect which is a prominent one in both the religious and political life of Northern India at the present day; but the reader who would rather remain in ignorance about *Niyoga* has only to skip the following five pages.

What Manu, the Hindu lawgiver, says about the matter is as follows:

"59. On failure of issue (by her husband), a woman who has been authorized, may obtain, (in the) proper (manner prescribed), the desired offspring by (cohabitation with) a brother-in-law, or (with some other) sapinda (of the husband).

"60. He (who is) appointed to (cohabit with) the widow shall (approach her) at night, anointed with clarified butter and silent, (and) beget one son, by no means a second.

"61. Some (sages) versed in the law, considering the purpose of the appointment not to have been attained by those two (on the birth of the first), think that a second (son) may be lawfully procreated on (such) women.

"62. But when the purpose of the appointment to (cohabit with) the widow has been attained in accordance with the law, these two shall behave towards each other like a father and a daughter-in-law.

"63. If these two (being thus) appointed deviate from the rule and act from carnal desire, they will both become outcasts, (as men) who defile the bed of a daughter-in-law or of a guru.

"64. By twice-born men a widow must not be appointed to (cohabit with) any other (than her husband); for they who appoint (her) to another (man) will violate the eternal law."[1]

Discussing this subject, Mr. J. D. Mayne, after citing instances of Niyoga from the Mahabharata and Vishnu Purana, observes:

"And so the law-books expressly sanction the begetting of offspring by another on the wife of a man who was impotent, or disordered in mind, or incurably diseased, and the son so begotten belonged to the incapacitated husband. No rule is laid down that the person employed to get offspring during the husband's life should be a near relation or any relation. In fact, in the instances just mentioned, the procreator who was called in aid was not only not of the same family, but one who was not even of the same caste, the owner of the wife being a Kshatriya and his assistant being a Brahman."[2]

These primitive practices had long fallen into desuetude in India, and their advocacy on a considerably

[1] Manu, chapter ix. paras. 59–64. G. Bühler's translation. "Sacred Books of the East," vol. xxv.

[2] John D. Mayne, barrister-at-law, "A Treatise on Hindu Law and Usage," p. 58.

extended scale by Swami Dayanand in the nineteenth century of our era on the authority of the Vedas created a sensation in Hindu society.

Swami Dayanand's teachings on the subject, as embodied in his book, "Sattyarth Prakash," naturally attracted a considerable degree of attention not only from orthodox Hindus, but from other Hindu reformers and from Christian missionaries also, with the result that Swami-ji was assailed vigorously from many quarters. Much bitterness was imported into the controversies, which were waged about Niyoga, the Vedas and the Bible, as well as Dayanand and his works, being criticized with great freedom by their opponents amongst the respective contending parties.

A literal translation into English of that portion of the Sattyarth Prakash which treats of the doctrine and practice of Niyoga was published in 1897 *by Lala Ruchi Ram Sahni, M.A.*, an able man, and a conscientious opponent of the Arya Samaj, and enabled me to learn what Dayanand taught in regard to Niyoga for the guidance of his followers.

Briefly, the reformer's dicta, although suffering from a certain degree of ambiguity, may, for my present purpose, be summarized as follows :

I. *A Hindu widow* who desires offspring may enter into a *Niyoga* contract with a widower of her own or of a higher caste for the procreation of not more than two sons.[1] As soon as this result is attained the relationship between them should cease, and the two children of the union will belong to the family of the widow's late husband, and must be reared accordingly.

The widow may, however, again enter into a second *Niyoga* alliance with another man who desires offspring *for himself*, and having borne him two children, may enter into other new connections of a similar kind. "In this way," to quote Lala Ruchi Ram's translation, "a widow may produce two sons for herself and two for each of four other men with whom she may have connection for such purposes. And a widower may similarly produce two sons for himself and two for each of four widows with whom he may have sexual connection."

In this way the Vedas enjoin the production of ten sons [2] by a man, and the same number by a woman who may have *Niyoga* connection.

---

[1] There is a peculiar vagueness throughout Dayanand's commandments in respect to Niyoga, as to whether the numerical limitations apply to sons or to offspring generally.

[2] *Vide* note above.

II. *A married woman* may, *with the consent of her* "*husband* who is unable to produce children," enter into *Niyoga* contracts similar to those recommended for widows. A married woman is moreover authorized to do likewise under particular circumstances, apparently *without reference to the wishes of her husband.* For it is enjoined that, "if the husband of a married woman has been absent from home for the sake of dharma (religion), then she should enter into the *Niyoga* connection with another man and produce issue after waiting for him for *eight years;* if he has been absent for acquiring knowledge and fame, then she should wait for *six years;* if for earning a livelihood, then for *three years* only. And when the husband returns home, then she should leave the man with whom she had *Niyoga* connection."

A married man has his Niyoga privileges too, which are thus laid down :

"In the same manner, if a wife be sterile, then at the end of the eighth year; if the children born of her do not live long, then at the end of the eleventh year; if she produce girls only, then at the end of the eleventh year; and if she be quarrelsome, then without delay, the man may leave her and enter into a *Niyoga* connection with another woman and produce issue from her."

If I understand aright, the married man may enter into other Niyoga connections as well, until he is the father of ten children.

It may be noted that neither a man nor a woman, whether in wedlock or out of it, is authorized to have more than *ten children in all.*

As regards a *second marriage*, Dayanand lays it down, always relying upon the Vedas for his authority, that such is not permissible. The "Sattyarth Prakash," which is written in the form of a dialogue, thus states the case :

"*Question.* Why should a man enter into a *Niyoga* connection, as he can marry a second time?

"*Answer.* No. We have mentioned above that the Vedas and other Shastras allow a man or a woman of the Dwij castes (three highest castes) to marry only once, but not a second time. Justice requires that a spinster should be married to a bachelor. It is unjust and therefore illegal to marry a widower with a virgin girl, or a bachelor with a widow. As a bachelor does not like to marry a widow, in the same way a virgin girl also would not willingly marry a widower. This will inevitably give rise to *Niyoga.* This is the true law (dharm), that is to say, all should be suitably connected."

Though claiming no authority whatsoever to pronounce any opinion on the obscure subject which has been engaging our attention, I must say that, judging from the arguments and objections advanced by his opponents, it seems to me that Dayanand greatly exceeded the Hindu law-books in his liberality to would-be Niyogists of both sexes, and thus unmistakably afforded encouragement to lasciviousness under the decorous mantle of religious authority. But as against this view it is necessary that I should state that the Niyoga system as expounded and prescribed in the "Sattyarth Prakash" was justified on *grounds of morality and expediency* by the reformer himself, and by his followers has been defended, with great warmth and subtlety on *religious and social* principles, against the attacks of Christian missionaries and others.

The Swami himself, a man of wide experience, says: "In their youth, all who are anxious to have issue, or who are licentious, will indulge in their vicious deeds in secret, if they are prevented by either the laws of the land or the rules of the caste from doing so openly. To put a stop to all this adultery and vice, the only successful way is this, that those who can control their passions, that is who do not wish to marry or to enter into *Niyoga*, may be considered as the best; but those who cannot control themselves should marry, and, in case of necessity, they should also enter into the *Niyoga* connection. This will lead to the diminution of adultery, while at the same time the children will be brought up in love. They cannot, besides, fail to multiply. Abortion will also be altogether avoided. In addition to these, the following evils are removed by having recourse to the marriage and *Niyoga* connections, viz. the illicit intercourse of a high-born woman with a man of low origin, and that of high-born men with low women like the prostitutes, the disgrace of noble families and their utter extinction, the evils arising out of ill-assorted matches and of abortion, etc., etc. For these reasons the system of *Niyoga* must be adopted."

When the controversy was at its height several long articles appeared in "The Arya Patrika," an English weekly organ of the Arya Samaj, on the subject of *Niyoga*, as well as the criticisms thereon of the missionaries, Messrs. Williams and Allnutt. The articles just referred to in support of Niyoga, written by educated Hindus, are highly interesting as indicative of the feeling in certain quarters of undisguised animosity towards Christianity, an animosity due, of course, to the perennially and aggressively hostile attitude of the missionaries towards Hinduism in all its aspects. That Christian missionaries, generally good and conscientious men, and professedly bearers of a gospel of peace, do in their zeal help to stir up evil passions in the hearts of the "heathen" is an undoubted fact, and this result, whether unavoidable or the reverse, should certainly not be blinked.

The clamant denunciations, by Christian missionaries, orthodox Hindus and the leaders of certain contemporary Hindu reform movements, of Dayanand's *Niyoga* doctrines filled the ears of the public. The matter even came before the law courts in a suit brought by some Arya Samajists against a Hindu detractor, with the result that the courts pronounced the tenets of the Arya Samaj in regard to *Niyoga* to be undoubtedly immoral.

What effect the Niyoga system prescribed by the founder of the Arya Samaj would, if it were practised by members of the society generally, have upon the character of the sect is too obvious to need discussion. The extreme and novel sexual freedom enjoyable under Dayanand's *Niyoga* system might certainly attract many members to the Samaj, but the corruption of family life within the society would soon be complete and the character of the Samaj become a by-word.

I believe that public opinion has as yet acted as a restraint upon the practices sanctioned by Dayanand's teaching, but, human nature being what it is, it is too early to judge to what lengths the Samajists may go if only out of devotion to their great leader—the founder of the new Vedic cult.

Most of the important beliefs and tenets of the Arya Samajists have now been brought before the reader, but it may be well to reproduce in this place the following statements of their principles, as formulated by themselves in what they are pleased to call their decalogue.

"I. God is the fountain of all true knowledge, and the primeval cause of all things knowable.

"II. Worship is alone due to God who is All-truth, All-knowledge, All-beatitude, Boundless, Almighty, Just, Merciful, Un-begotten, Infinite, Unchangeable, without a Beginning, Incomparable, the support and the Lord of all, All-pervading, Omniscient, Imperishable, Immortal, Eternal, Holy, and the Cause of the Universe.

"III. The Vedas are the Books of true knowledge, and it is the paramount duty of every Arya to read or hear them read; to teach and preach them to others.

"IV. An Arya should always be ready to accept truth and renounce untruth when discovered.

"V. Truth arrived at after consummate deliberation should be his guiding principle in all actions.

"VI. The primary object of the Samaj is to do good to the world by improving the physical, intellectual, spiritual, moral and social condition of mankind.

"VII. Due love for all and appreciation of Justice, an Arya should manifest in his behaviour towards others.

"VIII. He should endeavour to diffuse knowledge and dispel ignorance.

"IX. He should not be content with his own improvement, but look for it in that of others.

"X. In matters which affect the general social well-being of our race he ought to discard all differences and not allow his individuality to interfere, but in strictly personal matters every one may have his own way."[1]

Notwithstanding their decalogue there is still a good deal of uncertainty and vagueness about the tenets of the Arya Samaj, and no doubt this very vagueness helps at present to swell the ranks of its followers. But there are rocks ahead. Dayanand's mantle has not fallen on the shoulders of any one. No successor was appointed by the master, and it is more than probable that the sect will disintegrate into sections, each with its own special and peculiar views. There are some points, however, regarding which we can speak with tolerable confidence. The members of the Arya Samaj are Hindus inasmuch as they retain and observe those most essential peculiarities of Hinduism, veneration of the cow, the distinctions of caste and belief in the necessity of having a son. They also believe in the transmigration of souls, though the Vedic hymns contain no allusion to this doctrine, "which is a conspicuous characteristic of the Hindu creed in the later system."[2] But they are unorthodox Hindus,

[1] "Arya Magazine," vol. i. p. 3.

[2] Professor Sir Monier Williams, "Hinduism," p. 31.

inasmuch as they condemn idolatry and reject a large portion of the later scriptures acknowledged as sacred by their co-religionists. They also manifest a strong hostility to the Brahmans; their preachers in the bazaars endeavouring to enlist popular feeling against the hereditary priesthood by directing attention to the heavy pecuniary burden they are, and have always been, upon the Hindu community.

Section III.—The Lahore Arya Samaj up to 1888

We have seen that in April 1877 Dayanand visited Lahore, and that in the month of June of that year an Arya Samaj was established in that city.

In November 1879 a young native gentleman who was well aware of the lively interest I took in the movements for religious and social reform which had for some time past been agitating Hindu society through the length and breadth of India, placed in my hands a programme of the proceedings to be observed on the occasion of the *second anniversary* of the Lahore Arya Samaj, or Aryan Society. A glance at the paper showed me that besides the usual reading of reports and election of officers, appropriate to the occasion, there were to be hymns and prayers, lectures in Hindi and English, and the celebrations of the "Hom."

As the opportunity was one well worth improving, I made up my mind to be present during a portion, at least, of the ceremonies of the day, particularly the "Hom" [1] sacrifice.

By 7 a.m. of the appointed Sunday, I arrived in my carriage at the Shahalmi gate of the city.[2] There I was

[1] "Homa—a sort of burnt-offering which can be made by Brahmans only. It is only made on special occasions, such as the celebration of a festival, the investiture of a young Brahman with the sacred thread, marriages and funerals. The method of making it is as follows: During the utterance of Mantras, five species of consecrated wood, together with the Dharba grass, rice and butter, are kindled and burnt, and the fire is then kept burning as long as the festival or ceremony lasts. Great efficacy is ascribed to this rite."—Garrett's "Classical Dictionary of India."

[2] The "city" is the native town, outside of which lies the European quarter of Lahore.

joined by several of those bright-faced intelligent youths to be found at the present day in every town of British India, who, under the stimulus of Western education, are in a state of intellectual restlessness, eager for reforms and innovations in what they feel is a backward state of society, and who, with the generous ardour and confidence of boys, hope to be able to recast, upon an improved model, institutions which are the outcome of a hundred influences operating through many an eventful century. But however crude the ideas of these would-be reformers, however utopian many of their schemes, it is impossible not to sympathize with their earnest aspirations for the intellectual and social advancement of their countrymen, and it was with much pleasure that I found my young friends awaiting my arrival at the city gate. Here I had to quit my carriage, for it could not go into the narrow crowded thoroughfares of the native quarter which lay within the gate, and, with my companions, I walked up the lanes which led to the premises of the Arya Samaj. On the doorway was a board bearing, in large English characters, the words "Arya Samaj," and below that, in smaller characters, the same words in Hindi and Urdu.

Ascending a flight of stairs and passing through a narrow passage, we entered an open space or court, bounded on one side by high and on the remaining three sides by low buildings. The place of meeting was a very humble one, with unsightly walls all round and the open canopy of heaven overhead. In one corner was a recess, perhaps six feet square, roofless like the other portions of the court. Here preparations had been made for the performance of the *Hom* sacrifice. Floor-cloths had been laid down for the visitors to sit upon, and festoons of leaves had been hung in great loops right round the enclosure. The entrance to the little recess where the *Hom* was to be performed was specially adorned in homely but not ungraceful style. A green plantain tree had been placed on each side of the entrance, and garlands of leaves and flowers had been hung between them. These simple attempts at decoration gave the meeting-place something of a holiday look. At one end of the open court was placed a small table covered over with a white cloth of English manufacture. Upon it were ranged three brass vases containing flowers. At this table the lecturer stood when, in his appointed turn, he addressed the audience "on the wants of our country." Somewhat in advance of the table, *i.e.* a little nearer to the centre of the court, there was a small carpet, and a very low table, just a few inches high. These were for the use of the guru when he read to the audience out of the Vedas.

At the other end of the court three or four musicians were squatted tuning their instruments in a listless fashion. A little way behind them I noticed the Society's charity-box, marked in English and two vernacular languages, the uppermost line and the largest characters being English. There were not more than twenty-five persons in the place when I entered it, but the number gradually increased to about one hundred and fifty men and children. No women were present in the assembly, but I was told that there were a number of them congregated in the upper rooms overlooking the courtyard. None, however, were visible, and I dare say most of the fair ladies behind the purdahs understood little and cared less for the new-fangled proceedings of the Arya Samaj. Those of them who comprehended the matter were, in all probability, opposed to a movement which, if successful, would isolate them from the pomp and excitement of the polytheistic idolatry in which they had been reared. Indeed the women of India, brought up in the seclusion of the Zenanas, are, as I have often been told by respectable Indian gentlemen, an insurmountable obstacle to reforms which would simplify the ritual of their religion or lead to the abolition of objectionable but time-honoured rites, ceremonies, and festivals.

The reader who has followed me thus far will not need to be informed who the members of the Arya Samaj are —what distinctive doctrines they profess, and what common objects they have set before themselves? Yet the following passage from a letter which appeared in a Lahore newspaper over the signature of "An Arya," will not be without some interest to him :

"The Arya movement in the Punjab began with the advent of Swami Dayanand Saraswati in the beginning of 1877. This learned pandit, who is regarded by the people of India as the greatest Vedic scholar of the age, in that year delivered a series of lectures on the ancient civilization of the country. The eyes of the educated community were at once opened. They saw that the reforms which they were advocating, and to which there was so much opposition in the land, could easily be carried out by throwing off all the accumulated excrescences which had grown upon their religious and social systems during the lapse of ages, and by falling back upon their pristine books of authority, *the Vedas.* Dreading still further the growth of materialistic and atheistic views in the country, it was considered expedient to establish places of congregational worship where all should meet once a week to pray and hear lectures and sermons delivered.

"Within the last two years these Samajes which exist in the Punjab, the North-west, and the Deccan have acted as so many safeguards of public morals. They admit among their body all who believe in one God, discard idolatry and regard the Vedas as the original revelation given to man. Their meetings are open and resorted to by the Hindus and Muhammadans and Christians *all alike.* Such are the aims and such the scope of this useful institution."[1]

The religious writings known as the Vedas to which the members of the Arya Samaj have turned as the original, and perhaps sole, revelation given by God to man are four in number, the earliest being a collection of over a thousand hymns, which, according to our best authorities, date from 1500 to 1000 B.C. The hymns of the *Rig Veda* are of various dates and separate origins, and were, for centuries, preserved orally in different priestly or minstrel families, till finally brought together and embodied in one comprehensive collection such as has been preserved to our own day.[2] Older than the poems of Homer, older than the psalms of David, these venerable hymns are amongst the earliest yearnings of the human heart towards the Deity, which have been preserved to later ages in the records of the past, and must ever possess a special and unique value in the eyes of the student of the evolution of religious thought. The Vedic hymns embody the simple prayers of a pastoral people addressed to the clouds, the storm, the sun, the sky, the dawn, and other such objects and natural phenomena, and reflect, as in a mirror, the grand and ever-

[1] "Civil and Military Gazette," March 6, 1879.

[2] Prof. Max Dunker's "Ancient History of India," p. 28, on the authority of Prof. Max Müller's "History of Sanskrit Literature."

varying features of the giant snow-capped mountains over which the wandering Aryans had found their way from "the roof of the world" to the plains of Northern India. In the Vedic hymns the gods are invited to come down and partake of the sacrifices offered to them, and, in return, are called upon to provide pasture for the cattle and horses, to fill the udders of the cows, to bestow health, wealth, and long life, to afford protection to man and beast against the evil spirits, and to grant their worshippers victory over the enemies of the tribe.

The second, or *Yajur Veda*, prescribes the forms and ceremonies to be observed in the performance of the sacrifices appropriate to different occasions. The third, or *Sama Veda*, consists of a selection of hymns from the *Rig Veda*, to be sung when the juice of the Soma plant was the principal offering made to the gods. The fourth, and last Veda, called the *Atharva Veda*, is a collection of spells, charms, and incantations against sickness and death.

Although the Vedic hymns are plainly the outcome of a very primitive society which had not emerged from the tribal condition, and, although the religion of the Sanskrit-speaking Aryans was chiefly *physiolatry*, or the worship of the forces and phenomena of nature, yet there is in the hymns ample evidence of the fact that, at a very early date, polytheistic, pantheistic, and monotheistic conceptions had all been arrived at by the Aryan *rishis*, and had found expression in immortal song.[1] Indeed, the fact that they lend themselves to all forms of religious thought is what gives to the Vedas their wonderful vitality. Add to this that it was in the Punjab that these songs of the foreworld first rose to heaven with the patriarchal sacrifices of the earliest Aryan settlers in India, and there is no room for wonder that the Vedas, and the literature that has grown out of them, are objects of especial and fervent veneration to the Hindus of the Land of the Five Rivers, or of the *seven* rivers of the Vedic poets.

The members of the society, which is the subject of

[1] Edgar Quinet's "Le genie des Religions," p. 119. Prof. Sir Monier Williams' "Religious Thought and Life in Inda," p. 7.

this paper, professedly desire to revive in these days the long extinct Vedic religion, or, as they prefer to call it, *Vedic Theism* of the Sanskrit-speaking Aryans. What the religion of the Vedas really was it may be no easy task to make out now. A competent authority—the late Professor Sir Monier Williams—wrote :

> "Although the majority of the Hindus believe that the four Vedas contain all that is good, great, and divine, yet these compositions will be found, when taken as a whole, to abound more in puerile ideas than in lofty conceptions. At the same time it is clear that they give no support to any of the present objectionable usages and customs for which they were once, through ignorance of their contents, supposed to be an authority. The doctrine of metempsychosis, or transmigration of souls, which became an essential characteristic of Brahmanism and Hinduism in later times, has no place in the religion of the Veda. Nor do the hymns give any sanction to the prohibition of widow-marriages, the general prevalence of child-marriages, the tyrannical sway of caste, the interdiction of foreign travel, and the practice of idolatry." [1]

Any way, the Aryas of our day under the leadership of Dayanand Saraswati, have agreed to put their faith in the *Rig* and *Yajur* Vedas with the commentaries upon them, written prior to the date of the Mahabharata. But as the reader already knows, Dayanand's view and opinions are rank heresies, stoutly opposed by the orthodox pandits, who, at a large and influential meeting held in Calcutta in the year 1881, placed on record, for the benefit of the Hindu public, their own decision in regard to what books were to be regarded as authoritative scripture, and affirmed very plainly their approval of practices which had been condemned by the reformer. And ever since that time a most active opposition to the new sect has been kept up by the orthodox Hindus, who are not insensible of the mischief which the new society is capable of doing to the established forms of Hinduism.

The *Hom* had not been commenced when I entered the premises of the Arya Samaj. Through the courtesy of certain native gentlemen connected with the ceremonies of the day, I was assigned a seat quite near the place where the sacrifice was to be offered, and had the best possible opportunity of witnessing all the arrangements for, and the entire details of, the interesting performance.

[1] "Religious Thought and Life in India," p. 18.

The fuel (neatly cut pieces of dry wood) was arranged in a little square sacrificial pit. At each of the four corners of the pit stood a small black candle, if I may call it so, about six inches in height, made up of fragrant gums and other combustibles. Round the sacrificial pit were placed five brass vessels, one containing *ghee* (clarified butter), and the other four a mixture of various grains and spices moistened with *ghee* and milk. A young *sanyasi*, learned in Sanskrit-lore, presided at the ceremonies. He was well and warmly attired, and wore on his head a conspicuous turban of orange-yellow cloth.

The firewood and the four odorous candles were ignited, and then the priest commenced to recite Sanskrit *mantras*, each of which ended with the word *svaha*, which served as a signal for pouring a ladleful of *ghee* upon the fire, and casting into it a small quantity of the other offerings.

The language of the golden-tongued *rishis*, the dead language of the dead gods of a long-past age, sounded strange, as the *sanyasi* rolled out in slow and measured tones the mystic texts appropriate to the occasion. When the whole string of selected mantras had been repeated, some portion of the oblations still remained in the plates. In a whispered consultation amongst the officiating priests it was arranged that the leader should repeat the *Gayatri* [1] over and over again, while the five assistants kept feeding the flames with the offerings, until the whole quantity that had been provided should be duly consumed.

It is hardly necessary to say with what interest I watched this ceremonial which the Sanskrit-speaking Aryans had practised so many centuries ago at the very dawn of the historical period. But I could not help feel-

[1] The *Gayatri* is a form of prayer, consisting of ten Sanskrit words, which should be used by all Hindus daily, both morning and evening. It is translated as follows by Prof. Monier Williams: "Let us meditate (or we meditate) on that excellent glory of the divine vivifier. May he enlighten (or stimulate) our understandings" ("Hinduism," p. 61). In the translation of the Mahabharata by Pratap Chunder Roy (Calcutta: Bharata Press), the following rendering of the *Gayatri* appears: "*Om*, the Earth, the Firmament, the Heaven! I meditate on the adorable effulgence of the God who created them and who guides our intellect" ("Vana Parva," p. 612).

ing that the ancient rite had quite lost what significance it might have had in the old time, and that, as performed in my presence that day, it was but a lifeless ghost, a hollow ceremonial, meaningless to the spectators and entirely uncalculated to awaken in them any feelings of enthusiasm, of reverence, or even of solemnity. The attendants, it is true, performed their office with decorum, but I looked in vain for any indication of deep feeling or genuine interest on their features. As for the onlookers, they watched the performance as they might have watched a small bonfire, and listened with dull unconscious ears to the *mantras*, the Sanskrit language being quite unknown to nearly all of them. Some, indeed, were even less attentive than that. While the *Hom* sacrifice was being performed I noticed two or three young men leaning over the table in the reading-room looking through the newspapers.

In the old time the fire for such a sacrifice would have been kindled by the friction of two pieces of wood, and the goddess of fire (*Agni*) would thus have been mysteriously born again, under the hands of the operator, as the fire-drill (which, if we are to believe the philologists, gave rise to the myth of Prometheus),[1] gradually elicited the living, glowing flames from the dark inert timber. But the obtaining of fire by the friction of wood is a troublesome process, and so our modern *Aryas* preferred the simpler plan of igniting the fuel in the sacrificial pit by means of live charcoal brought from the domestic hearth.

I was amused and interested to find in conversation with several members of the Samaj, that they were disposed to deny the sacrificial character of the *Hom* and to maintain that it was intended to purify the air, for here, as elsewhere, the *Zeitgeist* is too strong to allow of the revival of the old worn-out religions, except as solemn mockeries of things long dead.

At the termination of the *Hom* the musicians struck up a hymn, singing, in a clear but subdued tone, to the accompaniment of their instruments. In regard to Hindu, or any other music, I am not competent to give a critical

[1] Fiske's "Myths and Myth-makers," p. 64.

opinion, but the hymns sung on this occasion had certainly a plaintive sweetness of their own, which was exceedingly agreeable to my ear. The hymns for the day, some in Hindi and some in Punjabi, had been selected from a collection which had been made and printed for the use of the Samaj. But the choir, strange to say, consisted of hired singers of the *Muhammadan* religion, with no faith or heart in the ceremonies or the beliefs of the Aryas. This fact alone would indicate the artificial character of the entire arrangement, and would serve to show how utterly futile is the attempt to revive, for any beneficial purpose, the obsolete practices of a long-past age. As soon as the selected hymns had all been sung, the lecturer took his place at the table. He first repeated the *Gayatri* in slow devout tones, and, in a quavering voice, pronounced the mystic *Om* with marked solemnity. So much had I heard and read about the pious horror of the orthodox twice-born Hindu, at the mere thought of uttering this sacred word in the hearing of an outcast or an unbeliever, that I was not a little surprised to hear it pronounced so often, as on this day, before a mixed audience, consisting of Hindus of all castes without distinction, and of many persons altogether outside the pale of Hinduism.

The lecturer in his discourse took up what may be called the stock questions of the Indian reformer. He dwelt upon the weak points of the system of early, or rather infant, marriage. Unaware, apparently, of Dayanand's opinion in regard to the inadmissibility of a second marriage, he alluded to the evils that inevitably spring from the cruel rule of Hindu society, which refuses to permit a widow, even a virgin-widow, to wed a second time. He pointed out the urgent necessity that exists for general and technical education, and, above all, for *national union* and self-help. Turning to more strictly religious topics the lecturer declaimed against idolatry, and scornfully pointed out, apparently with reference to a real existing evil, the absurdity of uneducated people becoming *sanyasis*. In denouncing idolatry the lecturer stated that in Vedic times men who bowed down to images made of wood or stone would have been punished like ordinary malefactors—in fact, like thieves and robbers. I am not aware what, if any, historical authority there may be for this statement, but this was the only part of the lecture that met with general applause, indicated by the clapping of hands in quite a European fashion. For some time past there has been in Hindu society an almost feverish desire for social reforms of all kinds. No objectionable practice, however old, or however trifling, escapes the keen criticism of men leavened with new ideas from the West.[1]

At the conclusion of the lecture the musicians again struck up a hymn, and, while they were chanting it, two or three men went round casting flowers over the visitors, and throwing garlands of flowers about their necks. One was placed in my hand, with the remark in English, "Of course, *you* need not put this on." And thus ended the proceedings announced for the forenoon of that day.

Three years later, in November 1882 (or, as the public notice put it, in "the Aryan era, 1,960,892,983"), I again attended the anniversary celebration of the Samaj. There was not much to note in the way of change. Even the Mussalman musicians were in attendance, as in 1879. But such changes as attracted my attention were in the right direction. The meeting-place, the same as on the occasion previously described, showed some well-meant attempts at decoration. I noticed that a couple of small-sized wall-mirrors had been hung up, and that something

[1] A Hindu's strong protest against "the custom of using obscene language on the occasion of marriage ceremonies," and the singing of immoral songs in the streets by women of respectable families and good position, on the occasion of Hindu festivals, appeared in the "Regenerator of Aryavarta," 22nd of December, 1884; and I was told by a young Hindu friend of mine that the *Khattris* in Lahore had taken up the matter in an earnest, practical spirit, and that the *panchyats* of the caste had determined to impose a fine upon any *Khattri* whose wife indulged in obscene songs in the streets of Lahore. Even trifling matters are not above the notice of these energetic reformers, *e.g.* it has been the custom, at all seasons of the year, to carry, as a present, on the occasion of a visit from the bridegroom's family to the bride's family, two large earthen vessels containing curds. Now, in the hot weather in India, these curds are usually an utter abomination of bad odours, but the practice was still rigidly, I may say religiously, maintained. The Lahore panchyat have now pronounced the observance of this custom unnecessary.

had been done to cover the bare, unsightly, and dilapidated surrounding-walls. The gathering, moreover, was larger than on the occasion of my previous visit, and there were not wanting signs of a healthy and more extended interest in the work of the Society. In fact, the Arya Samaj was clearly getting on in the world. But as clearly also it was experiencing the fate of all more or less successful movements. It was struggling against the opposition aroused by its growth at the expense of older institutions. There appeared to be a controversial tone in the addresses delivered, and it was considered desirable to affirm frequently (evidently in reply to objectors) that the *Hom* was not a religious observance, that it was not a worship of *Agni* (fire); but was carried out from purely sanitary considerations; since the products of the combustion of the particular substances used diffused through the atmosphere of a crowded assembly were of a distinctly healthful character. In private conversation with me a member of the Samaj supported this view with some warmth, referring to the common practice of disinfecting barracks, hospitals, and infected places generally by sulphur fumigation. But the reader does not need to be told that even if the products of the combustion of the substances burnt on such occasions happen to be of a healthful character the *Hom*, accompanied as it is by the solemn recital of sacred Sanskrit mantras, carried out in the open air, at a professedly religious gathering, is not, in any sense, analogous to the ordinary process of purifying an unwholesome place by disinfectants. Besides, it is well known that to *Agni* (fire) the greatest number of invocations are addressed in the hymns of the *Rig Veda*, and that the idea involved in the ordinary Vedic sacrifice is that the gods are gratified and nourished by the aroma of the burnt-offering.[1] Indeed it would be impossible for a religion based on the Vedas to get on at all without *sacrifices*, which seem to be the very essence of the Vedic religion.[2]

[1] Prof. Sir Monier Williams' "Religious Thought and Life in India," p. 12.

[2] On this subject the reader may consult "Cosmology of the Rig Veda," by H. W. Willis, 1887. Williams and Norgate, London.

The truth, apparently, is that at the formation of the Samaj, when idolatrous rites were proscribed, the *Hom* was retained on account of its Vedic origin, and also, perhaps, as a sort of connecting link with Brahmanism, from which ancestral religion the members of the new Samaj (either through prudence, or from feelings of tender association) could not quite break away. But opponents, both orthodox and heterodox, having taken exception to the *Hom* as being inconsistent with the purely theistic pretensions of the Arya Samaj, it has become a stumbling-block to the Society. It remains to be seen whether the reasonable objections of opposing sects will make the Samaj abandon a ceremony which is admittedly not of religious significance, or whether it will arouse a spirit of obstinate conservatism, tending to the retention of the *Hom* at all costs.

The anniversary meeting of November 1882 was the subject of an article in "The Arya Magazine." Here is an extract from it :

> "The long, spacious, and lofty hall of the Samaj was tastefully carpeted on the occasion. Silken and laced hangings adorned the windows. Large mirrors in magnificent frames, principles of the Samaj, written in letters of gold, and other mantras from the Vedas in variegated hues, made the room sumptuous with glowing colours. Two grand tables stood east and west of the hall; on one were arranged books for sale, and on the other prizes for girls. Between these two there was another table covered with precious cloth for the lecturer. Bunches of flowers in slender marble vases were arranged on either side of the table, and a highly valuable time-keeper stood in the middle. *Parterres* of flowers of every form and hue were arranged alongside the walls, and beauties of blooming nature were surrounding the hall. In the north a *Hom* (Kund) altar was made which was surrounded by grown-up plantain trees, and a long chain of flowers of different colours encircled them all. Wreaths of flowers entwined with evergreen were adjusted on the borders of each window. The whole hall presented a scene more enchanting than a poet's dream of Eden—a Puranic-man's vision of paradise. It was a rapture merely to sit there and breathe, though every other faculty were suspended.
>
> "The entrance was also as much beautified as the inner hall . . ."[1]

As the above glowing description seems to have been intended seriously, one can only wonder at the writer's unbridled imagination which could transform the whole scene so completely. Possibly for persons whose ordinary

[1] "The Arya Magazine," vol. i. p. 236.

surroundings are unlovely in the extreme, the simple and not inappropriate decorations of the meeting-place may have had an exceptional charm; but there can be no excuse whatever for writing of an open court, roofed only by the canopy of heaven, as a "*lofty* hall." The entire description, reproduced above, is instructive as a bit of unblushing exaggeration, and as an example (only too common) of that predilection for brag and disregard of strict accuracy which so constantly and disagreeably obtrudes itself upon the attention of the real friends of India. It is proper to add that the Arya Samaj cannot be held responsible for the description which I have criticized above, as "The Arya Magazine," although devoted to the interests of the Samaj, is, I understand, a purely private undertaking.

Within twelve months of the anniversary celebrations which I have just described, Swami Dayanand's untimely death at Ajmere, in October 1883, recorded in the preceding section, connected as it was with painfully suspicious circumstances, awakened in the breasts of his zealous followers and ardent admirers a fervour of deep and indignant sympathy. These feelings of sorrow found practical expression in a proposal put before a public meeting at Lahore on the 9th of November, 1885, to perpetuate the revered memory of the late reformer by establishing a college at Lahore to be named the Dayanand Anglo-Vedic College. Committees were formed, subscription lists opened, funds raised, and on the 1st of June, 1886, was opened, as a part of the scheme, the Anglo-Vedic *High School*.

In November 1886 I was present at a portion of the anniversary celebration of the Arya Samaj. The business extended over two entire days. As on previous occasions the sacrifice known as the *Hom* was duly provided for; also much singing of hymns (partly to the accompaniment of a harmonium), reading of reports and lectures. Of these last one was to be given by a woman. A Hindu woman lecturing in public! This was a real attraction; an opportunity not to be neglected.

The premises of the Samaj I found very much improved, and the place of assembly, although the same, looked very much changed. The area was more restricted, as a part of the open space I had seen before was now built upon, forming a quadrangle, bounded by double storeyed buildings with picturesque balconies. As on the other occasions, all present, with the exception of myself, were natives. The female lecturer did not give me a chance of writing a description of her charms, for she stood behind a screen, and poured forth, from her place of concealment, a long discourse in Hindi on women's rights.[1] She began by maintaining the thesis that women were quite as capable of education as men, and, to prove her contention, sent forward a little girl of about six or seven years of age, who recited a long Vedic poem the Mai had taught her. Mai Bhagwati, the lecturer, then proceeded to refer to the admirable manner in which everything in nature was ordered. She drew special attention to the important function of maternity. She told us a story, with the inevitable Raja in it, to prove or give emphasis to her statement that each one would receive according to his deserts. To the oppression of women in the Zenanas of Hindustan she attributed the subject condition of the country, adding that the blows, illtreatment, and abuse her countrymen received from the English were the just retribution of their acts in the Zenana. This remark called forth some applause and merriment. Of course Mai Bhagwati's remark was pointed against the unmanly domestic tyranny of her own countrymen, the English being, in her eyes, but the unconscious avengers of the wrongs of the harem. Following up these remarks, our invisible advocate of women's rights said that the husbands who beat and ill-

[1] The *purdah* system amongst Hindus is said to have been adopted during Muhammadan domination. However that may be, the purdah is now looked upon as a mark of gentility, and will not easily be lifted, even by the reforming spirit of the age. One might think that the spread of education will soon release women from their present seclusion, but in some cases it produces the very opposite effect. The cheap education now available in most parts of India raises a great many persons out of their natural humble sphere of life. The wives of such men, who once enjoyed the privilege of moving about freely in their own village, are converted into *purdah nasheens*, the seclusion of the women being an indication of superior rank.

used their wives here would be born again as dogs to be kicked and beaten in their turn, that those who ensnared women would be fishes who would be duly entangled in the meshes of the fisherman's net, and so on, statements which may, for anything I know to the contrary, rest on Vedic authority, but which were received with incredulous smiles by her male audience.

Later on an Indian gentleman addressed us in Urdu, advocating, in a very excellent speech, the claims to national support of the Anglo-Vedic College proposed to be established in memory of Dayanand, and to such good purpose did he speak, that at the end of his discourse a goodly stream of rupees for the establishment of the college came pouring in. One elderly man advanced to the table, and, divesting himself of his gold bangles (was it by prearrangement?), presented them as a contribution to the college. He then, with great deliberation, took off his earrings, one by one, and handed them over also, together with a small sum of money. His action was received with much popular applause, and he was showered with flowers by the sympathetic onlookers. Before retiring, he stipulated that the present he had made should be applied specially towards the building of a room in the boarding-house of the college to be named after his wife. His example stimulated many others to offer their ornaments, and many a ring and silver *Kurra* was handed up, with the name of the donor, amidst the plaudits of the assembly. But one gift more particularly brought the house down—a subscription of sixteen rupees and two annas from the inmates of *the Christian Mission boarding-house*.

Two years after the meeting I have described the Anglo-Vedic College for preparing students for Indian university degrees came into existence, and this institution, under its able principal, Lala Hans Raj, B.A., has, I believe, grown and prospered.

LALA HANS RAJ, B.A., PRINCIPAL ANGLO-VEDIC COLLEGE

To face page 166

SECTION IV.—THE LAHORE ARYA SAMAJ SUBSEQUENT TO 1888

Notwithstanding the apparent prosperity of the Samaj, as indicated by the establishment of its school and college and the increased membership of the society, disruptive forces were at work, and in November 1893 the Arya Samaj split up into two sections, the Vegetarians and the Meat-eaters being, for various reasons, unable to work amicably together. A division of the property owned by the society was the immediate result. On the 25th of November, 1893, the rival parties held their anniversary meetings separately, the Vegetarians in the Arya Mandir in the city, the Meat-eaters in the Dayanand Anglo-Vedic College. I attended at both places, and heard one lecture in each. Notwithstanding the recent rupture in the camp, both meetings were conducted with a studied and commendable moderation.

At the Arya Mandir of the Vegetarian, or *Mahâtma* party, where was prominently displayed on the walls the motto

> "Take not away the life you cannot give
> All creatures have an equal right to live,"

the lecturer to whose address I listened was a Bengalí, who indulged in a good deal of gesture and grimace bordering on buffoonery. He was on the whole more an advocate for social than for religious reform, and brought into his harangue, which was in Hindustani, a large number of English words and phrases. I noted, with surprise, that he enforced his views by constant reference to Durga and Kali, Seta Debi, Mahadeb, Parbati, etc., etc. I recalled to mind that the Aryas had professedly gone back to the venerable Vedas for their religion, accepting what Swami Dayanand had discovered in these ancient scriptures; but the orating Bengali moved in quite another and later world, and amongst Puranic divinities ostentatiously repudiated by the Aryan Reformer.

At the Anglo-Vedic College, where the Meat-eaters held their meetings, the speaker I heard was Lala Mulraj, M.A., a man of an altogether different stamp from the

Bengalí just referred to. Lala Mulraj had spoken at the inaugural meeting of the Samaj, and now recalled to the memory of his hearers that the Samaj had been in existence for fifteen years, that it had many difficulties to contend with in its infancy, and after a period of prosperity had arrived at a critical moment in its existence.

His statements, based as they were on intimate knowledge of the inner history, working and condition of the society, are of great interest, and may well be reproduced here in his own words. Referring back to the state of the Samaj in 1878 Lala Mulraj said :

"Its very life was doubtful at that time. There were adverse forces and opposition on all sides. The orthodox among the Hindus and especially the Brahmans were its determined enemies. The followers of other religious denominations also did not look upon it with favour. There was fear of petty persecution on more sides than one. Excommunication from caste was a threat which was by no means uncommon at that time. Sometimes the masses were ready to take the law into their own hands, and to wreak their vengeance on the members of the Arya Samaj by using physical force. Becoming a member of the Arya Samaj was sure to bring down upon a man the wrath of his whole family—father, mother, brother, sisters and even wife. The number of members was small. The funds at the disposal of the Samaj were very limited. It had no building of its own. It had no important institutions to control. There were at that time very few Samajes in other towns of the Punjab and in India.

"Now the case is different. There are at this time Samajes in all the important towns in the Punjab. Samajes have sprung up in several villages also. Throughout the North-Western Provinces there are Samajes in all the principal towns. Important Samajes have grown up in Rajputana. In the Bombay Presidency there are Arya Samajes in many towns. Bengal also has a few Arya Samajes.

"The Arya Samaj has important institutions to control, the most important being the Dayanand Anglo-Vedic College. This building in which we are now assembled is, as you know, consecrated to that institution. There are several schools for boys and for girls also, which have been established by the Arya Samaj. There are more than one orphanages managed by the Arya Samajes in India. There are some presses attached to the society. There are several papers in different languages which are being issued by the Samaj or its members. The funds under the control of the Arya Samaj amount to several lacs. All the important Samajes have buildings of their own. The members of the Arya Samaj are numerous. There is now not much fear of persecution from the outside world. There is no danger now of a man being turned out of caste for being a member of the Arya Samaj. Nor is there any fear of the members of the Arya Samaj being attacked by the masses. A man by entering the Arya Samaj now does not generally bring down upon himself the wrath of his family. On the other hand, in several families the relations take as great an interest in the Samaj as the man who is a member. The wives of many members share with them their views in Samajic matters. Some of them have joined together to found Samajes for females in more towns than one. The home life of a man does not become miserable by joining the Arya Samaj.

"But where there was harmony in the Samaj in 1878, now there is friction. The members have not the love which they used to feel for one another before. They are not now united, but are split up into sections and parties. There is unrest in the Samaj throughout India. The life of a man who is an active member of the Samaj knows no rest. He is talking all day of Samajic matters and of his opponents in the Arya Samaj, against some of whom he is very bitter. His great quarrel now is with his brothers of the Arya Samaj, with whom his views on some points do not agree. The differences in the Arya Samaj are not now discussed with closed doors and in whispers, but in public and loudly. Week after week the papers are full of angry discussions between the members of the Arya Samaj. The attention of the general public is being forcibly drawn to differences in the Samaj, and the people are alarmed about the safety of the Arya Samaj and of the valuable and useful institutions which rest upon it. There are some peace-loving members who are cutting off their connection with the Samaj as they have become sick of the quarrels in it. There are many men who are thinking that the Arya Samaj has proved a huge failure, and that the day is nigh when it will cease to exist.

"I think the differences which have taken place in the Arya Samaj are a great misfortune. It pains me very much to find one brother arrayed against another. I am sorry to find discord where there should have been harmony. But I am not despondent of the future of the Arya Samaj. I am as confident of its success now as I was in the year 1878. I believe there is a great future in store for the Arya Samaj, and that it is destined to remove superstition and ignorance and to introduce a purer form of worship in India at least, if not in other countries."[1]

As regards the religious side of the Arya Samaj the speaker insisted upon its liberal and *national* character, belief in the Vedas and in *one unincarnated God*, as laid down in the ten *Niyams* or principles formulated by Dayanand, being all that was necessary for admission into the Samaj, which did not pretend to prescribe what theories or philosophical systems its members should favour nor what articles of diet they should use.

The anniversary celebration on the 25th of November, 1893, was the last occasion on which I attended a meeting of either branches of the Arya Samaj.

When an open schism occurs in any sect or society, we

[1] Mulraj, M.A., "A Lecture on the Arya Samaj, delivered at the sixteenth anniversary of the Lahore Arya Samaj."—Anglo-Sanskrit Press, Lahore, 1894.

may safely expect some expressions of ill-feeling to be publicly indulged in by one or both parties, and we may also trust those who are equally hostile to both the contending factions to direct attention to their mutual recriminations.

In this connection the following passage written by a Christian missionary will be found both significant and instructive.

"One naturally asks, 'What was Dayananda's motive in making this wholesale perversion of the Vedas?' NO ONE WHO SEES HOW DELIBERATELY DAYANAND AND HIS FOLLOWERS DO DO THIS CAN BELIEVE FOR ONE MOMENT THAT IT IS RELIGION *QUA* RELIGION THAT IS THE MOTIVE! The first requisite in a religious reformer is sincerity. Such a man must deal reverently and honestly with the Shastra he puts forth as authoritative. With the Veda Dayanand dealt neither reverently nor honestly. Religion therefore was not the motive.

"The real motive is suggested in the following extract taken from the 'Arya Pattrika' of April 20, 1894.

"'This political teaching may prove of great use in deluding the ignorant people of Marwar that should they eat goats' flesh, thus proved from the Vedas, they would conquer irreligious men's countries. We hope that our readers will easily perceive the hidden desire of the publishers of the book—the flesh party—between the above Hindi lines. How they spoil the Holy Vedas to justify their dark designs.'

"The proverb 'Put a thief to catch a thief' is here well exemplified. In this passage the Non-flesh-eating party of the Arya Samaj accuses the Flesh-eating one (this schism has lately split up the Arya Samaj, dividing it into two pretty equal parties) of doing what they have done, from POLITICAL motives. But in point of fact POLITICAL MOTIVES are at the bottom of the whole Arya Samaj movement, whether the members be flesh-eaters or non-flesh-eaters. A religious character was given to it by Dayanand simply as a means to this end. Political motives are really those that have attracted even the rank and file. The members of the Arya Samaj are not one whit more religious—rather less so in my opinion—than their *confrères* of the old system. The reply usually given by the Aryas as to why they follow Dayanand is that he sought THE ADVANCEMENT OF THE COUNTRY (mark, not THE ADVANCEMENT OF THE RELIGION!). It is, I repeat, a political movement, and Dayananda sought to bind all his countrymen into one compact whole by giving ONE Shastra and ONE Religion, even though he had for this purpose to forge them both."[1]

In 1897 a preacher or missionary belonging to the Vegetarian (or *Mahátma*) branch of the Arya Samaj, Pandit Lekh Ram, was murdered under peculiar and painful

[1] Rev. T. Williams, "A Farce—a religion professedly based on a book, which, as translated for that religion, has no existence." A pamphlet published in 1894.—(S.P.G. Mission, Rewari.)

PANDIT LEKH RAM, PROTOMARTYR OF THE ARYA SAMAJ

To face page 171

circumstances by a young Muhammadan. It may be mentioned that for some years past an able and learned Mussulman, Mirza Ghulam Ahmad, of Qadian in the Punjab, and founder of the Ahmadiyyah sect, had assumed the *rôle* of a divinely-commissioned prophet; that in the fulfilment of his *mission* he was not particularly regardful of the feelings and beliefs of the followers of other creeds, and that he had a respectable following of almost fanatical partisans in the province where he was established.

Now Pandit Lekh Ram, in his endeavour to propagate the Vedic creed of Dayanand, seems to have constituted himself the special opponent of Islam, his speeches and writings being chiefly, though not exclusively, directed against the Muhammadans. At Delhi the pandit delivered some particularly violent speeches against Islam, and the Muhammadans brought two complaints against him in the law courts, but failed to secure a conviction or obtain any satisfaction. A month later a young man of some twenty-four or twenty-five years of age, came to Lekh Ram and represented himself as a recent convert from Hinduism to Islam; but already repentant and most anxious to be readmitted to the religion of his fathers through the gate of the Arya Samaj. Pandit Lekh Ram naturally welcomed him, and they went about together for about three weeks, when one evening—6th of March, 1897—the pretended disciple treacherously stabbed the pandit in the abdomen, as he lay on a *charpai* in the house of the vice-president of the Samaj at Lahore. The murderer made good his escape.

This event, the first martyrdom in the new Church of the Aryas, created a great sensation, mingled with deep resentment against the Muhammadans. Seven or eight thousand Hindus joined the funeral procession and followed the flower-laden bier of the martyr through the streets of the city, and about half that number were present in the grounds of the crematorium to witness the last rites.

A little while before the body was placed upon the funeral pyre, stirring speeches were made by several leading members of the Samaj, giving expression to their profound grief on this most unhappy and momentous occasion. It was represented by the speakers that their religion was in danger, that their lives were evidently not safe, and that their wily and implacable opponents were taking full advantage of the regrettable dissensions prevailing amongst the Arya brethren. Under the influence of the passionate emotions of the moment, proposals were made and accepted, but never carried out, that the two parties in the Samaj should reunite their forces and offer a solid front to their bitter foes. It was agreed that the moment was not one for tears or idle lamentations; the situation had to be faced promptly and boldly if Hinduism were to be vindicated. The same evening, therefore, while the ashes of the martyr were still warm, a crowded meeting of Hindus took place in the quadrangle of the Dayanand Anglo-Vedic College, when it was resolved that a sum of fifty thousand rupees should be raised to fittingly commemorate Pandit Lekh Ram's devotion to the cause for which he died, and that his various writings should be reprinted and distributed over the length and breadth of the land.

The excitement created by the tragic death of the Arya missionary was not confined to Lahore. Meetings in connection with Lekh Ram's dastardly murder were held in all the principal towns of the Punjab and in a few places outside that province. As a matter of course, the relations between the Mussulmans and Hindus, which of late had been of a somewhat unfriendly nature, became greatly strained. At Rawal Pindi an attempt was made, apparently by a Hindu dressed as a Muslim, to poison a number of Muhammadans by presenting them with sweetmeats after prayers in the Musjid. From amongst those who partook of these sweetmeats fourteen were taken ill and two died. Reports of similar attempts on the lives of Muhammadans at other places, with the view of avenging the murder of Lekh Ram, were also circulated. At this time, presumably at the instigation of the Hindus, the houses of the leading Muhammadans in Lahore were searched by the police, with the object —so it was believed amongst their enemies—to get information about a book on jihad (religious warfare with unbelievers) which the Amir of Cabul was said to have circulated in India.[1]

Religious animosities being, as a rule, deep-seated and long-lived, it is not surprising that time does not seem to have weakened the hatred between the "Aryas" and the Muslims, heated as it was to the highest degree by the treacherous murder of Pandit Lekh Ram and the equally treacherous acts of revenge which followed that event. Accordingly we find that as recently as August 1907 the hostility of the "Aryas" to the Muhammadans was sufficiently aggressive to induce the Government of the North-West Frontier Province to expel from the district the President of the Abbotabad branch of the Arya Samaj for violently abusing the Prophet in the open Bazaar, and thereby provoking religious disturbances.

Acrimonious dissensions within the Samaj and open enmity towards the followers of Islam did not, however, exhaust the energies of the Samajists, who discovered other fields wherein to exercise their reforming ardency. A dire famine in Northern India, the pitiful plight of the starving children, *and more especially a full realization of the benevolent work which Christian missionaries, in the interest of their own religious propaganda were carrying on in rescuing from starvation and heathenism the infant flotsam and jetsam of the terrible visitation*, aroused the Arya Samaj to action in a new direction. Influenced, no doubt, by feelings of compassion for the sufferings of the little ones, and stimulated by zeal for the preservation of Hinduism, the society made very notable efforts to snatch from death, and *from the tender hands of the Christian missionaries*, the infant victims of the famine which was devastating the land. To this end a Hindu Orphans' Relief Movement was first started in February 1897, and was subsequently maintained with creditable persistence and liberality. I have before me a Report, written by Lala Lajpat Rai, of the work done for the relief of famine-stricken orphans from October 1899 to

[1] For the particulars connected with the murder of Pandit Lekh Ram and the subsequent happenings, I am indebted to a Hindu friend of mine who was present at all the meetings, and took a deep interest in the proceedings.

November 1900, from which it appears that the rescue work was carried on over a considerable area in Rajputana, Central Provinces and portions of the Punjab. Agents of the Samaj, it appears, waited upon high officials in several Native States, " and tried to impress upon them their duty towards the orphans and other destitute children of their own territories, explaining to them how necessary it was, in the interests of the States themselves, to keep the children of their subjects on their own soil and to protect them in that trying season, not only from death by starvation, but also from being carried to distant places *for purposes of conversion into alien faiths.*" [1]

Hindu orphanages were opened through the exertions of the Arya Samaj, and a great many children brought into them. Applications were also made to the Government officials that Hindu destitute orphans might be entrusted to the care of those institutions. A certain measure of success rewarded the appeals to the authorities; but in some cases a deaf ear was apparently turned to them. For example I find it stated in the Report that :

> " We memorialized the Chief Commissioner, Central Provinces, to the effect that our claims to take charge of Hindu orphans might be considered favourably, and that we were prepared to take charge of as many as might be made over to us. We renewed our application from time to time, but to no purpose. Large numbers were made over to Christian missionaries, who sent them far away to different parts of India, but not one was given to us."

This method, persistently followed, of increasing the number of native Christians by the appropriation, through agencies well supplied with funds, of Hindu orphans or destitute children in times of national distress, and bringing up these waifs and strays as Christians of various denominations, raises an extremely delicate question not without an element of real danger, for it arouses feelings of grave discontent amongst the subject peoples against both the officials who dispose of the destitute children and the Christian missionaries who receive them. On the other hand any attempts to thwart the Christian missionaries in their self-imposed task of caring for the famishing children, *and giving them a new religion as well*, awakens, somehow or other, the strong resentment

[1] The italics are mine.—J. C. O.

LALA LAJPAT RAI

To face page 175

of these philanthropic gentlemen who, after all, are only human, and besides have to show some *results* for the money contributed towards their own support and the Christianization of India.

Now as the European and American missionary organizations, armed with long purses and favoured by the European officials, naturally score in this contest for souls, their success has suggested to the losing side the desirability of opening, in the hitherto well-guarded defences of Hinduism, new gateways for the re-admission of such "converts" as we have been considering, into the religious fold of their fathers. In this effort for the preservation of Hinduism against the aggressive missionaries, the Arya Samaj has taken a leading part. Referring to this matter, Mr. Burn in the last Census Report writes as follows: "Converts are usually made from orthodox Hindus, but special efforts are directed to reconverting as Aryas persons who have themselves been converted from Hinduism to Christianity or Islam, or the descendants of such persons."[1] And so the long-standing conflict goes on, not without serious irritation and dangerous possibilities.

When I was contemplating the issue of a revised edition of the present book, I wrote to Lala Hans Raj, B.A., Principal of the D.A.V. College (who had graduated from the Lahore Government College), asking him to put me in the way of sources of information which would help me to bring my paper on the Arya Samaj somewhat up to date. With great courtesy that gentleman placed a number of publications at my disposal, which have proved very useful, and he also informed me that Lala Lajpat Rai, a prominent member of the Arya Samaj, who was on a visit to England, would be pleased to call on me in person and give me what further information I might require. Lala Lajpat Rai, also at one time a student in the Lahore Government College, was not unknown to me, so I was glad to see him and to obtain the advantage of his intimate knowledge of the Samaj of which he had been an active member for many years.

[1] "Census of India Report," p. 367.

I reproduce below the questions I put to Lala Lajpat Rai at one of our interviews, and the answers thereto, as I believe the information thus obtained is of value for the comprehension of the aims and methods of the Arya Samaj.

I. Is the Arya Samaj an exclusively *Hindu* sect?

A Muslim was admitted by Swami Dayanand himself, but was never able to secure a social footing amongst the Hindus, though he was allowed to be present at the ceremonies and festivals of the Arya Samaj. He is still living, and is recognized as an Arya, having renounced Islam. The Arya Samaj, Gujranwallah, have admitted a Muslim graduate to the Samaj, and freely eat and drink with him. A few other Muhammadans have been admitted elsewhere. Muzbi Sikhs have also been received into the Samaj, and are freely eaten with. Many families of Christians and Muhammadans (converts from Hinduism) have been admitted into the Samaj. The intermarriage of these with the other Aryas has not been yet satisfactorily arranged.

II. Is there any formal ceremony of initiation into the Arya Samaj? If so, what are the details of such ceremony?

With Hindus merely signing the declaration of faith is sufficient. In the case of non-Hindus a *shuddhi* ceremony of a simple kind is obligatory though not necessarily carried out by a Brahman. Yet, of course, such Pandits are usually employed. After fasting, bathing, shaving and changing his clothes, and after the *Hom* ceremony has been performed, he accepts the *Gayatri*.

Those who were originally (as Hindus) entitled to wear the sacred thread are again invested with it. In the case of men who are not Hindus by origin the thread has also been conferred, and this has, as might have been expected, given rise to some objection and opposition.

III. Are the ordinary rules of the Hindu caste system set aside in the Samaj? Do Arya Samajists intermarry or even eat with one another irrespective of caste?

In the Punjab eating in common is usual; but hardly yet in the United Provinces. As regards marriage the position is very delicate and quite experimental. Marriages between members of sub-castes have occasionally been carried out, and it is the policy of the Samaj to encourage such, leaving the castes to be dealt with later on. In *theory* the Samaj does not recognize hereditary castes. In the case of the marriages of orphan girls adopted by the Samaj, the usual caste rules have been set aside and such marriages have come to be accepted, or, at any rate, have not been objected to.

IV. Idolatry, I know, is condemned by the Aryas; but do they repudiate the Hindu gods, Vishnu and Siva, and deny them worship?

These names, Vishnu and Siva, are accepted as names of the one God; but the reputed consorts of Vishnu and Siva—Durga, Kali, Devi, etc.—are not regarded as divinities.

V. Do the Aryas conduct their birth, marriage and funeral ceremonies without the help of the Brahmans?

Generally Brahmans are employed, but qualified persons who are not Brahmans often officiate in the performance, particularly of birth and funeral ceremonies.[1]

Cremation is practised, but no post-funeral rites are carried out, beyond the purification of the house where the dead body lay, by the performance of the *Hom* with all the prescribed mantras.

VI. I am aware that the Aryas profess belief in the transmigration of souls and that they venerate the cow; but are their ideas of a future life and hell and heaven those of the orthodox Hindu?

Yes, the doctrine of reincarnations is believed in, and the cow is venerated by the Aryas. Heaven and Hell, in the Hindu or usual sense, are not believed in by the Arya Samaj.

The Arya Samaj holds with Swami Dayanand that there are three entities, the Supreme Soul, the Soul of Man and Matter.

---

[1] Here we have an example of Brahmanical functions usurped by *non-Brahmans*, whose descendants may, at some future time, claim to be of genuine Brahmanical stock.

VII. The Samaj is said to be aggressively anti-Christian. Is this so?	Certainly, *on the defensive.*
VIII. The teachings of Swami Dayanand in regard to *Niyoga* is, I understand, taken by all his followers as an essential part of the Master's doctrines. Am I right?	The Samaj does not consider *Niyoga* an essential doctrine.
IX. After the murder of Pandit Lekh Ram there was, I know, an attempt to bring about a reconciliation between the two sections of the Samaj. What was the result?	The division still exists. The Mahátma Samaj made good progress, but is now suffering from internal strife.
X. Have there been any other schisms in the Arya Samaj since 1893?	No.
XI. Some time back it was given out that Swami Bhaskara Nand Saraswati had established a branch of the Arya Samaj in Philadelphia, U.S.A. Is this true?	Not credited by those who knew him best.
XII. What are the *political* aims of the society?	None at all.

In connection with the last point I may here reproduce, without comment, the following manifesto published in June 1907, by the President, Vice-President and leading members of the Arya Samaj:

"We are much grieved to learn that several people have insinuated that the Arya Samaj is connected with the political agitation, constitutional as well as unconstitutional, that has been going on in the Punjab for the past few months. This is entirely without foundation. The Arya Samaj is a non-political body, and as such, it has no connection with any kind of political agitation. It cannot be denied that some members of the Arya Samaj, along with their brethren of other communities, Hindus, Sikhs, Mahomedans and Christians, have taken part in the constitutional and political agitation, and that of late a few fanatics, drawn from different classes, have been preaching and writing sedition, and have brought troubles even upon those who were for constitutional agitation. We as members of the Arya Samaj and as subjects of the British Government, strongly disapprove of the conduct of those fanatics and declare that we have no sympathy for their doings.

"It is unfortunate that Lala Lajpat Rai, Lalas Hans Raj, and Gurdas Ram of Rawalpindi, prominent members of the Arya Samaj, have been suspected of unconstitutional agitation. We believe that these gentlemen were advocates of constitutional agitation only, and that sedition had no place in their minds. They have suffered terribly, and we pray to God that their innocence may be soon proved to the satisfaction of the Government."

How far the profession of the creed of the Arya Samaj will lead the members of the sect to abandon Hindu rites and customs hallowed by time, is a point of interest which may profitably occupy us for a moment. As far as I have been able to ascertain, not many Aryas have dared to openly set at naught the hereditary customs in which the Brahmans play a part, though an attempt has been made to modify some of the hitherto recognized ceremonies. For instance, in the early days of the Society, two young men were invested with the sacred thread at Lahore under the auspices of the Arya Samaj. A Brahman pandit was induced to officiate on the occasion, but all rites of an idolatrous character were omitted. The Brahman's fee for the double investiture and the other necessary expenses came up to fifteen rupees, so that the cost to each of the young men was a moiety of that amount. For a long time the two young men in question were objects of ridicule to their orthodox fellows, who proposed, in derision of the irregular ceremony which had been performed with the countenance of the Arya Samaj, to invest any sweeper with the thread on his paying the now recognized fee of seven rupees and eight annas. It is, I understand, a rule of the Arya Samaj to abandon the custom of early marriages. Yet a prominent member of the sect, a university graduate, and a minister of a foreign state, broke the rule in the case of his own son.

I was once present at a wedding conducted, according to the reformed ritual of the Arya Samaj, without idolatrous rites and without any display. Instead of marriage songs, *bhajans* or hymns were sung by the women, and notwithstanding some very simple attempts at decoration the affair, with its symbolic scented candles, bundle of sticks and lotah of milk, was plainly lacking in interest. The bride's face was, as usual, carefully concealed from view. I asked a friend whether the bridegroom had ever seen her, and a young fellow crouched at my feet volunteered the remark, "He may have seen her photograph." "Is that allowable?" I queried. "Yes, in these days," was the reply, with a knowing snigger.

A painful instance of the trouble arising from the desire

on the part of an earnest young reformer to carry out the principles of the sect on the occasion of the death of his own father, came to my knowledge. It appears that when news of the critical condition of his father reached the reformer in question, he hurried to Multan, where the old man was, and arrived just in time to see him expire. Bent on keeping strictly to his newly-adopted principles, the young man staunchly refused to have any Brahmanical rites performed on the occasion, nor would he consent to have his own head and face shaved in accordance with orthodox practice. The result was that the *bradri* (brotherhood) refused to help in the cremation of the dead, and angrily held aloof. Deceased's son as obstinately declined to yield a point, and the poor old man's body lay, hour after hour, in the open court of the house, to the horror and dismay of the family, particularly the women-folk. At length the Arya reformer's persistence influenced a few of the younger men to stand by him in his determination to abide by the much-vaunted arrangements of the new sect; and the old man's body was carried to the cremating ground attended by a score of youths amidst the unconcealed disgust and contempt of the multitude. No Brahman was allowed to have anything to do with the obsequies. As he would have done under ordinary circumstances the son lighted the pyre, and in due course the corpse was reduced to ashes. "What but disaster could follow so foolish an abandonment of time-honoured customs or divine ordinances?" argued the weeping, outraged women, and so also said the orthodox pandits, and it came to pass that the young reformer was not long in following his father to the unknown land.

Another case connected with funeral rites may be referred to. A native gentleman holding a superior Government appointment and vice-president of one of the more recently-established Arya Samajes lost his father, and on this sad occasion performed the funeral rites according to the ritual prescribed by his Samaj, exposed the while to the execrations of the women and the taunts of the orthodox. Immediately afterwards the vice-president started on a visit to his native town Behra. In defiance of orthodox custom he had not shaved his face and head as a sign of mourning, but on the journey home he had this operation carried out in order that he might appear before his relatives and friends at home as a Hindu mourner is expected to do. His secret plan was to stay away in his native place till his beard had grown again, and then to return to his *confrères* of the Samaj just as he had left them. But his artful doings came to be known. At home he was obliged by the clamour of the family to repeat the post-funeral rites for his father in accordance with the orthodox practice, and then, of course, his brethren of the Samaj created a hubbub which long agitated the Society and amused the scoffers. Both the Arya Samajists and the orthodox Hindus denounced his duplicity, and no doubt our humiliated vice-president had ample reason to regret having set up as an unflinching reformer of social and religious customs.

Section V.—Concluding Remarks

The influence of the spirit of scientific rationalism which, with the diffusion of European education, has for years past been making itself felt throughout India, rendered it inevitable that various attempts should be made for the reconstruction or reform of the ancient creeds of the country. That a new and a rationalistic interpretation of the Vedas could be made by Dayanand, a Brahman unacquainted with any European language, shows to what a depth below the surface the modern spirit has permeated. The persistent and organized aggressiveness of Christian missionary effort has also forced the Hindus, particularly the educated and priestly classes, to reconsider the foundations of their faith, while creating a strong feeling of opposition to their well-meant efforts at evangelization. Between the unanswerable truths of science on the one hand, and the uncompromising attitude of condemnation taken up by the Christian missionaries on the other, the leaders of native thought in India felt that something had to be done, and done quickly. The old strongholds had become untenable, the greater portion of the land was clearly defenceless, so the Arya, retiring before the enemy and practically surrendering the whole country, has taken refuge behind the bulwarks of a little-known and very ancient fortress in the recesses of the mountain.

Viewed broadly, and without a too close reference to its more or less settled tenets and opinions, the Arya movement is an acknowledgment on the part of a section of the Hindu community of the intellectually unsustainable character of popular Hinduism; and it is also a patriotic demonstration against Christianity. In this last respect lies its real influence as a factor in the future of native society, but to me it seems to possess too little vitality to make a successful stand against Brahman and missionary, although I am assured that the enthusiasm for the Arya cause is so great that many men give to the Samaj a month's pay every year and others as much as *half their entire salary*. Others, again, put aside, in a separate vessel, a handful of meal out of every supply taken for their daily food, and sell the accumulated store for the benefit of the Samaj at the end of each month. Widows, who have no further need of their jewels, have been known to present them to the Samaj.

In one respect the Arya sect is in the first of the many stages through which the Brahmo Samaj has passed. It pins its faith upon the Vedas as did the earlier Brahmos;[1] but there is this difference—the Arya Samajist has a new interpretation of the Vedas to go upon. It is the Vedas not as usually understood, *but as interpreted by Dayanand*, that he believes in. But this, on the face of it, is not a very stable foundation upon which to rear a new religion. The men who have become the disciples of Dayanand are, with a few exceptions perhaps, by no means competent to understand or critically appreciate the soundness, or otherwise, of his interpretation of the Vedas. They have been drawn to him, not from a scholarly conviction of his genuine knowledge, but by the personal influence of the man, and by his offering them a *national* religion without idolatry. The Arya may think

[1] In the early days of its existence the Brahmo sect held staunchly by the Vedas, but after a deliberate and critical study of those ancient books, under the leadership of Debendra Nath Tagore, it formally rejected them as being at variance with true theism.

he has found, or may profess to find, in the *Rig* and *Yajur* Vedas a purer and more reasonable faith than that preached by the Christian or Muslim missionaries, but there is strong ground for believing that as long as he clings to any form of Hinduism he will not be able to free himself from the hereditary priesthood who have guided and ruled the social life of India for so many centuries.

After a careful consideration of the matter, I am inclined to think that the Arya Samaj is at most destined to form one inconsiderable sect amongst the innumerable sects into which Hinduism is divided. But even as a numerically inconsiderable Hindu sect, the Arya Samaj, composed as it is mostly of men who have received an English education, will probably be an important factor in the regeneration of India, whilst its open abandonment of idolatry and its public profession of monotheism cannot fail to have a healthy influence on religious opinion in India. As we have seen, the Arya Samaj has from its foundation manifested a tendency to take a share in the political agitation which has been very active in India during recent years; a fact which, I think, shows that the Society owes its existence quite as much to national as to religious aspirations.

In this respect it differs strikingly from the religious movement which found expression in the Brahma or Brahmo Samaj of Bengal. Of the two sects, both professedly monotheistic and non-idolatrous, one is national, militant and practical; the other and older one, which originated in Bengal, is cosmopolitan, dreamy and emotional.

According to the Census Report of 1901 the Aryas numbered 92,419 and the Brahmas only 4,050 souls. In regard to the geographical distribution of these sects we learn from the same source that the Aryas were to be found almost exclusively in the Western districts of the United Provinces and in the Punjab; in those portions of India, indeed, where, as we have seen, Dayanand's commanding personal influence had been exerted and had made a deep impression. While the Brahmos, followers of Bengalí reformers, were, to the extent of 75 per cent. of their entire number, resident in Bengal.

PART II.—SOCIAL

I. AT THE PLAY
II. AT THE FAIR
III. BAZAAR GUP
IV. MENDICANCY AND MENDICANTS OF SORTS

CHAPTER I

AT THE PLAY; THE NEW INDIAN THEATRE

THE old Sanskrit dramas — unintelligible to the masses or even to the cultured classes in these days —have been appreciatively described by European scholars;[1] but of the plays which interest and amuse the modern Indian very little has, as far as I know, been recorded, therefore I venture to hope that an account of my experiences and observations in this field, limited though they be, will be acceptable to my readers.

There is perhaps less difference between London and Lahore than there is between a play like "The Sins of Society," at Drury Lane, and one like "Indur Sabha" on a Hindu stage in Anarkali.

[1] R. W. Frazer, LL.B., "A Literary History of India," chapter xii. Prof. H. H. Wilson, "Theatre of the Hindus," 2 vols.

The performances which I am about to describe took place in mere temporary sheds, simply because there were no permanent theatres or better accommodation for such theatrical representations existing in the capital of the Punjab, or probably anywhere in Northern India. At Calcutta, I understand, the Bengalís have got two or three theatres of their own, but I regret to say I have not visited any of them.

The play of Aladdin, or the Wonderful Lamp.—On an evening in March I went, accompanied by a friend, to witness the performance by a Parsí dramatic company of "Aladdin, or the Wonderful Lamp," in the temporary theatre erected not far from the Mayo Hospital at Lahore. The theatre was a huge shed, very dimly lighted by a single chandelier of only four lamps, suspended in the centre of the room, and a couple of wall-lamps with reflectors fixed against side-posts. These six lamps, with the row of foot-lights on the stage, constituted the entire lighting arrangements of the theatre, and, as might be readily imagined, every part of this big shed, with the exception of the stage, was in semi-darkness. When my friend and I arrived, about twenty minutes before the time appointed for the commencement of the play, the place was already thronged with an audience representing all ranks of the native community except the highest. There were also present, occupying for the most part the front rows, a small number of Europeans and Eurasians of the lower classes, including a sprinkling of respectable representatives of the gentler sex, some of them in demi-toilette and evidently dressed for the occasion.

The stage, as we soon had an opportunity of learning, was got up after the European model, and was provided with an abundance of trap-doors and lifts, so necessary for the sudden appearance and disappearance of the genii who figure in the story of Aladdin.

The piece was performed in the Urdu language, and the whole of it, with trifling exceptions, was sung to the accompaniment of a *sárangi* and a drum. I had not been prepared for this musical performance, and found it rather more difficult to follow the words as they reached us not a little disguised by their passage through the nasal organs of the performers.

The troupe consisted of ten Parsí men and one young European woman, whom a strange fate had brought into association with this roving company of men of an entirely alien race and creed.

The curtain rose to discover a black, thickly-bearded, well-featured man standing at a small table, with alembics and crucibles in the background, engaged in some magic rites. In his hand he held an hour-glass. This was the famous magician of the story. After consulting the hour-glass attentively once or twice, he fired a pistol below the table, and immediately up rose a fairy, from whom, after a short colloquy, he received a ring. The fairy then vanished as suddenly as she had appeared. Rubbing the ring, and again discharging the pistol, brought up, this time, the venerable king of the genii, from whom the magician learned particulars as to how possession of the wonderful lamp might be secured.

During these proceedings, there lay unnoticed a dark figure prostrate on the floor. A kick from the magician brought the sleeper to his feet in apparent confusion, and introduced to the audience a dumb half-witted Abyssinian slave, who henceforward played a part, more or less irrelevant and absurd, in every succeeding scene.

This character has, as far as I remember, no warrant whatever in the "Arabian Nights." It is apparently introduced as a concession to the rules of the modern Indian theatre, which, "like the ancient, has its *bidushaka* or privileged buffoon, the companion of the king; who generally unites great shrewdness and mother-wit with love of creature comforts."[1]

The next was a street scene.[2] Aladdin and a number of youths were playing at ball, and quarrelling and fighting over their game, when Aladdin's old mother came

[1] 'The Modern Hindu Drama,' by Babu Kissory Chand Mitra: "Calcutta Review," vol. lvii.

[2] To appreciate the fact of the use of scenery in these popular representations, it should be remembered that as Professor Wilson says, writing on the Indian theatre, the Hindus probably never knew what scenes were, and substituted curtains for them.

upon them, and not without some little trouble got her wayward, petulant boy away from the others, advising him to give up childish frivolities, and to learn wisdom at last. The acting in this scene, of both mother and son, was good, that of the old lady particularly so, and gave me a favourable opinion of the histrionic talent of at least some members of the troupe.

As scene after scene of the well-known story, which has delighted many successive generations of young people in the West as well as in the East, was presented to us, as "old lamps for new" was being cried in the streets of Bagdad, as the wily magician gradually got Aladdin into his toils, as the genii came and went in obedience to the possessor of the lamp, I felt somehow that this story, so entirely in keeping with the genius of the East, enacted thus in an Eastern tongue, before an Oriental audience, and with appropriate natural surroundings, lost much of its improbability, and seemed to be a presentment of what might have actually happened. In fact I was for the moment under the spell, as it were, of the mystic genius of Asia.

As I mentioned before, there was but one woman in the troupe, and she a European. Women, I am informed, have only very recently begun to appear on the regular stage in India, though they have always taken part in the *panchaly* performances in the Bengal zenanas. Nor need we be surprised at this, when we recollect that it was not until the Restoration that females appeared on the boards of an English theatre. But I should add that, according to Professor H. H. Wilson, female characters were generally represented on the old Hindu stage by females, although it was not uncommon for men or lads to personate females in certain cases. No native women were, as far as I could see, present at the performance of Aladdin; not even *hetæræ*, who, it is certain, frequented the Greek theatre, from which respectable females were excluded.

Indur Sabha.—Very different from Aladdin, and performed by an entirely different company, and in another place, was the play I now proceed to describe, a very popular modern drama, "Indur Sabha," composed, it is said, by a Mussulman poet, by command of Wajid Ali Shah, ex-king of Oudh.

The theatre was a huge framework of bamboos, badly put together and covered with thin cloth or canvas sheeting. The stage was good enough, and was lighted by some fifteen lamps with reflectors. There were no other lamps in the big enclosure, but a tropical moon shining through the ceiling-cloth gave a subdued light which was far from disagreeable. The reserved seats consisted of two rows of chairs, the first class of a similar double row a little further back; then came a barrier, and behind it a rude arrangement of seats for the bulk of the spectators. The charges for seats varied from three rupees to four annas each, and there was a special place reserved, at eight annas a seat, for "native females"; but I did not see any there, or anywhere else in the theatre. The performance was advertised to commence at nine. At about two minutes to that hour, I took my seat in what appeared an almost empty house. A quarter of an hour went by; I ventured to inquire of an attendant connected with the theatre when the performance commenced. "At nine," he said, but added significantly, "You see they don't come till late"—referring, as I understood, to the audience. "And so you wait for them?" I observed. "Yes," he replied, "we *must* wait for them." Twenty minutes past nine, the half-past nine gun, and no sign of business nor the slightest indication of impatience on the part of the audience, which had now increased considerably. This, at any rate, gave me time to study my company. In the first row of all, and just before me, was a young Eurasian woman in a yellow satin dress, evidently got up for the "opera"; a portly companion in a serviceable stuff dress chaperoned her; a little boy about twelve years of age and a native girl, perhaps a trifle younger, dressed in a *sari* of flaring red, completed the party. The little girl took her seat quite naturally with her beautiful big eyes riveted, in mute wonder, on the glories of the drop-screen, when she was rudely awakened from her fairy dreams by one of the attendants, who told her to go further back and not to sit with the *sahibs*. Very reluctantly the little girl, whose "first opera" this evidently was, retired, without withdrawing her eyes from the stage, where evidently she expected something wonderful to take place. A quarter to ten—tinkle! tinkle! tinkle! and up goes the screen to reveal to a delighted audience a sort of fairy palace-garden, where, on a comfortable sofa, lay a sleeping prince, Goolfam of Hind. Bang! and behold a fairy all in green, and glittering with tinsel, floats down from the upper air on cords, alas! too visible. The prince does not awake, and Sabz Parí—for that is her name—hovers round him enamoured of his beauty. In song and dance (the slow voluptuous measure peculiar to the East) she gives expression to her tender feelings, to the accompaniment of an unseen orchestra of stringed instruments and *tablas*.

The next scene reveals the court of Indur. Seated on his throne, with courtiers and attendants about him, appears the King of Heaven, against a striking background of forked lightning, stars and suns, with the most impossible of mountain ranges that scene-painter ever put on canvas. Stiff, uncomfortable, and very much bored looked poor Indur—"one of the principal deities of heaven" according to the playbill—as he sat in state upon his tinselled throne, and it did not surprise me when he ordered a demon attendant to summon a heavenly *nautch-girl* to amuse him. Immediately there appeared, from a trap-door, a *parí* all in gauze and glittering tinsel, with enough clothing on to satisfy the most prudish taste, decked with jewellery of various sorts, amongst which tinkling anklets and wristlets were not omitted; but there were no shoes on her feet. She danced, or rather glided, with clinking anklets, before the king to a sort of slow measure, never lifting her feet more than half-an-inch off the floor, swaying her body about gently, and moving her uplifted arms in a graceful manner. Nothing in the world could be more in contrast than the dress, the movements, and the manner of this *bayadère* and those of a spry, pirouetting ballet-dancer in silk tights on the boards of a European theatre, which contrast will not be lessened by the fact that the graceful *pari* was after all a man, who figured in the play-bill as "Master Homi." The audience highly appreciated the

Photo by W. Bal

A NAUTCH-GIRL, WITH HER ATTENDANTS

To face page 102

parí's performance, and the King of Heaven was also so well pleased that he wanted more entertainment of the same kind, and had three other parís in succession dancing before him, the last of these being the too susceptible Sabz Parí, who on her way to the court had seen Goolfam asleep in the garden. Dreary and puerile appeared to me the protracted scene, as parí after parí, introduced by trapdoors from below, came forward and sang and danced to please the King of Heaven. To my untutored ear, the measure and the music seemed always the same, and the sentiments, as far as I could understand them, not very novel. But tastes differ, and the audience, I am bound to say, viewed the performance with very different eyes from mine, and were highly pleased with it.

The glories of Indur's reception-hall gave place to a small room, in which the poor green parí, madly in love with Goolfam, persuades a demon of the court to bring the prince to her. Hardly has the demon consented to carry out her wishes, when lo! suspended in mid-air, appears the couch of the still slumbering Goolfam. The demon awakes him, and then conceals himself. The mystified and astonished prince, lost in wonder at his new surroundings, feels, as one would feel quite naturally in the East, that he is in the toils of some magician. The green parí appears and attempts to reassure him, offering him her love in the most forward, unblushing, and disagreeable style,[1] but the prince cannot reconcile himself to his new situation, looks regretfully towards his native Hind, and repulses her with cold disdain. Learning, however, that the parí comes from Indur's court, he is carried away by a desire to see the wonders of the celestial kingdom, and promises to return her affection if she will only take him there. But to introduce a mortal amongst the celestials was a serious business, beset with the gravest difficulties, and Sabz Parí protests her inability to gratify his whim. To gain his point, the prince

[1] This is not an uncommon feature of the plays which delight a modern Indian audience. Women in love are frequently represented as pursuing the object of their passion in the most unblushing manner, notwithstanding the rudest rebuffs. See the story of Puran Bhagat, at the end of this chapter.

hints that far from being a parí of Indur's heaven, his admirer must be, at best, only the mistress of some wretched demon; an insinuation which Sabz Parí resents by giving him a smart box on the ear. In vain she declares that no human being could gain admittance to Indur's court; Goolfam is obdurate, and in the end Green-parí—poor enamoured parí—yields to his importunities, and conceals him in a place from which he can view the glittering spectacle he so longed to see. Here in the midst of the usual enjoyments, the singing and dancing of the celestial *nautch-girls*, a demon attendant smells the human intruder and drags him before the king. All is now apparent to an indignantly virtuous court. The wanton parí, with wings clipped, is banished, and the Prince of Hind sentenced to pass his life in a solitary cave. In the last act everything is put right. The fame of the beauty and power of song of a certain wandering female devotee reaches King Indur, and he requests her presence at his court. She comes, and charms the god with both her person and her voice. To reward her, Indur offers her one costly gift after another, but she declines them all. He then offers to give her whatever she might ask for. "Give me Goolfam," says the happy *yognee*, who is, of course, no other than Sabz Parí, and the Prince of Hind is duly restored to her loving arms.

Of the two plays I have just described, "Aladdin," though Oriental in its genius and surroundings, and with a large element of the supernatural in it, was acted by men who had, I fancy, formed their style upon European models, and who accordingly introduced a good deal of vivacity and human interest into the piece. The acting and singing in "Indur Sabha" was dull and stately, without animation, action, or expression; but, as I have already said, unquestionably suited the taste of the audience. The music was at times decidedly pleasant even to my ears, all untrained in the mysteries of Eastern harmony. The representation closed with a melody which certainly was not without a beauty of its own, and fairly carried the audience away.

Somehow the court of Indur, when the lifted curtain disclosed to our view the Olympians sitting in solemn state, reminded me forcibly of the final result of the *Katputlee ka tamasha*, an Indian performance of marionettes not unfamiliar to most Anglo-Indian children, which mainly consists in a lot of tinselled Rajas coming out and taking their seats, in solemn state, on a row of tinselled thrones. As each high and mighty Raja floats into the reception-hall, suspended by a fine wire which *ought* to be invisible, the manager announces the many grand-sounding titles which it is his happy privilege to possess, and the pompous grandee slowly subsides into his seat. The attendant musicians play vigorously on their *tablahs*, and another slow and solemn chief of world-wide fame enters; and so on, till at last the entire row of seats is occupied by the gaudy dolls, whose appearance, as they sit in state on their tiny thrones, is as ridiculous as their titles.

One more account of an Indian theatrical representation, and I have done. This time the play was acted at the expense of a successful tradesman, who hoped to acquire some religious merit by having a moral drama produced for the benefit of his fellow-townsmen. Admission being free, the audience was by no means select; but it was as orderly and well-behaved as the best-bred audience could have been. There was a stage for the actors; but there were no seats for the audience, who contentedly squatted down on a terrace floor before the stage, under the open canopy of a lovely starlit heaven—and a more suitable *auditorium* could not be imagined for a sultry night of an Indian summer.

The drama of Prahlad.—The play selected, known as "Prahlad," is a good sample of the most popular Indian dramas. I went to the performance at half-past nine and left at midnight, when the play was only half over. The first scene opened with a potter's oven. A few homely and very familiar articles of Indian pottery, *chiraghs* and *chillums*, were about to be baked under the superintendence of a woman, who was dressed very much better than women of her station in life usually are. In the potter's oven a cat had placed four of her kittens, and Prahlad (the king's son), who happened to come that way, observing them, told the woman that she should remove the helpless creatures or they would be burnt to death. "If it is the will of god (Rama) that they should live, they will be safe enough in the oven!" said the woman. "Rama!" replied the lad; "why, my father is greater than he,[1] and my father himself could not save them alive in the blazing furnace." "Let us see," was the answer. For four days the fire was allowed to glow, but, strange to say, the kittens were none the worse for it. Prahlad, upon this, became a devoted and fanatical follower of Rama, who he confessed was a greater being than his father the king. His devotion to the worship of Rama roused the indignation of his mother, who, curiously enough, made him over to a Brahman schoolmaster to be taught better ways. Nothing, however, could shake his reverence for Rama, whose name was always on his lips.

The scene in the Brahman's school, brought on the stage before us, was intended to be a humorous one. The boys cuffed one another behind the master's back, made faces at the pedagogue when he could not see them, and so on. Prahlad himself took no great part in the pranks and horseplay of the other boys, but frequently exclaimed "Rama! Rama!" for which unseasonable interruption the master would give him a taste of the cane. He was, however, incorrigible. Tired out by his refractory pupil, the Brahman went to the king, who took the boy in hand himself, and, after trying argument and persuasion in vain, ordered him to be put to death. The pious young prince, the devoted adorer of Rama, was taken out to be hanged—was, in fact, actually hanged before us, but the rope broke; he was thrown from a hill, but not hurt; he was struck by the executioner's sword, but remained unharmed. Enraged beyond endurance, the father drew his own mighty sabre upon his obstinate son. At this critical moment the ground opened, and Rama (Vishnu), in the form of a formidable tiger, appearing upon the scene, tore the impious king to pieces. Could anything

[1] Prahlad's boast was not without some good foundation, as his father, "Hiranya-Kasipu, in his wars with the gods, had wrested the sovereignty of heaven from Indra, and dwelt there in luxury" (Professor Dowson's "Classical Dictionary of Hindu Mythology").

in the world be more religious, more tedious, and more utterly Indian?

As for the acting in this very serious and moral piece, it was enough to make one laugh outright; though the audience, to judge from their almost reverent attention, seemed very much impressed by it. In the opening scene, when the dialogue took place between the prince and the potter's wife, the speaker, whichever it happened to be, always stood near the left-hand corner of the stage, behind which the prompter was concealed. The prince, about to take up the dialogue, would step slowly to the left and the potter's wife would go, as slowly, to the right-hand corner of the stage. After he had said his say, they would change places, slowly and majestically, and the woman would repeat what the prompter told her from behind the curtain. Although this ridiculous interchange of places went on for ever so long, not a soul amongst the audience appeared in the least degree amused by it.

As my object in this short chapter has been to give an idea, however inadequate and imperfect, of the popular modern Indian drama, at least in the Punjab, I make no apology for reproducing here the argument of the favourite opera, "Puran Bhagat," as given in the play-bills, since it will perhaps afford some insight into the conditions of Eastern life and the taste of the people in regard to the subjects best suited for dramatic representation.

Puran Bhagat.—The play-bill says, in regard to the opera, "Puran Bhagat":

"This piece, which is in the mouth of every one in the Province, is expressly translated with some alterations from a Punjabi domestic true story. It gives an example of the proverbial saying 'Murder will out,' and the author has no doubt intended to intimate that though secrecy may veil the deed of the murderer for a time, 'Providence,' that suffers not a sparrow to fall to the ground unnoticed, will by some means or other both expose and punish the evil-doer. The triumph of virtue over vice is also represented in an affecting manner.

"ARGUMENT OF THE OPERA.

"In Sealkote (Punjab) there was a King called Saliwan who had a Queen by name Lona (daughter of a cobbler), she was both accomplished and fair, but equally cruel and incontinent. The King had no issue by her.

"He had a son called Puran by his first Queen. The King was very fond of Lona, having never loved his first Queen since espousing her. One day the King ordered his son Puran to visit his stepmother. The Prince wished to obey the command of his royal father, but was advised by his mother to avoid Queen Lona, as she was a woman of an intriguing nature. However, he obeyed his father's orders, and was received in a very kind manner. Queen Lona fell in love with him, and there and then declared her passion. Puran refused her proposal with disdain; she, disappointed and thwarted in her desires, accused Puran of dishonourable conduct and of attempts against her honour and constancy. King Saliwan entering the palace finds his wife in a sorrowful mood, and believing her words to be true, orders Puran to be kept in close confinement. Lona, mad with love, again wishes to persuade Puran, and after obtaining permission from the King, visits him in prison on a pretence to advise him to desist from such immoral conduct, and instead of advising urges him again to satisfy her passion. The Prince refuses, and she on seeing the King and Puran's mother eavesdropping, pretends her love to Puran as that of a mother, but Puran was still bad and wanted to love her as a mistress; the King gets incensed beyond measure, orders the poor Prince to be thrown into a well. The Queen mother tries to get him pardoned, but the King gets angry with her also, and turns her out to the jungles.

"Some hermits discover Puran in the well; relieve him from his confinement; he joins them as a Faqueer. Puran enters a city as a Dervish and asks charity in a house, where the owner is a beautiful orphan lady called Soondra, she pities him and falls in love, and urges Puran to accept her proposal. He advises her to abstain from such a bad passion. She supplicates. At this time Puran's Saint enters, and advises Puran to desist from this world's pleasures. She in disappointment goes after Puran in the disguise of a Nun.

"One night King Saliwan dreams, and sees Puran's Saint revealing to him the intrigues of Lona and Puran's innocence. The Saint by his power, as a punishment makes him blind, and as the only cure to his malady, recommends the King to wash his hands in Lona's blood.

"On one hand the Queen mother, and on the other hand Soondra, wandering encounter each other in a jungle, where after mutual explanations they recognize each other in disguise. But here we must digress a little.

"The King having now become aware of his folly, intends of revenge and to bring an end Lona's life. At this juncture Puran enters, and requests his father to pardon her. The Saint presses him to end her life, but at the urgent solicitation of Puran, Lona is forgiven. Lona apologizes sincerely for her crime. The Saint promises the King to cure him, sends Puran in search of his mother, who after surmounting vast difficulties finds them in a jungle, and a happy meeting takes place. The disconsolate King is relieved from all pains, unites Puran with Soondra, and the curtain falls to the strains of a pleasant song."

So much for the plays popular in Northern India. I may add here that I have also been present at an "up-to-date" temperance play, to which I have made allusion in another book.[1] I am moreover aware that various adaptations in Urdu of Shakesperian dramas have been prepared to suit Indian taste, and have been duly performed under new names and with a new setting.

As for the lively and quick-witted Bengalís, they are particularly fond of dramatic representations, and rejoice in a very popular form of mythological drama known as the *Yatra* or *Jatra*.[2] They have also the *Panchaly* represented only by actresses for the amusement of the secluded inmates of the zenanas.[3] With regard to the modern drama in Bengal we learn from a Bengalí writer that it owes its origin entirely to the vivifying influence of English education which led to a revival of Sanskrit studies, and that it can date only from the eventful year 1857, when, for the first time, a Bengalí version of the Sanskrit drama, "Sakuntala," was performed at Simla in the house of Babu Asutosh Dev.[4] In fact it was the study of Shakespeare and English dramatic literature in the state and missionary colleges which, in the first instance, stimulated the Bengalís to bring out vernacular versions of the old and almost forgotten Sanskrit plays, and subsequently led to the composition of original plays both tragic and comic. With the birth of the modern Bengalí drama, theatres, both private and public, constructed after the modern European type, came into use.

As I stated at the commencement of this chapter I have had no firsthand knowledge of the Bengalí theatre; but a play-bill of one of these playhouses which came into my hands is so interesting and informing that for the benefit of my readers I reproduce it here exactly as it appeared in a Lahore newspaper. There are, unfortunately, some obvious misprints in it, but I have not ventured to make any alterations.

[1] "The Brahmans, Theists and Muslims of India," pp. 172–3.

[2] "The Yatras, or popular Dramas of Bengal," by Nisikanta Chattopadhyaya. Trübner and Co.

[3] "The Hindoos as They Are," by Shib Chunder Bose, p. 19.

[4] 'The Modern Hindu Drama,' by Kissory Chand Mitra: "Calcutta Review," vol. lvii.

SATURDAY AND SUNDAY, 28TH AND 29TH MAY.

NATIONAL THEATRE, 6, BEADON STREET.

Saturday the 28th May, 1881.

At 9 P.M. will be repeated with necessary improvements and additional grandeur, that new and original historical drama by Babu Grish Chunder Ghosh

ANUNDO ROHO, OR AKBAR.

This new drama is no stale story told in dull monotonous dialogue, nor is the work crammed with tremendous tiring octavo speeches and soliloquies. The greatest statesman and mightiest monarch Akbar is portrayed with a truely histrionic pen.

The dying speech of Rana Pratap will bring tears from every human eye!

The scene where Akbar suffers from the effects of poison, falling a victim to his own malicious machinations, that monarch of monarchs whose single breath could one day change the fortune of this vast Indian Empire suffering all the untold tortures of hell in his secluded pavilion in the centre of a tank, and now so poor as so console his burning soul or pour a drop of water on his scalded tongue, this awfully grand scene we say will have an impression in the mind of the spectators never to be effaced, and impart a lesson illustrative of the Truth, that the crooked path of *policy* is always perilous!

BETAL.—A quite original and strictly national character, sublime and magnanimous, will be played by Babu Grish Chunder Ghosh.

Soul dissolving songs—where religion and love are harmoniously blended together—will even for the instant inspire confidence and love for Good in the heart of the most ungodly!

SCENES.—As for our scenic grandeur, we need only say "Come and see!"

NEXT DAY, SUNDAY, AT 6 P.M., THAT SPARKLING MELODRAMA,

MAGIC STATUE.

All the local papers have spoken very highly of this piece, both as a practical production and stage play.

☞ *Please note.*—This is that well received play in the *finale* of which marble statues are transformed into living beauties.

G. C. GHOSH,
Manager.

This characteristic Bengalí play-bill with its distinctly moral tone speaks for itself, and does not call for any special commentary.

Photo by W. Campbell Oman

THE EKKA OF NORTHERN INDIA

To face page 201

CHAPTER II

AT THE FAIR

SECTION I.—INTRODUCTORY REMARKS

FAIRS, or *melas*, are a very common, agreeable and picturesque feature of Indian life, exhibiting as they do in their every aspect, the characteristic amiability, temperance and reasonableness of a people whose civilization is not of yesterday.

Everywhere, in towns and villages, on commanding hill-tops, in the wide plains and by the sacred rivers, everywhere there are temples and shrines of sufficient importance to justify a periodical gathering to which people, both young and old, flock in their hundreds or thousands, often from miles around, to crave the favour and protection of the tutelary divinity, and at the same time to enjoy an inexpensive yet delightful day's outing, whole families, from grand-sires to babies, making holiday together.

There are some religious *melas* of almost national interest, held yearly, or at fixed intervals of years, at all the more sacred spots in the country. To this class belong the periodical fairs held at Sonepore, Hardwar, Allahabad and Benares, which are attended by such multitudes that special administrative arrangements have to be made for their proper regulation. But the fairs held at the lesser town and village shrines have their special attractions for folks who are not able to wander to far-distant places in quest of the blessing of the gods; not because such folks do not value the spiritual advantages, or do not covet the pleasurable excitements of such pilgrimages, but because they are not possessed of the means wherewith to defray the unavoidable expenses of long journeys. Hence the local temple fairs all over the country are amply patronized year after year, and the custodians of these shrines derive a modest income from the donations of the happy visitors.

SECTION II.—THE BHADARKALI MELA—A HINDU FAIR

One hot evening in May my *chaprási* (messenger) presented himself before me asking for leave of absence to go to Bhadarkali mela the following day. "Why do you go to melas?" I inquired. "What good do you get by going to them?" "Oh, huzúr," he replied, "I wish to go to Bhadarkali to bow my head (*matha tikáná*) at the feet of the goddess, who is propitious to her devotees." A few further inquiries on my part elicited the following particulars regarding certain experiences of my devout chaprási. On one occasion he went to the Bhadarkali mela promising himself a good time. He carried with him in a small *batwá* (purse) four four-anna pieces, making in all one rupee, and, for greater security, tied the purse under his arm; but a cunning thief in the crowd had managed somehow to purloin the *batwá* and its four silver coins. The disconsolate chaprási, robbed of his expected pleasures, approached the Devi's shrine, and prostrating himself before the goddess complained that she had been unpropitious to her servant who would now have to go hungry away. He returned to Lahore, attended to his ordinary duties, and in the evening went for a dip in the canal near by the City wall. After his plunge in the cool stream he noticed, lying on the canal bank, a dirty rag of a handkerchief, and on examining it found, tied up in one corner of it, just four four-anna pieces. He slipped the rag and its contents into his pocket, and thanked the gracious Devi who had been pleased to restore to him in this way the money he had lost at the fair. It was in the chaprási's eyes an unmistakable case of prayer answered, for which he was grateful to the goddess, and he therefore desired to return thanks for the favour which she had vouchsafed to extend to him.

Photo by W. Campbell Oman

CONFECTIONERS' STALLS AT THE FAIR

To face page 203

I granted the man the leave of absence which he wanted, and told him, at the same time, I should be at the fair myself on the morrow, an announcement he received with undisguised pleasure.

About seven miles from Lahore, near the village of Niaz Beg, is held annually the largest of the fairs which take place in the neighbourhood of the capital of the Punjab. It is attended by multitudes of Hindus of both sexes. Muhammadans in numbers also frequent the gay scene. Here in a temple with a domed roof is the Devi, or goddess, whose presence gives sanctity and importance to the place. Near her shrine is another domed structure, larger than the one she occupies and built expressly for her, but through the medium of dreams the goddess made it known to her priests that she had no desire to leave the abode she had long occupied, and consequently the new building came to be used for other purposes, in fact as a place for storing the properties of the shrine and the belongings of the *pujáris* or attendant priests.[1]

To visit the fair I started from Lahore at 5.15 in the early morning, while there was still some little freshness in the air, and driving at a tolerable pace arrived at Bhadarkali in about an hour. Along the entire route the road was being watered from temporary tanks fed by means of furrows leading from the ordinary irrigation channels, quite an army of men being busily employed in carrying out this very necessary precaution against our being suffocated by the dust which lies deep on Punjab roads in summer time.

One living stream of visitors to the fair filled the highway along which I drove. Seated some in *ekkas*, many in bullock-carts, some in dog-carts, others in hackney carriages or hired phaetons, the moving crowd made its way to Bhadarkali as fast as the nature of the conveyances would allow. However, the majority of the pleasure-seekers were on foot, shuffling along in the easy unconstrained manner which enables Indians, whether old or young, to cover long distances with a minimum of fatigue.

Gay colours, conspicuous amongst the women's gar-

[1] Syad Muhammad Latif, "Lahore: its History, Architecture and Remains," pp. 198–199.

ments, gave to the scene a decidedly bright and cheerful aspect, and so did the smiling faces of the good-natured occupants of the over-crowded vehicles, on one of which (an ekka) I noticed a young child literally hanging on to the rope-netting behind, just as a monkey might do; and, if one may judge from appearances, quite as securely. Occasionally there were exhibitions which excited momentary mirth, as when a small boy came into view trudging sturdily along carrying above his head a very antiquated English parasol of white material, garnished with a deep lace frill. The little fellow had, obviously, no intention to provoke smiles or laughter; but evidently felt important, and was convinced that he looked imposing under his handsome sunshade.

Against the inevitable effects of the heat and dust of the trying summer day, provision had been made at many places along the route in the shape of stalls for supplying water, sherbet and sweets to the thirsty and hungry wayfarers. These stalls were set up under *shámiyánas*, or in tents of sorts, decorated sometimes with half-a-dozen Chinese lanterns swaying in the breeze, and provided with three or four rush chairs and a wooden bench or two. Amongst these welcome resting-places, I noticed at least one of more artistic pretensions than the others, fitted with cloth panels so cleverly worked as to resemble perforated stone; though tainted with deceit the little structure certainly looked neat and pretty, and did credit to the designer's ingenuity and desire for effect. At many of these places (*sabils*, or *chabils* as they are more commonly called) water, or sugar-and-water, was supplied freely at the expense of some wisely generous soul, who hoped to acquire merit by supplying wholesome drink to the thirsty on this auspicious occasion.

At Bhadarkali the scene presented to the eye was interesting and animated. An extensive encampment made up mostly of shámiyánas, or canvas pavilions, and tents, occupied a considerable space in the neighbourhood of the temple, and gave shelter to various stalls where food or pretty trifles could be purchased. Sweetmeat stalls were much in evidence, displaying varieties of Indian confectionery, often ornamented with silver-leaf, neatly arranged

JHÚLÁS—AT THE FAIR

To face page 205

in tasteful designs. Fruiterers were well represented, their stalls pretty with green and yellow melons, plantains and other fruits of the season. And there were also flies in myriads, not at all shy, and keenly appreciative of both sweets and fruits. How ever did they contrive to congregate here in such swarms? Probably along with us; in fact, in our very conveyances there must have journeyed flies galore, riding at their ease to the feast provided for them at Bhadarkali. Any way, they were undoubtedly present there in countless numbers, and fairly busy all the time seeking what they could devour.

Along with the stalls for the sale of sweets and fruits there were others containing cheap toys, and tin trumpets, for the little folks; soap, small looking-glasses, bangles and beads for girls and women; all these pretty things affording ample opportunity to the generous husband or father for the acquisition of fairings for his women folk or children.

Amusements, too, were provided, but not on an extensive scale. At the door of one tent I read the inviting legend: "This is the skittle alley, try your skill," but I was not tempted to look in. Out in the open, however, one could not fail to see the jhúlás at work; for, as is usual at Indian fairs, these well-patronized merry-go-rounds, creaking on horizontal axes, were in full swing, carrying the young people of both sexes, seated in oblong boxes or cradles, round and round in vertical circles as in the famous but slow and now dismantled great wheel of Earl's Court. That the jhúlás gave great delight to their patrons was evident to every spectator, and the pleasure was purchasable at the moderate cost of probably *one pice* (farthing) a ride or bout.

Then there was the *theatre*, where an *opera* was going to be performed. This was an attraction for me, so I paid the entrance fee of one anna (one penny), went in, was provided with a stool to sit on, and witnessed the performance. The *dramatis personæ* consisted of a king, a green *pari*, also a red *pari* and a giant. A *sárangi* or violin and a *tabla* or drum constituted the orchestra. There was no raised stage, but attempts at scenery were not wanting, and there was quite an ambitious drop-curtain on which was painted the façade of a building that somewhat suggested the Royal Exchange. As the performance went on it appeared that the giant was very much in love with the green parí; but unfortunately the king was also enamoured of the same adorable sprite, a situation which gave occasion for much singing and some dancing. I did not quite understand the *dénouement*, but I think the fickle king transferred his royal affections to the red fairy, and then all parties were supposed to be happy. The audience was not large, consisting of about twenty-five or thirty persons in all; but I presume there was a succession of audiences sufficient to provide the players with what would in their eyes be adequate pecuniary reward for their musical and histrionic talent.

I asked and obtained permission to photograph the actors (for even the parís were men) in their paint and finery.

As I strolled about the fair seeking knowledge with amusement, I came across many most charming groups of figures and arrangements of colour which would have delighted any eye, and it was more particularly so in and near the large tank surrounded by a grove, where numerous bathers of both sexes enjoyed a cooling immersion before presenting themselves at the Devi's temple. This tank had steps leading into the water from all four sides, and an elegant white building standing at the middle portion of each side. Within one of these was the women's bathing-place, for such as cared to use it, into which the water flowed from the tank through a perforated stone screen, which sheltered the bathers from observation. Though there was much of interest to tempt one to use the camera, I had to forgo taking any photographs, as my doing so would naturally have given offence, and probably been resented.

Near by the tank, in the shade of a spreading tree, an artist was offering his coloured pictures for sale. I stopped to inspect them, and found that our artist's handiwork had for the most part a moral purpose, for you see nearly everything in India is somehow connected with religion. The pictures exhibited were certainly not expensive—just a halfpenny each—and recognizing that

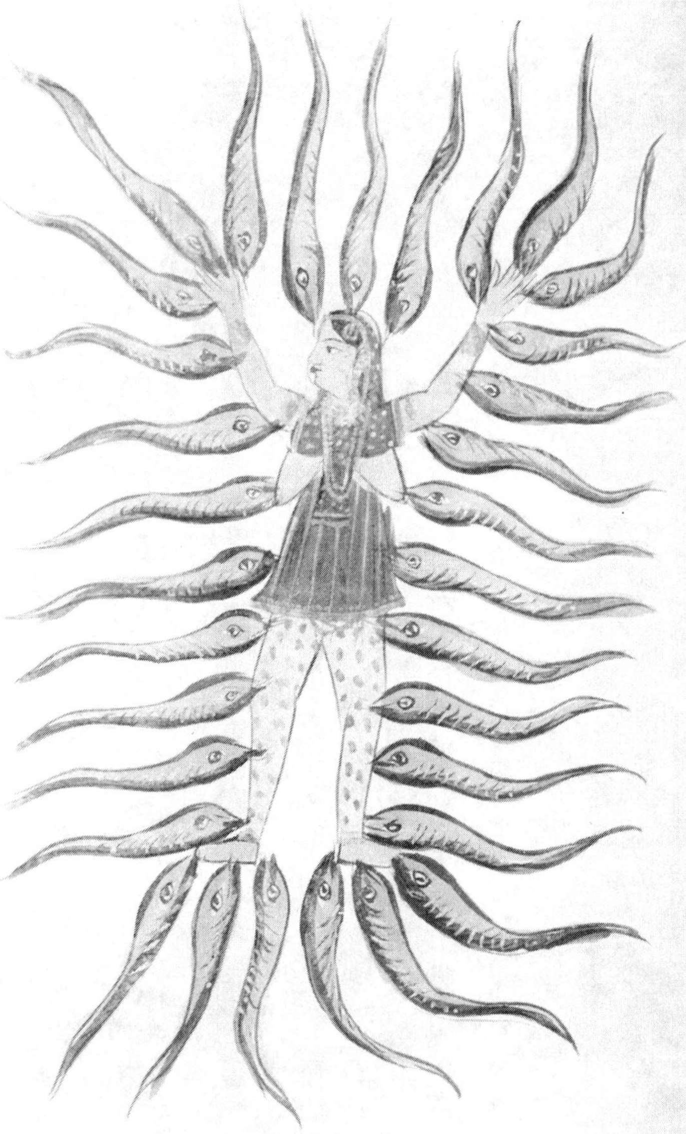

THE UNFAITHFUL WIFE—HER PUNISHMENT IN THE NEXT WORLD

To face page 207

they were well intentioned, I purchased a few devoted to illustrating in a forcible way the specific torments which offenders of various kinds will have to endure in the next world. Art being what it is, we need not doubt that the virtuous artist felt a glow of righteous pleasure—what artist would not?—at the thought that his productions would deter some men and women from sin, because of the dreadful tortures to be endured hereafter by transgressors, as depicted in unmistakable colours by his cunning brush. As I have already mentioned I purchased a few of these moral pictures, and at the same time invested in a portrait of Bhairon, attended by his dog, for my collection.

Leaving the artist's stall my eye was caught by the following in conspicuous characters: "Welcome to the chabil of the cloth merchants of Lahore," and I reflected that these good merchants, practical business men, were here earning merit for themselves collectively by providing clean water, perhaps sweetened with sugar, for the thirsty multitude at the fair. "Well, let them have the merit," thought I, "since the thirsty souls who drink the water they supply will willingly bless them for it."

Under an awning at a spot within the most frequented part of the fair, I came upon a small model of a temple made of coloured paper and tinsel. Incense burning in it diffused a sweet perfume around, while two or three men near the little structure beat drums in a rhythmic fashion, and a small crowd of tired people sat within what I may call the odour of sanctity grouped about in picturesque ease.

A yard or two away from this miniature temple four men were playing a game of cards.

The ascetic sects or orders were not well represented at this fair—I only noticed two evil-looking Kanphati Yogis, wearing huge jade earrings, wandering about in a rather suspicious way. And in a retired spot I found an Udasi sádhu seated by himself in the conventional attitude of contemplation. Why he came to the *mela* for the practice of religious abstraction I could not imagine, unless it was to test his own training or to offer himself as a living example to worldlings.

A stream of men and women flowed towards the temple, and I went with it. The crowd was rather packed near the sacred edifice, and some policemen, evidently anxious to assert themselves, and *perhaps* to maintain order also, though they did not go about the business in the right way, *hustled* the people in a rough and apparently quite objectless manner. In the press one woman knocked up, or was pushed against me, and made a wry face, and uttered some words to indicate that I had hurt her. I apologized in my best manner, and with my blandest smile, while the injured one received my excuses with an expressive twinkle in her wicked eyes and still affected pain. Reflecting that the daughters of Eve are much the same all the world over, I thought it best to set my face resolutely towards the temple. And a peculiarly interesting sight did the temple present on this occasion. The shrine itself is a small domed building, contained, as it were, in a somewhat larger structure, so that the outer one affords a wide covered way or verandah all round the sanctuary for the customary circumambulation of the shrine by the worshippers. I stood by this iron-barred verandah and watched the worshippers passing along inside.

Transversely across the verandah were wooden beams, and to each of these four or five bells were hung. And they were there for use, the worshippers eagerly ringing them with uplifted hands as they passed along circumambulating the cella which contained the image. Perched on one of the beams I noticed a *pujari* or temple priest, who received their gifts from the visitors, and handed them to other priests to carry within the shrine and presumably lay them before the idol. Some acknowledgment of these offerings, which were most likely *ex votos*, had to be made to satisfy the worshippers; so the Brahman on the perch handed some trifle or other to each donator; such trifles, flowers mostly, having presumably come from the inner chamber where the goddess was enthroned in state. It was real worship, and there was nothing flippant or perfunctory about it, the worshippers declining to move on till their eagerly uplifted hands had received something, however small, which had come

THE ADULTERER–HIS PUNISHMENT IN THE NEXT WORLD

To face page 208

from the inner shrine and been sanctified by the presence of the Devi. Observing me standing outside, a pujarí came forward and presented me with a small basket of sweets and a few flowers; a servant of mine in attendance appropriated the gift, and I handed the pujarí a rupee.

As far as my observation went, there was but one discordant note in the fair, due to the rampant fanaticism of a Muhammadan, who loudly denounced the idolaters, proclaiming emphatically that the god who made the heavens and supported them without pillars, would assuredly send all these *Kafirs* (infidels) to *jahannum*. He himself was, no doubt, on the way to paradise, and I trust he was induced by the police to leave the idolaters to their fate.

I left the *mela* quite early, and so also did thousands of respectable natives with their families. Of course those who had arranged to pass the night at Bhadarkali looked forward to more excitement and dissipation than was possible or permissible in the daytime.

Section III.—The Chiragan Mela, a Fair of Lamps—A Muslim Festival

This fair originated with the lighting of lamps (*chirags*) at the tomb of a Muhammadan saint, known as Madho Lal Husain, which stands in the village of Bhagbanpura about a quarter of a mile from the famous Shalimár Gardens. "People staid at the saint's *khangáh* for the night," says a Muhammadan writer, "and used to walk to the garden of Shalimár next morning for the sake of recreation. In course of time, however, the gathering at the Shalimár quite eclipsed that of the mother-place, and although lamps are lighted at the *khangáh*, the fair itself is held in the Shalimár, and after the original name is known as Chiragon-ka-mela." [1]

The legend of Madho Lal Husain is curious and interesting. It appears that the saint who lived in the time of Akbar, the famous Mogul Emperor of Delhi, took a violent

[1] Syad Muhammad Latif, "Lahore: its History, Architectural Remains and Antiquities," p. 268.

fancy to a Brahman boy named Madho; but the object of his affection died, and the distressed saint besought the sorrowing parents to give him the lad's body, and having persuaded them to do so, he breathed life into the inanimate form and subsequently converted the resuscitated youth to Islam. The saint and his *protégé* are buried near one another. "Many stories are told," says the writer already quoted, "of the miracles performed by Lal Husain. It is said he spent his nights in repeating the Korán by heart in a standing posture in the Rávi. He died in 1008 A.H. (1599 A.D.), and was buried at Shádera. A few years after, as predicted by the saint, the grave was swept away by the overflow of the Rávi. Madho exhumed the corpse, and, with due formalities, buried it in the present locality."[1]

Whatever we may think of these "miracles" it is worth noting here, in passing, that the saints of Islam buried in India are multitudinous, and their legendaries replete with marvels—to which, of course, they owe their sainthood. In the case of the saints of Christendom, their miracles, before or after death, have to be established to the satisfaction of the Holy See as a preliminary to their canonization; but I hardly think any such formal proceeding is thought of in connection with the saints of Islam now in question. In other respects, however, the Christian and Islamic saints have much in common.

About the tomb of Madho Lal Husain there is nothing very striking except that near it is a tower in which is preserved, as a sacred relic, a footprint of the prophet Muhammad (Kadam-i-Rasul), which, of course, confers a peculiar sanctity on the site. The lighted chirágs and the assembly at the saint's *khangáh* are, as mentioned already, not particularly imposing; but the great gathering at Shalimár is worth a visit; one reason, and not the least, being the attractiveness of the extensive garden in which it is held, a remnant of the splendour of the spacious times of the Mogul emperors. Laid out in three successive terraced orchards differing in level by about twelve or fifteen feet, with a great reservoir of pure

[1] Syad Muhammad Latif, "Lahore: its History, Architectural Remains and Antiquities," p. 268.

Photo by W. Campbell Oman

A VIEW IN SHALIMÁR GARDENS

To face page 210

water reflecting elegant pavilions and kiosks, and supplied with artificial cascades and hundreds of fountains, this secluded spot, covering some eighty acres, enclosed within lofty walls, is an ideal pleasure garden.

What it must have been in the luxurious past, when in its prime of spotless marble it was prepared and lavishly decorated for the reception of the princesses and great ladies of the court of a Mogul emperor, would not be difficult to imagine. With the mind's eye we can see the costly hangings depending from the now rusty rings beneath the cornices of the pretty pavilions, the rich carpets and cloth of gold on the marble floors, showy groups of superbly dressed and bejewelled ladies strolling about the gardens or reclining in the pavilions upon soft silken cushions. We can see eunuchs in attendance and pretty slave girls carrying the iced sherbets in gold or silver vases and luscious fruits in costly salvers. We inhale the voluptuous perfumes of the roses of Basara, listen to the pleasing strains of Eastern music, and listlessly admire the gorgeous birds kept for the amusement of the inmates of the harem, while the hundreds of fountains throw sparkling jets of water into the sunshine.

But Shalimár has been the scene of other sights than royal pleasure parties; for it was here that Nadir Sháh, the Persian invader, encamped in 1739 and received the homage of Zikaríya Khán, the Delhi Emperor's Viceroy. Here, too, or in its immediate neighbourhood, thirteen years later, after a four-months' siege of Lahore and a pitched battle, Ahmad Sháh Durani assumed the sovereignty of the Punjab and appointed as his Viceroy, Mir Mannú, the gallant but unsuccessful defender of Lahore against the Afghan forces.

Even now Shalimár is a pleasant place when its myriad fountains are all spraying with a gentle murmur into the warm summer air, and the umbrage of its beautiful fruit-trees invite to otiose rest away from the glare and heat of the summer sun.

To Shalimár, then, let us wend our way to visit the great Chiragan mela.

Three miles of road lie between Lahore and the old Imperial Gardens, and on a Chiragan fair day the whole distance seems for hours to be almost blocked with the traffic. Driving along with the crowd of vehicles of many descriptions, carrying sight-seers or pleasure-seekers from the city to the *mela*, is certainly neither an expeditious nor an exhilarating business, but need not be unpleasant. Long before the end of the journey the kiosks which adorn the high walls of the garden become visible, and a perceptible block in the traffic is experienced. There is but one gateway to the garden, and as all comers have to alight there and enter on foot, a certain unavoidable delay is caused at that point, and the stream of vehicles becomes more or less congested. But each impatient holiday-maker in his turn arrives at last at the entrance, and passing under a stately gateway faces a long double line of fountains in full play, with wide paved footways on either side, flanked by groves of shady fruit-trees.

The vista is charming and inviting, while the motley crowd of Muslims is both picturesque and interesting. For my part I stood for a minute or two under the gateway to admire the holiday scene before joining the human stream which was setting towards the central pavilion. The fountains were in full operation, and alongside the paths, on both sides, were a succession of stalls—forming, indeed, an extended bazaar—in which were displayed sweetmeats and toys of many kinds, with cheap jewellery and tinsel ornaments. Here, besides the ordinary huckster, the cook was in evidence, filling the atmosphere with the odours of his "kabobs" and other culinary preparations; for the Muslim is not a vegetarian, and likes highly-seasoned meat dishes. On either side of the bazaar most of the available space amidst the trees was occupied by the tents of the native gentlemen who had come to the fair for a day's enjoyment.

The central pavilion when I reached it was thronged, and just below it lay shimmering in the sunlight the great reservoir, brimful and enlivened by scores of fountains within its ample surface throwing up jets of water, while a cascade from the upper terrace to the reservoir below fell in sparkling beauty over an indented marble slope.

Behind me lay the terrace I had just traversed, below

Photo by W. Campbell Oman

THE INDIAN BULLOCK CART

To face page 212

me the reservoir, and beyond that still another and lower terrace also furnished with rows of fountains.

Being a Muhammadan fair, the Chiragan mela has certain peculiarities which differentiate it from a Hindu mela; for example, the absence of women except of the freer sort is quite noticeable, whereas at Hindu fairs reputable women of all classes, at any rate of the lower and middle classes, are a prominent feature of the crowd. Then again, ceremonial bathing is no part of a Muslim fair; though this is, I should say, an indispensable accompaniment of a Hindu fair, which is always a religious assembly. Muslim fairs being, as a rule, gatherings for *amusement*, are characterized by a great deal more music and dancing than can be found at Hindu *melas.* The Muslims, indeed, on the whole appear to appreciate good living and the enjoyments of life far more than the Hindus do.

At one spot my attention was arrested by a singing-girl performing before an audience of admirers. For attendants she had an elderly man who played the sarangi (violin), and two others who helped him with small drums. These three accompanists formed her modest orchestra. The violinist was, of course, the leader of the band, and to him, for safe custody, the singer handed the presents which were made to her after each song by members of the audience. A Hindu in semi-European clothes sat opposite the fair performer, and was clearly her willing captive. He wore a sheepish expression on his face, for he was conscious that many eyes were upon him; but he could not move away. He handed out his money with liberality after every song, and looked the while things unutterable. The girl was certainly good-looking, with a pair of killing eyes, and lovely hands which were richly bejewelled.

Elsewhere from behind a screen of canvas walling came the dulcet sounds of soft music. Within, I presume, were some hired dancing-girls and a *select* party of friends enjoying themselves; but I observed that they were not quite private, for a prying youth had climbed a neighbouring tree, and from his lofty perch overlooked the show which was not intended for his eyes.

In the midst of these very mundane enjoyments the stricter Muslims would stop abruptly when one of the appointed prayer times came round, and spreading a small carpet or sheet on the ground, would stand upon it, turn their faces in the direction of Mecca, and repeat the prayers with the genuflections and other movements prescribed for such occasions, with the utmost fervour and decorum. It was indeed an edifying sight to see these Muslims, often in groups, at prayer, while the more worldly passed along but with a subdued manner and a deferential carriage.

As I made the round of the fair I came upon a man seated on a chair of European pattern at a small table, reciting, for the benefit of a small knot of attentive listeners, the story of the loves of Magnoon and Leila.

In the way of entertainments, suitable more especially for children, I may mention that I saw the usual performances of trained monkeys and goats; the former personating the exacting Morór Khán and his submissive wife Jahuran, the goats being their steeds. The dancing-bear was there, too, being *persuaded* to do his master's bidding by suggestions conveyed along a cruel cord passed through his tender nose, aided by sundry hard knocks from a heavy truncheon. Poor Bruin! one can see how he resents his treatment and longs for revenge. I wonder if he ever gets it? It is to be hoped he does.

Snake-charmers with baskets full of serpents, and tight-rope walkers—often women—contributed their share to the pastimes of the day; while quail-fighting (with, no doubt, betting at the back of it) attracted the sporting element amongst the visitors to the fair.

There were other performances also more peculiar than agreeable. One was a weird dance by villagers, the performers being for the most part poised on one leg with their arms carried in grotesque ways. The leader of the party had a lace curtain on his head arranged like a woman's chaddar, and he evidently fancied himself. The movements of the dance were slow and rhythmic, the faces of the dancers absurdly solemn. Yet on the whole the show was more unpleasant than ridiculous, and seemed like some relic of out-of-date savagery.

MARÓR KHÁN AND JAHURAN, AT THE FAIR

To face page 214

Several Muslim *faquirs* but no Hindu *sádhus* were about. One faquir wearing a most outlandish hat of cock's feathers sat in solemn state with a small gathering of respectably-dressed people about him. These, I dare say, were consulting "*faquir sahib*" on matters in which they were interested. Not far off two faquirs were dancing a curious whirling dance of their own, and might have been Indian representatives of the dancing dervishes so well known in Egypt, though they were habited quite differently. One faquir, a truculent fellow, roamed about with an iron instrument in his hand begging or rather demanding alms, and I was told that such as he, if ordered off by any stall-holder, would inflict some injury upon his own person with the instrument; and *then*, the sin of driving one of these idle fellows to hurt his worthless self would be terrible, so terrible, indeed, that no ordinary man would ever care to face it.

Before bringing this sketch to a close I must not omit to mention what the people speak of as "hál-playing," a peculiar form of religious excitement which seems to have an irresistible attraction for Punjabí Muhammadans. I stood to watch this for two or three minutes. A boy was on his feet swaying violently backwards and forwards, supported by another lad not much bigger than himself. A man seated on the bare ground was throwing himself about to a peculiar rhythmic throb of drums beaten by practised hands, while another man was writhing in painful contortions, with his hands clenched convulsively and his face almost distorted by suppressed excitement. It was a painful sight, but it was all genuine. As, however, I have dealt with this hál-playing in some detail in a subsequent portion of this volume (Part IV., Chapter I.), I shall not pursue the subject any further in this place.

Section IV.—The Kadmon-Ka-Mela

There is still one other type of mela to which I would draw attention, but as I need only dwell upon those peculiarities which make it deserving of notice here, my sketch will make but little demand upon the reader's time.

On the first Monday after the new moon of February I took a stroll to see the assembly for the Kadmon-ka-mela in and about Anarkali, just outside the city of Lahore. Crowds and dust were the predominant features of the scene. As usual, provision had been made in various ways for the amusement and requirements of the people. Here creaking *jhúlás* were rotating rapidly with their burden of young persons of both sexes; there an athlete was displaying the strength and quality of his muscles by lifting heavy weights, while itinerant vendors hawked toys, sweets and trifles everywhere amongst the throng. Notwithstanding these attractions, the temple of Setala, goddess of small-pox, situated in the neighbourhood, was, I noticed, being duly honoured by hundreds of devout and anxious visitors; for the dread disease was about, claiming many victims in the city. The fair, however, was held in honour of Sakhi Sarwar, a Muslim saint and patron of young children, whose tomb is in Anarkali; and here petty offerings were being given to the attendants at the *khangáh* and to any beggars that might be standing about. But the most interesting feature of the proceedings was of a special and peculiar kind. Here and there, grouped about two or three large and noisy drums, a few custodians of the tomb, known at the fair as *sheiks*, might be seen dancing a slow measure to the throb of the sonorous instruments, round which they circled slowly. To these men, women bystanders would approach and confide their babies, and the little ones, safe in the arms of the dancing *sheiks*, would be carried round the drums. After a round or two the mother would redeem her offspring with a few pice, feeling in her loving heart that the little one was fortified to some extent against the troubles of infantile life by the favour of the amiable saint whose followers had kindly accepted her money. Near each set of drums was erected a sort of short standard decorated with a big bunch of little pillows of various colours about two or three inches long, these standards with their adornments serving to attract attention as they were intended to do.

By W. C. O.

By W. C. O.

PROFESSIONAL AMUSERS, AT THE FAIR

To face page 216

Such examples of Indian fairs as I have given in this chapter will, I hope, serve at least to show that each has its own peculiar characteristics, and that the religious element enters into them all more or less. For the Hindus and for the Muslims of India, but more especially for the Hindus, religion is an essential of their daily life in a manner and to a degree quite unknown amongst the Anglo-Saxon peoples of the Western world.

CHAPTER III

BAZAAR GUP; OR, RUMOURS OF THE MARKET-PLACE

"When the oak is felled the whole forest echoes with its fall, but a hundred acorns are sown in silence by an unnoticed breeze." —CARLYLE.

THE stories that circulate in the bazaars of India, and find credence amongst the people, are perhaps a fair indication, if not a measure, of the intellectual condition of the masses, and afford, in addition, some idea of the standpoint from which they regard the actions of their foreign rulers. For these reasons I have thought it worth while to note down here a few samples of *bazaar gup* which have come to my knowledge.

My grass-cutter came to me one day and begged earnestly that I would get him a pass to cut grass in the Lawrence Park, as he dreaded going into the less frequented parts to obtain grass, since the *Mumiyai Sahib* was going about with his myrmidons.

The *Mumiyai Sahib!* I had never heard of him, and naturally inquired who and what he was, and why his presence in the neighbourhood should interfere with my getting grass for my horses as usual. My questions elicited the following circumstantial details:

The European in question, known throughout the country as the Mumiyai Sahib, has a host of agents who go about dressed in black, each armed with a short stick having the peculiar power of causing any person who smells it to follow its possessor, in spite of what friends and neighbours might say to dissuade him from so doing.

Under the spell of this magic wand the unhappy victim follows the Mumiyai Sahib's agent on and on until he is led to some solitary place, usually a distant tope or jungle, far removed from human habitations. Here the miserable man is seized, has a hole bored through the top of his skull, and is then suspended, head downwards, over a caldron of boiling oil, with a roaring fire under it. Into the hot oil the drippings from the victim's brain are allowed to fall and form a most valuable medicine, known as *mumiyai*, and also as *silajit*. This is bad enough, but mark! these proceedings are all carried out *by order of the Sirkar* (Government), as the medicine is much prized by Europeans.

All the servants in my establishment, except a Muhammadan cook somewhat above the average in education, could confirm the above statements, and were able to add some interesting details, as, for instance, that very black people were particularly prized for the manufacture of silajit. One of my informants had actually possessed a little of the precious medicine made out of the brains of black men. He got it from a servant connected with a state dispensary, and believed that what he received must have been stolen from the Government stock.

Latterly people have become wary of the dangerous men dressed in black; so the wily Sahib now employs women to carry out his nefarious object, who go about with flowers, *missie*, *soorma*, and such-like things, and, under pretence of selling these necessary articles of an Indian toilet, get their innocent victims to smell some of that fatal magic substance which leads to inevitable destruction. My servants were aware of one or two persons who had somewhat suddenly disappeared, and must have been kidnapped by the terrible Mumiyai Sahib, that strange pharmacist, tolerated, if not employed by, the British Government. In fact the fatal snares of this objectional gentleman appeared to them to be the rational and only explanation of the disappearance of the persons referred to. When I pressed my servants to say whether they really believed the Sirkar would authorize, would even allow such destruction of innocent people, one man promptly observed: "Why not, Huzzoor? the Mumiyai Sahib pays a special tax to the Sirkar for permission to carry on his business," and this seemed to settle the matter conclusively as far as the speaker and his fellow-servants were concerned.

Now it happens that there are such substances known

to the Indian druggist as *mumiyai* and *silajit*, black, hard, heavy, bituminous solids (*Asphaltum Persicum* and *Asphaltum silajit*), obtained from Persia or the Himalayas, which enjoy a great reputation for their curative properties, particularly in cases of bone fracture.[1] These rare and unfamiliar substances, brought from foreign parts, command a high price at Lahore, and afford to the ignorant a sufficiently substantial basis for the acceptance of the wild story about the *Mumiyai Sahib*. Desirous of knowing more about this curious popular belief, I inquired of some educated natives whether they had ever heard of it. Oh yes; it had been well known to them for several years. And this, no doubt, was true; for I find from Mr. Cust's "Pictures of Indian Life" (p. 135) that the belief was current during the Sikh campaigns.

My educated native friends also told me that it was commonly believed that the stray dogs killed every summer by order of the European authorities were required for the manufacture of a medicine out of their tongues, and that the water supplied by the Lahore municipality was expressly designed to deprive the people of their caste.[2] In connection with these mendacious

[1] Dr. Honigberger's "Thirty-five Years in the East," vol. ii. pp. 238–239. The word *mummy* is said to be derived from *mumiyai*, such bituminous substances being employed in the embalming of bodies.

[2] About the time of my inquiries regarding the Mumiyai Sahib, "The Madras Times" contained the following:

"Some of the ignorant natives have given credence to a report that men of the Lubbay caste are prowling about the streets of the town with the object of kidnapping children, who, it is said, are wanted to be sacrificed in connection with the Harbour works. So firmly is the rumour believed, that every Lubbay is looked upon with suspicion, and some ugly quarrels have taken place. Yesterday morning, in Popham's Broadway, there was quite a commotion on a Lubbay being suspected in the way we have stated. It would appear that while the man was walking along the Broadway he had accidentally touched a little boy, and it being supposed that he wished to get the boy under his power in some sinister manner with a view to kidnap him, a mob of men got together to assault him, and he had to seek shelter in a shop. A similar rumour was spread abroad, and generally believed in among the poorer classes of the natives, when the Madras Pier was in course of construction. It is an idea prevalent among the ignorant masses of the natives that no large works, such as the Pier or the Harbour works, can be carried to completion without the sacrifice of human life; hence the ready credence given to the rumour we have alluded to."

rumours many of my readers will probably call to mind the malign reports recently circulated in the Punjab by seditious persons to the effect that the authorities were deliberately poisoning the wells in order to disseminate the plague far and wide through the country.

Accustomed as they have been for centuries to government based on narrow selfishness, the mass of the people of India are not yet able to understand or appreciate the principles of British rule. It is vain to endeavour to persuade even the tolerably well-informed that the English authorities are honestly desirous of promoting the public good. They may acquiesce in the statement, but their manner shows too plainly how far they are from believing it. And, after all, this is not to be wondered at, in the face of the haughty and unsympathetic attitude of British officers and of Europeans generally towards the people of the country; for it is certainly hard to believe that men who shrink, almost nervously, from contact with the people really care very much about their welfare or happiness. Owing no doubt to this want of cordiality between the rulers and the ruled, malicious falsehoods are often circulated by designing persons with the object of making the English government unpopular.

During the summer of 1878, when small-pox was going about Lahore, I was told by one of my domestic servants, not without a touch of suppressed feeling, that the Sirkar had given orders that the native women should all be vaccinated, not, as usual, on the arm, but *on the breast*.

Not infrequently the Sirkar's name is used to serve some purely private end, as the following particulars, while throwing light upon other matters, will very clearly show. It appears that when a wedding is to take place in the family of a fairly well-to-do man, there collect to the expected feast, from many miles round, a host of idle and ignorant Brahmans; also a number of bards, who chant the praises of the family; strolling minstrels with dancing-girls, and wandering *sanyasis*.[1] All these self-invited guests are feasted by the host, and presented with money and other gifts, at an expense often very dispro-

[1] Men of any caste may join this sect.

portionate to his means. To add to the troubles of the bride's family, Muhammadans from the neighbouring villages and low caste people from all sides flock in for *backsheesh*. For the credit of the house the host will do his utmost to gratify these unscrupulous harpies, but it is not always possible to do so. At a village wedding at which my informant—a University graduate—was present, a number of sanyasis presented themselves, and insisted upon having not less than one rupee each. The host declared he could not afford so much as that, but offered to give half a rupee to each man. The offer was indignantly spurned. As the host held out, the sanyasis resorted to their usual tactics. One man beat his forehead with a sharp stone till the blood flowed. In this state he moved about amongst the assembled guests, while his companions commenced chanting a funeral dirge. Such a dirge at a wedding, and the disgusting aspect of the bleeding man, effected the purpose of the unscrupulous sanyasis, for, to get rid of them, their demands were satisfied as quickly as possible by the unwilling host. The evil is, of course, no new one, and it would need a deal of courage and concerted action to make a successful stand against the impositions of these worthless mendicants. Under the stimulus of Western ideas and feelings, some educated young men at Lahore formed themselves into a society for the purpose of regulating marriage expenses, which sometimes plunge a family into hopeless ruin. A tariff was drawn up. The maximum amount to be given to each Brahman was duly fixed, and it was decided that the bards, who on account of their sarcastic tongues are much feared, should receive twice as much as any ordinary Brahman, instead of, as hitherto, four or five times as much; the strolling minstrels, Muhammadans, and low caste people, were to be sent away empty-handed. The proposed scheme met with favour in many quarters, but fear of the Brahmans restrained a great many persons from openly accepting the proposed rules and scale of rates. To gain their object, the promoters of the scheme gave out that the rules had been framed by *Government*, and that any infringement of them would be punished with a heavy fine, thus deliberately setting afloat one more untrue report regarding the Sirkar and its doings.

Official records and the proceedings of the courts of justice abound in instances of the propagation, for fraudulent purposes, of false rumours regarding orders said to have emanated from the Government. Some years ago a subordinate state official was brought to trial in Assam for circulating a report that Government had directed the preparation of a list of good-looking and marriageable girls, who were to be given as rewards to the officers and men of a certain force engaged on the eastern frontier. Of course the official concerned intended making money out of the affair, by promising to obtain, for a substantial consideration, an exemption for any fair one whose name might appear on the list of eligible beauties.

The religious contentions of Hindus and Muhammadans, unfortunately too common, sometimes fill the air with false reports of sedition and disaffection, set on foot by one or other party, with the design of discrediting their opponents in the eyes of the authorities. As might have been expected, such cases have found their way into the law courts, and been sifted to the bottom by Indian magistrates.

Religious and other superstitions are also prolific sources of *bazaar gup*. When Mahárája Dhulíp Singh, sometime King of the Punjab, was about to visit India with the permission of the British Government, all sorts of rumours in connection with his coming were floating about the bazaars of his native country, not the least important of which was that the Mahárája was being sent out to displace the ruler of Kashmir, who was no longer in favour with the paramount power. It is needless to say how disturbing such gossip must have been to both Punjabís and Kashmirís, especially if it be remembered that Dhulíp Singh was the subject of a prophecy contained in the *Sakhee* Book of the Sikhs, to the effect that he would "drive his victorious elephant through the world," and would "be the emperor over all the kings." [1] I well remember with what excited eagerness

[1] "The Sakhee Book," translated by Sirdar Attar Singh, Chief of Bhadour, pp. 35–37.

I was cross-questioned about the Mahárája and his movements, when I went one morning to visit the tomb of the Sikh Guru Arjan, hard by the fort of Lahore.

As a matter of fact, Dhulíp Singh, instead of being made ruler of Kashmir by the British Government, was, on account of certain grave indiscretions on his part, not even allowed to land in India. And having gone to his long account, he will certainly never drive his victorious elephant through the world.

As a relic of the troubled times which preceded the British conquest of India, a belief lingers about the bazaars of Upper India that Delhi is fated to be "looted" every hundred years, Lahore every fifty years, and Multan every thirty years. Regardless of history and chronology, the people were persuaded a few years ago that the destined period had arrived for all three cities, and the Punjabí mind, I was told, was on the tip-toe of expectation, watching with anxiety for the inevitable bloodshed and disorder.

In war time the *bazaar gup* in an Indian town is especially interesting and significant. At such a time rumours of reverses or disasters are always in the air, are eagerly listened to, and perhaps maliciously kept afloat. Let me give one instance out of any number that might be cited. During the Afghan war of 1878–1880 we had, for a few days, no news of General Roberts and the forces immediately under his command. The bazaar was, as usual on such occasions, teeming with the most circumstantial accounts of what was going on at the front. The gallant General had been murdered near Cabul, and his little army totally destroyed by the tribesmen. Such was the story that found ready acceptance in the market-place, while in reality the General was making a quiet and completely successful entry into the Afghan capital, in company with Yakub Khan.

Sir John Kaye has dealt with this subject of bazaar news in a spirit of something like poetical exaggeration, which the real circumstances of the case by no means justify. This historian says :

"It is a fact that there is a certain description of news, which travels in India, from one station to another, with a rapidity almost electric. Before the days of the 'lightning post' there was sometimes intelligence in the bazaars of the native dealers and the lines of the native soldiers, especially if the news imported something disastrous to the British, days before it reached, in any official shape, the high functionaries of government. We cannot trace the progress of these evil tidings. The natives of India have an expressive saying that 'it is in the air.' It often happened that an uneasy feeling—an impression that something had happened, though they 'could not discern the shape thereof'—pervaded men's minds, in obscure anticipation of the news that was travelling towards them in all its tangible proportions. All along the line of road, from town to town, from village to village, were thousands to whom the feet of those who brought the glad tidings were beautiful and welcome. The British magistrate returning from his evening ride, was perhaps met on the road near the bazaar by a venerable native on an ambling pony—a native respectable of aspect, with white beard and whiter garments, who salaamed to the English gentleman as he passed, and went on his way freighted with intelligence refreshing to the souls of those to whom it was communicated, to be used with judgment and sent on with despatch. This was but one of many costumes worn by the messenger of evil. In whatever shape he passed, there was nothing outwardly to distinguish him. Next morning there was a sensation in the bazaar, and a vague excitement in the Sepoy lines. But when rumours of disaster reached the houses of the chief English officers, they were commonly discredited. Their own letters were silent on the subject. It was not likely to be true, they said, as they had heard nothing about it. But it was true, and the news had travelled another hundred miles whilst the white gentlemen, with bland scepticism, were shaking their heads over the lies of the bazaar." [1]

It seems a pity to pry too closely into this mysterious system of disseminating intelligence, which, some would actually have us believe, was carried on by the imaginary *mahatmas* of the Himalayas "by their own methods," [2] that is, if I am not mistaken, along strange magnetic currents in the atmosphere; but as the circumstance dealt with by Sir John Kaye is often referred to in India as something more or less inexplicable, and as the plain matter-of-fact explanation of the whole thing is so obvious, I cannot refrain from pausing a moment to consider it here.

In the time of the terrible Indian mutiny and rebellion to which Sir John Kaye's remarks apply, disaster followed disaster, and the predictions or guesses of the bazaar, *always hostile to the British*, were unfortunately too often verified; but, the circumstances of the case being considered, there was surely nothing strange or mysterious

[1] Kaye's "Sepoy War," vol. i. pp. 491–492.
[2] Sinnett's "Occult World," p. 21, foot-note.

in this. When a rising at any station was pre-arranged to take place on a certain date, it was obviously quite possible for any one in the secret to travel to a distance and declare on the appointed day, and even at the appointed hour, that a mutiny had broken out at such a station, and that the Europeans there had all been massacred; for indeed they had little chance of escape. There was nothing particularly mysterious in all this. If the rumours of the town did not tally with the facts as they were eventually known, the false reports were at once forgotten. Had the rumours current in Lahore, about the disaster said to have befallen Sir Frederick Roberts at Cabul, been to any degree borne out by events, we may imagine what an effect the coincidence would have produced, and how much some people would be disposed to make out of it. As it was, the events gave the lie to the rumour, and it at once dropped out of men's minds. Indeed, mendacious stories of disaster to the British arms have been current in the bazaars whenever our forces have been engaged in a war beyond our own borders, and Sir John Kaye has himself given several instances of such false rumours of reverses.[1]

How news is *manufactured* in the East we may learn from a Muhammadan historian.

"When the besieged were thus reduced," says Zian-d din Barni, "to extremities, and were suing for peace, very nearly a month had passed since any couriers had arrived from the Sultan, although the Khan had previously received two or three letters every week. This want of intelligence from the court caused some uneasiness in the minds of the Khan and his officers; they imagined that some of the posts on the road had been destroyed, and that consequently the couriers had been unable to prosecute their journeys with the news. It also caused apprehension and misgivings to spread among the troops, and stories were carried from one to another. Ubaid the poet, and Shaikh Zada-i Dimashki, two evil-disposed and turbulent fellows, who by some means had been introduced to the Khan, fanned the strife, and spread false reports among the soldiers to the effect that the Sultan was dead, that the government had been overthrown, that a new prince now sat upon the throne of Delhi, and that the way was quite closed against all couriers and messengers. So every man took his own course. These two malicious men trumped up another false story. They went to Malik Tamar, Malik Tigin, Malik Mall Afghan, and Malik Kafur, keeper of the seal, and told these nobles that Ulugh Khan looked upon them with

[1] Kaye's "Sepoy War," vol. i. pp. 35, 266, and 483.

envy and suspicion, as generals and nobles of the reign of Alau-d din, and as obstacles to his attaining the throne; that their names were written down in a list as men to be disposed of, and that they would be all seized at once and beheaded. These nobles were aware that these two treacherous men were constantly about Ulugh Khan, and so they credited their statements. They therefore agreed to take flight, and joining together their followers they left the camp. Through this defection a panic fell upon the army, trouble and tumult arose, and no man thought of another. This event was very opportune for the besieged Hindus, and saved them. They sallied forth and plundered the baggage of the army, and Ulugh Khan, with his immediate followers, retreated to Deogir. The soldiers were worn out, and fell in all directions. As they retreated, couriers arrived from the court, bringing news of the health and safety of the Sultan."[1]

It is unnecessary to remark that the rumour set on foot by the conspirators might have turned out to be true, as indeed it did in the following case :

"While the Emperor was on this campaign against Khan-Zainun, the author's father remained at Agra, in the performance of his duty to the Emperor, and the author himself was at Agra with him. Every day turbulent and designing men spread disastrous news. One day I said to one of my companions, 'Suppose we set some favourable reports afloat;' and he asked what we should say, and I replied, 'Let us say that news has come that they are bringing in the heads of Khán Zaman and Bahádur Khan.' I told this story to several persons. Three days afterwards, Abdullah, son of Murad Beg, brought in the heads of Khán Zaman and Bahádur Khan. The rumour was started in Agra on the very day they were slain."

There are some, I am quite aware, who regard the rumours of disaster which fill the bazaars in time of war as indications of the hostile feelings of the people generally towards their foreign rulers. I myself attach no such importance to the matter. The vast majority of the people know nothing and care nothing about political or military affairs. The picture sometimes drawn of our Indian fellow-subjects, or even of the Indian Muhammadans, watching the political horizon with keen and intelligent interest, is superlatively ridiculous. During that critical period, the early part of 1885, I often asked English-speaking natives about the news, and found that they were as ignorant and indifferent about it as if they had been dwellers in the Fiji Islands. The totally uneducated are, if possible, even more indifferent. No

[1] From the "Tarikh-i Feroz Shahi" of Zian-d din Barni. Elliot's "Muhammadan Historians of India," vol. iii. pp. 231–232.

doubt that with the changing political outlook the people are learning to take a greater interest in public affairs than ever before; but it is none the less true that the gossip in war time comes from the camp and camp-followers, and the rumours of disaster are circulated by malicious persons of the stamp of the political agitators of whom so much has been heard recently. Sometimes the *bazaar gup* originates with dishonest speculators, who hope to profit by a panic; and sometimes it is set afloat by wags and foolish fellows who wish to get up a little excitement. These rumours are, of course, not to be contemptuously disregarded, but at the same time it is not to be denied that there are in the English press itself elements sufficient to unsettle the minds of the Indian people. For how is it possible that the masses of the large towns in India should learn with indifference, through the distorting medium of the vernacular press, the complaints constantly made in England, for party purposes, of the naval and military weakness of the country, of the utterly unprotected state of the British Isles, and of the vast superiority of foreign nations in men and weapons?

There is no dearth of materials available to swell a paper on the subject of *bazaar gup* in India; but I have, perhaps, said enough to indicate the nature of the rumours which, originating in various ways and circulated for various purposes, float about the Indian bazaars in ordinary times as well as on special occasions. That such false rumours, however baseless and absurd, might at a critical moment be productive of grave consequences to the State, no one will question. There is, however, but one remedy—*education*. Much has already been done by schools, colleges, and universities, but a great deal yet remains to be done to enlighten the *masses*—not the country folks only, but the urban populations as well.

A DESCRIPTIVE SONG AND DANCE

CHAPTER IV

MENDICANCY AND MENDICANTS OF SORTS

IN all civilizations an essential characteristic is the keeping up of appearances, and the more complete and perfect the civilizations the more marked is this feature. Individuals as well as communities and nationalities are swayed by this sentiment, and consequently whatever is regarded as disreputable or tending to lower appearances is tabooed and sedulously kept out of view. All classes alike combine to suppress or hide away, as much as possible, all sores and blemishes in the social system; but there is a wide divergence in the judgment of different peoples as to what should be regarded as social sores and blemishes.

In English estimation the mere externals of poverty are so disreputable, so ignoble, that each and every poor man (or woman) not utterly lost to shame, endeavours to the best of his ability to hide himself and his miseries from the public eye; while tramps and bold-faced beggars who dare obtrude their unworthy condition before the world are summarily dealt with by the law, and helpless paupers are immured in penitentiaries—workhouses, asylums and such like—where they are indeed supported at the national expense, but under strict discipline and prisonlike restrictions of liberty. Yet notwithstanding all these checks and hindrances public mendicity cannot be quite suppressed even in England, and begging in transparent disguises goes on to a moderate degree in the sale by men and women of matches, boot-laces and other useful trifles; in street-singing, and in less objectionable ways; while in spite of severe laws [1] and strong public feeling, professional vagrants, tramps and unemployables may be reckoned in their thousands.

Disease, especially chronic disease, and all bodily infirmities of certain types, are regarded in England with a sort of nervous horror mingled with pitying contempt. Whether these feelings have their roots in æsthetic sentiment or in mere selfish dread created by the germ theories of the day, the effect is that the diseased, the infirm, the incurable are, whether in hospitals or in their own homes, kept carefully out of sight.

I am not at present concerned to discuss either the advantages or the ethics of these arrangements, for which much may be said. It is sufficient for my purpose to note that natural feeling in England, guided by its ideals and aided by its power of organization, forces poverty and bodily infirmities into the background of the social world, in order to keep up appearances and to maintain what it believes to be a proper standard of national respectability.

Turn to India and a widely different picture presents itself. There, as in sunny Italy and other southern lands, poverty even in rags is not a crime, is not odious, and

[1] Even to-day tramps who can show no visible means of subsistence may be sentenced to be flogged by magistrates, and are often so dealt with.

A RELIGIOUS MENDICANT

To face page 231

may show itself boldly in the light of day without being regarded with the contempt bordering upon detestation which greets it in England. Bodily infirmities, too, do not amongst Indians give rise to that almost terrified avoidance which is characteristic of the West. Besides, in India the State does not provide workhouses for paupers and but few asylums for incurables, with the result that the foreign rulers, who, although they must carry with them their English notions in respect to poverty and disease, are not able to suppress mendicancy with a strong hand.

In consequence, then, of the peculiarities and conditions just stated, the resident or traveller in India can hardly avoid coming across native beggars all over the country, and may, in the very unlikely event of his caring to do so, obtain from them many interesting glimpses of the ideas and practices of the people.

Religious mendicants are to be met with in considerable numbers everywhere in India, and at certain *melas* or fairs in troupes of remarkable proportions. In India many circumstances, both racial and climatic, have, from the earliest times, been favourable to religious emotionalism, contempt of the world and a repugnance to labour. And there, too, from the earliest times, begging has not only been treated with indulgence, but has been encouraged and even honoured.

"Now I will tell you a story of a faquir," said Guru Govind Singh to some of his disciples. "A faquir lived in the jungles and never asked anything from any one; once on a time the will of God was this, that for eight days he got no food from anywhere; then the faquir thought to himself, 'As God has given me hands and feet I will go into the city and beg.'"[1] Here we have a truly Indian solution of the difficulty in which the faquir found himself. The idea of *work* would never occur to him, he was a faquir, and labour of any kind was out of the question; but having realized, almost as one might think to his own surprise, that Heaven had blessed him with hands and feet, he determined to go and *beg*.

It is therefore not to be wondered at that the mantle of

[1] Colonel Court, "Sikhan di Raj di Vikhia."

religion—albeit materially a very scanty one—easily covers and dignifies to some extent the habitual, irreclaimable tramp, who elsewhere would be an outcast and a danger to society. In India inveterate vagrants of harmless instincts naturally get themselves initiated into, or irregularly assume membership of, a religious sect, and thus habilitated peregrinate the country as sádhus, supported by the willing charity of good Hindus, sometimes rising, step by step, to comfort and even affluence, as the heads of temples or religious houses founded by themselves, and sometimes, of course, dying in a state of neglected misery.[1]

Next amongst Indian mendicants may be considered the great army of *regular beggars*, who do not belong to any of the professedly religious *sects*, and in this class are to be found a great many Brahmans *who are too proud to do any kind of work*, and accordingly gain an *honourable subsistence* by begging.[2] Into this class also fall the poor and the weak, who are everywhere and always with us; poverty-stricken India having more than a full share of paupers whom the needs of the flesh, physical infirmities and advancing years drive to mendicity. Then we have also in this class the born vagabonds, who cannot but live upon the road, and the ordinary flotsam and jetsam of a population which numbers one-fifth of the human race.

In addition to the above two classes of mendicants, India has yet another, made up of a variety of beggars of a special type, who roam the country temporarily, actuated by motives peculiarly Indian. It is to this class and the one just preceding it in my classification that I desire to give prominence in this chapter, having previously devoted an entire volume[3] to the case of the religious mendicant sects or orders.

Some recent books have given us an insight into the lives and doings of beggars in certain European countries, laying bare the cunning deceptions practised by these

[1] Dr. J. N. Bhattacharjee, "Hindu Castes and Sects," pp. 360–3.
[2] Ibid. pp. 61, 75, 76, 79, 115, 118.
[3] "The Mystics, Ascetics and Saints of India." London: T. Fisher Unwin.

A RAJPUT GIRL ON A BEGGING TOUR

To face page 232

gentry and making us acquainted with the remarkably methodical arrangements and efficient organization upon which they rely for the purpose of exploiting to their own advantage the world of simple charitable folks upon whom they live. We read of contractors and agents who work the profitable mine of mendicity in Paris, and of directories containing the names, addresses, and peculiarities of benevolent persons, compiled for the guidance of mendicants;[1] but, though the Indian beggar is by no means devoid of intelligence, his environment, the warm climate of his native land, the very low standard of dress and comfort obtaining there, the religious and social opinions of his countrymen are none of them inimical to mendicity, and therefore the stimulus is wanting for the cultivation of that *'cuteness* which is absolutely necessary for the success of the European mendicant under quite other conditions of life and public opinion. At lies the Indian beggar will not usually stick, and he is not above deception; but combination involving discipline and obedience as well as organized effort for the attainment of an object is quite beyond him.

The Indian pauper, driven by stress of circumstances and by the absence of State provision for his maintenance to rely upon the public for his subsistence, is to be met with everywhere, and, to the credit of his countrymen be it said, is, except in times of widespread distress, cheerfully provided by the charitable with sufficient food to keep him alive and a rag, which is all he wants, to cover him. All over the country some of the destitute have hitherto been fed at religious houses on the bounty of more fortunate persons. On festive occasions, such as a marriage, or the birth of a son, something is commonly set aside for the poor, and thankofferings for recovery from dangerous illness or escape from threatened danger, for unexpected successes in business or unlooked-for windfalls, often take the form of feeding the poor—the exercise of charity being regarded as a most important virtue.

But even so, it is still obvious that the pauper must

[1] "The Beggars of Paris." Translated from the French of M. Louis Paulian by Lady Herschell. London: Edward Arnold.

obtrude himself upon the charitable public at every convenient opportunity if he is not to be overlooked; hence we find the beggar in India unblushingly importunate, sitting on the wayside and crying aloud for alms with a monotonous insistence which is truly wonderful; and wonderful too is the manner in which, day after day, the exiguous contributions of the passers-by mount up till they satisfy the beggar's needs and sometimes more than his needs; for I have known of cases in which the mendicant was able to amass quite a respectable reserve fund, discovered at his death.

At some sacred places solicitations for alms are so general and eager that they amount to positive annoyance and persecution. Of this I have a lively recollection in connection with a visit I paid to Ajudhya, sacred to Rama. Nor can I forget the unpleasant and degrading spectacle I witnessed on the *ghauts* at Benares of a crowd of healthy, able-bodied men fighting with each other and with women and children for food distributed in charity.

Bazaars are naturally the hunting-grounds of beggars able to walk about, and in times of general distress crowds of them may be seen tramping the streets and alleys of populous centres. A few years ago the deformed and diseased pushing their way amongst the ordinary pedestrians in their eagerness for alms was a common sight. I well remember seeing, years ago, leprous beggars forcing their unwelcome presence on shoppers in the China bazaar at Calcutta, but I believe that latterly there has, under police regulation, been some improvement in respect to this matter, which constituted a public danger. However, that the evil has by no means disappeared from Indian cities, even Calcutta, may be gathered from the complaints made on this point as recently as 1906 and 1907 in some Indian newspapers.

Indian beggars also go the round of the houses of the charitable, each having his special patrons, who, on fixed days, distribute relief to the paupers they have, so to speak, adopted. This custom is not entirely confined to Hindus and Muslims, for even Christians of the Roman Catholic Church may be found in many places to set aside a rupee or two each week for Sunday charity to the poor,

Photo by W. Campbell Oman

A TYPICAL HOUSE-TO-HOUSE BEGGAR

To face page 234

who come for the expected dole with a regularity which tends to establish a sort of tie between the giver and the receiver. Of the house-to-house beggars all, or nearly all, proclaim their presence by invoking a blessing upon the house and the dwellers therein, but more especially the children. Sometimes, though very rarely, a woman amongst these beggars will attempt a song or a mimic dance for the amusement of the little folks, if there happen to be any. I need not say that beggars are, as a rule, never allowed to pass the gates of the compounds of Anglo-Indians of any pretensions, and that should one happen to stray in unobserved he or she is soon driven out by the *sahib's* servants, roughly, perhaps with blows, but assuredly without a farthing.

Turning now to those *beggars who seek alms ostensibly for specific purposes*, many cases might be instanced. For example, in one of my wanderings I met a group of four or five persons begging from the charitable public to enable them, so they affirmed, to pay the land-tax due by them to the inexorable *Sarkár* (Government), and so save from public auction the fields that had come down to them through many generations of industrious ancestors. Whatever truth there may have been in their story I cannot imagine that they met with any success. Once, too, I came upon a Muhammadan appealing to his co-religionists to help him to give decent burial to one of their own faith, who had died near the shrine of a well-known saint in the neighbourhood, and contributions in the shape of small coins were dropped into his beggar's bowl quickly enough, so that I have no doubt that the stranger's obsequies were carried out in a decorous manner. The element of altruism in this case ought, perhaps, to exclude it from the category of *begging* as ordinarily understood; but it seemed to have a sufficient interest of its own to be included here.

To the above instances, which have their own peculiarities, I now add the following descriptive notes, which will, I hope, serve to show that there are types of beggars to be met with in India whose counterparts could hardly be found anywhere else.

The Hatyárá (Sinner).—At the meeting of cross-roads

in a populous thoroughfare I came upon a man whose appearance and behaviour excited my curiosity. His face was almost entirely concealed by wraps, leaving only his eyes visible. Hanging from a string fastened about his neck there was something queer-looking, which, on closer inspection, turned out to be the desiccated tail of a calf. With monotonous iteration the fellow repeated, as he sat in the shade of a tree, these words : *Main hatyárá, main hatyárá* (I am sinful, I am sinful). "That might very well be the case," thought I. "All of us could with truth utter these words ; but what particular evil deed was troubling this muffled mendicant, and why did he adorn himself with a cow's tail?" Giving utterance to my thoughts, bystanders readily explained that the beggar's cry was the one ordinarily raised by the contrite, if involuntary, cause of the death of a cow or a calf, and that it has to be constantly repeated by the transgressor as he proceeds towards the Ganges, where, after the performance of such ceremonies as may be prescribed by the Brahmans, he may wash away his sin in the waters of the sacred river. The miserable sinner himself explained very humbly that he had quite unintentionally killed a calf ; that ever since the commission of that sacrilege, misfortune had dogged his footsteps ; and that as his only chance of escape from his misery was to purify himself by bathing, under the direction of the Brahmans at the junction of the holy waters of the Ganges and the Jumna, he was proceeding thither. But to reach Prayaga (Allahabad) was not enough, he must arrive there with the means of satisfying the demands of the hereditary priesthood, without whose assistance his long pilgrimage would be infructuous, and that is why he appealed to public generosity. Would not the *sahib* out of his abundance help a poor man in trouble? Asked why he concealed his visage, the fellow explained that, after having committed such a heinous sin as he had been guilty of, it was quite unbearable to face the world unveiled. Perhaps so, but there may have been other reasons besides shamefacedness for this masquerade.

However, it is not only to obtain funds for religious ceremonies that a man placed as our hatyárá was may

Photo by W. Campbell Oman

MUHAMMADAN MENDICANT

To face page 237

have to beg. He is sometimes *required* to do so by the Brahmans *as a punishment*, as in a case which came to my knowledge of a well-to-do man, a sort of petty chief, who was condemned by his spiritual guides to beg for a certain number of years in expiation of the awful crime of killing a cow accidentally when out hunting.

The Qalandar.—In a convenient place in the vicinity of a grocer's shop, where men and women are continually passing, sits a Muslim faquir of the order of the Qalandars, well dressed and apparently well nourished. With a scrutinizing look he scans the faces of the passers-by as they saunter past him in the leisurely manner of the East, and presently beckons one of them to approach him. The man who is wanted usually obeys, although with a somewhat sheepish look and deprecating smile upon his face. "Why are you cast down?" says the Qalandar to him; "your trouble will soon pass away. Yes, it will soon pass away." Several persons, not pressed for time, stop to watch these proceedings. "Just take hold of this bamboo," says the Qalandar to his victim. "Squeeze it now, so" (showing the way it should be done). "That's all right. See, your hand is moist with milk from this *dry* wood. That's a *sure* sign. Go, brother, go, but do not forget the faquir who has made you happy." The man who has been made happy under the eyes of so many onlookers, fumbles about for what he can find rolled up in the waist of his ohoty, or loin-cloth, hands it to the Qalandar, and passes on his way to enjoy the good fortune that is coming to him.

Women at work.—It is the *Basant* or spring festival. Crowds gaily dressed and with cheerful countenances are gathering at the fair. All seem happy, especially the children, as, reluctant to move on, they admire with wide-open eyes the gaudy-coloured toys in the booths. Now, surely this is a proper time and a suitable place for collecting some money, so half-a-dozen women, by no means paupers, sit in a line on the roadside singing together an appeal for alms. They have a cotton sheet on the ground to receive donations, cowrie shells, pice or whatever else might be thrown to them by the charitable holiday-makers. And the burden of their song is this : " God has blessed thee with more than enough, share then His gifts with the poor and the needy."

The Hindu Astrologer.—" Har, har, popo! har, har, popo zabar jang!" Hullo! what's that? Only a Hindu fortune-teller announcing his advent to the women in the village. His words may have, for aught I know, no specific meaning, but they are understood as indicating his readiness to lift the veil that hides futurity from us. There he stands, smiling, the astute, experienced Brahman, clever enough to gauge the characters and, I should say, the weaknesses of the folks about him, if not wise enough to read their destinies in the motions of the planets he pretends to study. His services are soon in requisition, for who does not desire to anticipate the future? Yet not before the world at large can his secrets be revealed, and so the astrologer is invited inside the court, and there, with the aid of his astrological almanac he discloses in private the dangers, and with them the greater blessings, in store for his client in the years that are to come, and having worked upon her imagination, harrowed her feelings and excited her hopes, the seer regains the street, with a small pecuniary reward and many solemn promises of further gifts when the happy events predicted by him shall have come to pass.

Collecting money for a daughter's wedding.—On the margin of a beautiful tank, under the shade of a splendid old tree, sits a stranger in conversation with some of the townsfolk. He is an elderly man and a Brahman, who, I am told, had been travelling on foot for the past two months from some place on the Jumna near Agra, journeying by way of Delhi, Hardwar and Jwala Mookhi. His object was, not to see the world, nor to trade, nor even to perform a pilgrimage; but, as he explained to me, to collect money, by *begging*, for the wedding of his little daughter. The accomplishment of this marriage was for him so important a religious duty that the evasion of it involving, as it did, the most terrible consequences to himself, here and hereafter, was not to be thought of for a moment. A husband had to be found for the girl, that was imperative, and certain expenses were also unavoidable. According to the stringent customs of the clan to which he belonged nothing whatever could be received from the bridegroom's family, and, therefore, it was obvious that he, the girl's father, must go forth and *earn* what was needed by *begging* through the country. For shelter and subsistence he could reckon upon thákurdwárás and shivalas (Vishnu and Siva temples), scattered as they are along the highways of the land, and so he had been very *busy* for the previous three months working out his plans for his little daughter's benefit. The Brahman admitted that he had received the *mantra* of a Bairagi, but it did not suit him, good easy man, to conform to the practices and customs of the sect. He carried with him a brass *lotah* for water, and explained that as he could not eat bread cooked by others he had to prepare it for himself. I wished to know how he managed his culinary operations, seeing that he carried no cooking-pots with him. The explanation was simple. Having got some water in his *lotah* all our Brahman had to do was to knead some flour and water into dough *in a corner of the sheet which covered his shoulders*. Now for the oven! To prepare this he would select a smooth piece of ground, and spreading a lot of dry cow-dung cakes upon it, set them alight. In a short time the fuel would thoroughly heat the ground, then what fuel still remained, and the ashes, would be swept away, and behold the extemporized oven. The dough, patted into flat cakes between the palms of his hands, would now be laid on the heated ground, and soon be converted into well-baked and excellent unleavened bread. "When a little *ghi* is mixed with the dough, the bread so baked," said my informant, "is better than a *púri* (a cake)," and at the thought of the appetizing delicacy his mouth literally watered, and he smacked his lips. Truly, man *needs* but little here below, and the Hindu has discovered, and often is quite content with, the irreducible minimum of human requirements.

In regard to the object of his wanderings our Brahman had already been so far successful that he had been able to remit home *ten rupees* towards the amount required to meet the expenses of the wedding; and for so good a cause he did not disdain to accept a rupee from my unhallowed hand.

A Muslim fan-waver.—The day is sultry, not a breath of air seems to be in circulation. Men and women move about listlessly in the narrow street taking little heed of one another. Near a shop, where from time to time purchasers stop to buy the usual daily necessaries, stands a slender, venerable, long-bearded Muslim, dressed in a coat of faded green and with several strings of large beads hanging about his neck. He does not utter a word, but he heaves a sigh now and again, as with the palm-leaf fan in his hand he fans the faces of the people who pass by, or who arrest their steps near the shop. Very few notice his sighs or his attentions, but occasionally a benevolent person passes a *half-pice* or a handful of rice to the faquir, who repays the gift with the blessing, *jíta raho!* (live on!)

Driven from home by a curse.—A party of men, women and children came to me requesting my help under rather strange circumstances. They really formed a family party, and were wandering about, at the expense of the charitable public, in earnest quest of a *sádhu* who had cursed them and brought utter ruin upon them all. If they could only meet the sádhu and appease his anger the burden would be lifted from their miserable lives, and they trusted that the generosity of the public would enable them to realize their anxious hope.

It all came about in this way. The family were giving a feast to their friends and neighbours in their village home when a sádhu presented himself at the house with importunate demands for a share of the feast. The unbidden guest was told to wait his turn, but not heeding this very reasonable injunction continued his irritating demand for early attention. Losing his temper the head of the house told the troublesome fellow to be off, adding that he might content himself afterwards with the remnants of the feast when they were cast into the drains. Stung to wrath by his contemptuous treatment the sádhu heaped dire curses indiscriminately on the house and its inhabitants, on the food provided for the feast, on the guests and the entire village. He then left the place and

Photo by W. Campbell Oman

A FAMILY OF TRAMPS

To face page 240

was seen no more. Hardly had he disappeared when it was discovered, as indeed he had predicted, that the food provided for the entertainment was putrid and alive with worms; then, not long after, followed, according to his maledictions, the total destruction of the village by fire, the utter ruin of the offending household, and the lamentable plight in which I met them, as wanderers on the face of the land. Oh! if they could only find the good man and obtain his forgiveness all would yet be well with them.

As the family party had been on the tramp for a couple of months or more when they came to me, it was apparent that they had a sufficient number of good Hindus to support them while engaged in their important search for the insulted, irate and undoubtedly formidable *sádhu.*

Concluding remarks.—The facts and details given in this chapter furnish, I believe, quite enough material to satisfy the reader that in the matter of mendicancy the mental latitudes and longitudes of India are far removed from those of England.

To understand mendicity in India one must bear in mind that, for ages past, to beg for about twelve years of his life was the common lot of every person of superior status.

"Boys at an early age were made over by their parents to the *guru* or teacher. They lived with their teacher, begged from door to door for his maintenance and support, tended his cattle, swept and cleaned his house, served him menially, and acquired from him from day to day that knowledge of the Vedas and of religious rites which was the heritage of all Hindus in the ancient days. . . . And after the students had thus spent twelve years or longer in acquiring knowledge, they made suitable presents to their guru, returned to their longing relatives, married and settled down as householders."[1]

Again, as we have seen, Brahmans in distress, or for the accomplishment of a purpose, do not disdain to live upon the willing contributions of their co-religionists, while all Indian sects—the professional religionists—have resorted to mendicity for their own support; and in this way have given the stamp of respectability to begging as a vocation.

With the modern apotheosis of wealth in India, which

[1] Romesh Chunder Dutt, I.C.S., "Brief History of Ancient and Modern India," p. 14.

necessarily involves an increase of selfishness, the support of a large mendicant community is becoming irksome to the classes whose unstinted generosity could in former years always be fully relied upon by the poor, the needy and the religious. To-day the standard of respectability coming into favour amongst the upper-middle strata of Indian society is one in which fine clothes and the display of worldly possessions are—as in the West—the prime factors. Poverty in rags—respectable for ages in India—now clashes with new ideals, and is an offence in the eyes of an increasing number of well-to-do persons. Mendicity, the usual concomitant of poverty, is beginning in these days to be contemned as it never was at any previous period in Indian history; and there can be no doubt that State intervention on a large scale for the maintenance of the helpless poor will be demanded by considerations of humanity.

PART III.—DOMESTIC

LEAVES FROM THE LIVES OF THE LOWER CLASSES

LEAVES FROM THE LIVES OF THE LOWER CLASSES

I.—Introductory Note

In his "Short History of India," Mr. Talboys Wheeler wrote :

> "As a matter of fact, plots and intrigues of one sort or another are the daily life of the natives of India. There are more plots and intrigues in a single establishment of native servants than in a hundred English households. An Englishman in India, who chooses to study the character of his servants, will know more in a few months of native thoughts and ways than he can learn in books from the study of a lifetime."[1]

No one who knows anything about the matter will hesitate to endorse this opinion, with the very necessary caution, however, that although native servants in the households of Europeans in India possess, to the full extent, the general characteristics of their fellow-countrymen, they form, after all, a very small class out of the vast population of the country regarding whose domestic life, whether in the hut of the peasant or the *zenana* of the gentleman, Europeans in India have little direct knowledge. At the same time it has to be borne in mind that the native servants of Europeans in India form a class very considerably above the average of their fellow-countrymen in intelligence and experience of the world. So that however ignorant and superstitious they may appear in these pages, the bulk of the Indian people—the agricultural population—must be placed upon a decidedly lower intellectual level.

The following sketches of the domestic life of the lower orders are, in every case, based on full notes jotted down at the time at which the events described actually

[1] Note at page 628 of Mr. Talboys Wheeler's "Short History of India." Macmillan & Co., 1880.

occurred or the anecdotes were related to me, and, whatever their value, may at least claim to embody, as accurately as possible, the facts which came under my observation.

Of the persons who figure in the following narratives I did not find any reluctant to communicate facts about the lives of themselves and others, or regarding their religious and social customs. This was more especially true of the women, who were always eager to tell their mistress of their joys and sorrows; and it is due to the confidence engendered by my wife's great sympathy with her servants in their troubles, and her unfailing tolerance of their many shortcomings, that I was enabled to gather the materials for not a few of the sketches included in the remaining portions (Parts III and IV) of this volume.

II.—Old Fakeerah and his Conjugal Troubles, with Some Account of that Nefarious Fraternity the Thugs, and Stories illustrating the Antagonism between Muslims and Hindus

Long years ago, when I was quite a child, our old home of pleasant memories was broken up, and the numerous servants of a comfortable Anglo-Indian household had, nearly all of them, to be discharged. Amongst those who were told that their services would not be required any longer was Fakeerah, who had been my father's "bearer," or valet. He was a Muhammadan of Colgong, or Kahalgaon, and owned a small bit of land in his native village. When the time for settling up accounts arrived he came, with tears in his eyes, to receive his well-earned wages. Palm joined to palm, he stood before my mother and respectfully said, with unfeigned emotion, "For years I have eaten the sahib's salt, and now that he is gone shall I desert the children? You cannot do without servants. Some you must have, however few in number. I will stay with you for small wages, or even for none at all. Have I not my bit of land at Colgong?" The man was thoroughly in earnest, and, true to his generous resolve, remained in our service on much smaller wages than he had had before. He accompanied us to Calcutta, was in all things entirely honest and trustworthy, evinced a genuine affection for us children, and seemed contented and happy. But as years went by a home-sickness came upon him. The picturesque little village, under the shadow of the low hills, on the banks of the Ganges, where the noisy river rushes madly amongst the noble granite rocks he knew so well, seemed to draw him with irresistible power, and so one day he explained, in his usual deferential way, with many apologies and much hesitation, that he wished to visit his *mulk* (country), and begged leave of absence for three months. According to Indian custom he brought us a *badli*, or substitute, and arranged to proceed on his journey with some companions who were going towards the same part of the country as himself. There were but a few miles of railway open in India at that time; the journey to Colgong was to be performed on foot by easy stages. As *Thugs* and other highway robbers were unfortunately too common in those days, no traveller would make a journey without companions; few would venture on the road without arms.

The appointed day arrived. Fakeerah came to make his farewell *salaams*. He was a slim man, a little over five feet in height, with fine, well-cut features, and a clean brown complexion. His moustache, except at the two ends, was clipped close and partly shaven, so as to leave a clear narrow space immediately over the upper lip. This is the orthodox Muhammadan style of dressing the moustache, and has for its object to prevent food eaten by the believer from being contaminated by contact with the hair. The beard, however, is allowed to grow in full luxuriance, and in Fakeerah's case attained a length of several inches without the slightest curl or irregularity, although now largely sprinkled with grey.

He was ready for his journey, with his loins girded up, and well do I remember his appearance as he came to take leave of us. A small bundle of clothes was tied across his back; a strong bamboo stick rested on his right shoulder, carrying his quilt slung easily upon it, and at the extremity of the stick was his pair of shoes. One would think that the feet, and not the end of the stick, was the proper place for the shoes; but the poor native, accustomed from infancy to go barefooted, reserves his shoes for rough ground, and willingly removes them when treading smooth roads or plodding through mud and slush. At his side was a *tulwar*, or curved sword, in a leather scabbard, purchased for the occasion, and from his left hand, by a strong cord, hung his brass *lotah*. The sword was, of course, for his protection from Thugs, *dacoits*, wild beasts, and other dangers of the highway; the lotah and string were to enable him, during his long and dusty march, to draw cool water from the roadside wells; what money he had was carefully secreted in the folds of his waistband. Thus fully equipped, Fakeerah departed on his journey to Colgong, between which place and Calcutta there lay some two hundred and fifty miles of road, passing for long distances through dreary jungles tenanted only by wild beasts or robbers.

Three months passed away, four and five months passed away, and yet Fakeerah did not return. We began to speculate amongst ourselves whether he had been detained by the charms of home, or whether sickness was the cause of his prolonged absence. We even began to fear that he might have fallen into the hands of Thugs and been strangled by them. Many a story of these dreadful assassins had we heard and remembered only too well, for Colgong (Kahalgaon) was a noted centre of their criminal practices at the time of which I write, and, indeed, had enjoyed an unenviable notoriety in this respect at least as far back as the days when the Chinese pilgrim, Hiuen Tsiang, visited India (A.D. 637).[1] So much was Thuggee in our thoughts in connection with the prolonged absence of our faithful old servant, and so interesting, for many reasons, is that unparalleled system of assassination and robbery that I trust the reader will pardon a short digression on the subject in this place.

Thuggee is an institution peculiar to India. Amongst the customs of most barbarous races there have existed practices of a character revolting to our modern ideas; but nothing more repugnant to feelings of humanity could be imagined than the cold-blooded assassinations which, for

[1] General Cunningham's "Archæological Survey of India," vol. xv. p. 35.

purposes of gain, *but under religious sanctions, and with religious ceremonies*, were systematically committed by the Thugs in a land where civilization had already made considerable progress. Thuggee was not confined to any one part of India, but extended far and wide, and, curiously enough, embraced both Hindus and Muhammadans in the great brotherhood of crime. A secret dialect and a set of secret signs facilitated intercourse between the initiated from different parts of the country, while a share in the spoils of their murderous expeditions, or the superstitious awe inspired by their mysterious calling, secured for them the protection of the Zemindars, or landholders, and the native police. Strange to say, the members of the Thug fraternity belonged to many grades of society, to different castes, including *Brahmans*, and generally followed some peaceful and respectable avocation. They were artisans, agriculturists and traders, a fact which seriously hindered the British authorities in their endeavours to bring the criminals to justice; for when a suspected gang was followed up it soon disappeared in the mass of the apparently respectable population.[1] Whenever a plundering expedition was to be undertaken, a number of the brotherhood assembled by appointment at some convenient spot, and travelling along the road in various disguises and for various ostensible objects, fell in with travellers along the highway. Trained in every artifice required to promote the success of their horrible trade, the Thugs easily gained the confidence of the unsuspecting wayfarers with whom they fell in along the dusty high-roads of the country, and when a suitable opportunity—for instance, a secluded

[1] "Dr. Cheek had a child's bearer, *i. e.* a he-nurse, who had charge of his children. The man was a special favourite, remarkable for his kind and tender ways with his little charges, gentle in manner, and unexceptionable in all his conduct. Every year he obtained leave from his master and mistress, as he said, for the filial purpose of visiting his aged mother, for one month; and returning after the expiry of that time, with the utmost punctuality, resumed with the accustomed affection and tenderness the charge of his little darlings. *This mild and exemplary being was the missing Thug!* Kind, gentle, conscientious, and regular at his post for eleven months in the year, he devoted the twelfth to strangulation."—Tayler's "Thirty-eight Years in India," p. 194.

locality—presented itself, treacherously strangled their victims in cold blood. No feeling of pity ever stayed the fatal noose when once the omens were propitious. What mattered it to the Thugs that the companions who trudged by their side were, after years of absence, returning to their distant village homes, and to their expectant wives and children? What mattered it to them that the men they wished to murder were fellow-countrymen and co-religionists? Had not the goddess Kali delivered the victims into their hands? and were they not bound, under penalty of incurring her displeasure, to take their lives with the consecrated *roomal*, or handkerchief? The deed accomplished, the murderers at once secured the property of their victims, even to the clothing on their persons, and then with the *sacred axe* buried the bodies out of sight as quickly as possible. In most cases an impenetrable mystery shrouded for ever the fate of the unfortunate wayfarers, and the Thugs, emboldened by success and immunity from punishment, pushed their cruel trade with greater audacity than before. There was a method in the perpetration of these revolting crimes, and an observance of religious ceremonies, which excites astonishment and lends special and peculiar interest to the practices of this extraordinary sect of assassins. It is difficult to tell when the Thuggee system first began to develop itself in India.[1] It can undoubtedly date back to a distant period; but it was not till 1829 that the British Government made a serious and systematic attempt to suppress the widespread evil which seemed to have become naturalized in every part of India.

[1] Sir R. Temple thought "it arose from the disregard of human life caused by scenes of incessant bloodshed during wars and revolutions, and from the demoralizing effects of the ruthless system of spoliation established by the Mahrattas and continued by the Pindaries" ("India in 1880," p. 196). Probably these causes helped to encourage the spread of Thuggee, but it undoubtedly existed long before the time of the Mahrattas and Pindaris. We have an account of the capture of about a thousand Thugs near Delhi in the thirteenth century (Elliot's "Muhammadan Historians of India," by Dowson, vol. iii. p. 141). The grave of one reputed founder of Thuggee, Shah Nizamaldin, who lived about six hundred years ago, is still to be seen at Delhi. But the system, as already indicated in the text (p. 248), can probably claim a far higher antiquity.

The legend which enshrines the origin of Thuggee relates that at some remote period a terrible demon, named Rukut Beij-dana, who was so gigantic that he could stand in the deepest part of the ocean with his body above the waves, was busy destroying the human race when the goddess Kali interfered to save mankind, and with her mighty sword severed him in two pieces. But from his blood other demons sprang into existence, and as fast as Kali disposed of them more monsters were generated from the blood of those who had perished by her sword. Weary of her fruitless labour, the goddess created two men out of the sweat which trickled from one of her arms, and giving them *roomals* or handkerchiefs directed them to strangle the demons. When they had duly accomplished their allotted task, and came to give up the *roomals* to Kali, that grateful goddess bade them keep those serviceable weapons and hand them down to their descendants with instructions to use them, for their own profit, in the destruction of all men who were not of their kindred.

To the goddess Kali, therefore, the Thugs looked for protection, and they believed that if they carried out their horrid murders only when the omens were propitious and the proper rites and ceremonies had been observed, they would enjoy both safety and prosperity. With what revolting indifference their cold-blooded and wholesale assassinations were carried out, and afterwards talked over with pride and pleasure, became known to the world when the task of suppressing Thuggee was taken in hand by the East India Company, and the secret doings of the nefarious fraternity were dragged to the light of day.

Once attacked with vigour and determination, the timidity and treachery of members of the infamous brotherhood helped the Government officers materially towards the suppression of the abomination. Many Thugs apprehended upon suspicion, losing faith in their patron goddess, turned king's evidence and revealed the secrets of the fraternity, their slang vocabulary, their private signs, their religious ceremonies, superstitions, and methods of procedure. From the mouths of these approvers particulars were obtained which, while enabling the police authorities to track the criminals and bring them to justice, afforded the British officers the opportunity of unfolding a page in the secret history of human institutions which could hardly be surpassed in gloomy interest.[1]

However, although the perils of the road beset with Thugs and haunted by wild beasts were real enough, Fakeerah did come back at last, and presented himself at the door well and hearty. His face, which was naturally light-complexioned for a native of India, was burnt black by the sun, his grey beard looked ragged, and his moustache over-grown; but he was not much the worse for his long journey, and in his undemonstrative way appeared pleased to see the "baba logue" (children) again. We wanted to know what had kept him away so long, and were forthwith admitted to a tale of domestic woe. When he reached his village his old friends were resolved upon giving him a wife. Probably he was not reluctant to get one, although he protested that such was not the case. A wife was found for him, and, evidently pleased with his partner, he determined to bring her with him to Calcutta. This time the journey was to be made by water. A boat bound for Calcutta was found at Colgong, and Fakeerah engaged places in it for himself and his wife. There were several other passengers for the capital and intermediate places; but Fakeerah's wife was the only woman on board. Hardly had the boat proceeded a day's journey from its starting place when a storm arose, and it was completely wrecked upon a sand-bank in the river. Either because she was the only woman on board, or on account of some unlucky marks about her face or person, Fakeerah's wife was fixed upon by the travellers as the cause of their misfortune. Her husband apparently shared this opinion, and, reluctantly we may presume, conducted her back to her village, whence, after some delay, he started once more for Calcutta, but this time alone. It was useless to argue with the old man about the absurdity of supposing that

1 For a short account of Thuggee the reader may consult Mr. James Hutton's "Thugs, Dacoits, and Gang-robbers of India." W. H. Allen & Co., London.

his wife could possibly be the cause of the wreck of the boat. His reply was that all the passengers said so, and that seemed to settle the matter for him. With the lapse of time, his opinion in regard to the blame attributable to his young wife for their mishap on the Ganges seems to have undergone some modification, for he asked and obtained permission to go and fetch her. The long journey home and back was this time successfully accomplished, and the couple arrived at Calcutta apparently quite well and happy. The wife was rather good-looking, and attracted some attention by her costume, which was that worn in her native village; a full skirt and short bodice, with a sheet or *chudder* thrown gracefully over the head, quite unlike the saree of Bengal. She was very shy, and kept her face concealed as much as possible, whilst she made the very best use of a pair of handsome black eyes. However, the treacherous chudder revealed enough of her face, from time to time, to enable us to say that it was decidedly bright and pretty. Absorbed in her domestic duties, we saw and heard little enough of Fakeerah's wife. But after a few months the climate of Calcutta began to disagree with her. She was constantly ill. Her husband grumbled. "What was the use," he said, "of a wife who could not cook his rice, and who needed to be nursed and looked after? She would be better at home." So he sent her back to her village.

Fakeerah himself did not think very much of Calcutta. He used to pronounce it a perfect Babylon, the very soil of which was demoralizing, and, to give point to his opinion, related the following story to me:

An old woman, a native of a remote village in the west, came to Calcutta to pay a visit to her son, who was employed in that city. She was very infirm, and so old that she had not a tooth left in her head. After being two or three days in Calcutta, the old woman said to her son, "Do you happen to know any suitable person to whom you could get me married?" The son, unwilling to expose his mother to ridicule, recommended her not to mention her wish to any one, promising, at the same time, to make every necessary inquiry in person. He thus put her off for some days. Unable, at length, to withstand her importunities, he told her that he was himself anxious to get married, but desired to take a wife from amongst his own people. He advised her to select a husband in the same quarter. In order to carry out this object they started homeward the next morning, the son carrying a bag containing something which he was very careful to conceal from his mother. When they had travelled for two days, the son told the mother that they were approaching a village where he had many friends and acquaintances, and he knew of one at least who would be delighted to marry her. "Fie! my son," was the reply, "thus to jest with an old woman like me —your mother too—tottering, as I am, on the brink of the grave." The son said no more. That evening he carefully spread the contents of his bag under the mat on which his mother was to sleep. In the course of the night she said to him, "Son, I have been thinking over what you said to me to-day. True, I am an old woman, but not so very old after all, and, if I married, I would be no longer a burden on you, my dear boy. Do you know anybody in this village who would make an eligible match for me?" "I shall see about the matter to-morrow," said the young man. On mentioning the proposal to the old woman next day, she looked rather foolish and disconcerted, but treated the affair as a mere joke. "You surely did not think I was in earnest?" was all she said, and the son heard never a word more about the matter. At Calcutta she had been eager for marriage, but away from the naughty city the desire had passed away, except when the long-extinguished fires were temporarily revived by the proximity of the mere soil of the Indian Babylon, which the son had carried in his bag and spread under the old woman's mat by way of experiment.

To return to old Fakeerah himself. Whether his wife died on her return home I am not aware, but the lonely "bearer" suddenly consoled himself with a new wife. We were at this time living at the little French settlement of Chandernagore. The new wife was stout, and by no means young according to Indian notions, a fact which seemed to require some explanation. It was no use, the garrulous old man said, to marry a mere girl who knew nothing, whose thoughts would run upon finery, and who would neglect the house and his interests; nor would it do to seek a wife from amongst his own people, for the air and water (*hawa, pani*) of Calcutta would not agree with the up-country woman, as he had already found out to his cost. The new wife was a native of Bengal, was not too young, and in all probability would keep good health and be useful. Keep good health she did, and proved it by having a remarkably good appetite. Being in her own country and amongst her own kith and kin, she had many friends and visitors, and rather liked to entertain them and show her hospitality. Poor old Fakeerah was in despair. All this was more than he had bargained for. What he wanted was a thrifty wife who would save him from some domestic duties, look after him when he happened to be sick, and save money. Great was his disappointment. At the end of the first month of his wedded life he came, with tears in his eyes, to relate the details of the consumption of rice, dáll, ghí, etc., that had taken place in his household, and protested that he must certainly get rid of the woman, who was no better than a voracious glutton and would assuredly land him in jail if he kept her much longer.

Just at this time we removed to Calcutta, and, taking advantage of the opportunity, Fakeerah gave his wife the slip, and congratulated himself upon his fortunate release from such a terribly extravagant woman. However, he never dared to show his face in Chandernagore again, for fear of the personal vengeance of the relatives of his deserted wife. Legal proceedings he seems never to have dreaded or dreamt of.

All alone again, the old man went on quietly enough for a little time, but presently set up a constant complaint of the hardship of having to cook his own food. After our past experience we could guess pretty well what all this would lead to, and one fine day Fakeerah asked a week's leave to get married again.

A young woman of a rather flashy appearance was his new partner. She was quiet enough, and apparently the couple got on fairly well together. One morning the old man came with a very mysterious look on his face, and kept muttering to himself as he went about his duties. Inquiry elicited the whispered statement that his wife had the extraordinary habit of stealing out on moonlight nights into the garden, and collecting flowers. There was no doubt about it; he had watched her himself over and over again and could not get rid of the idea that she was a *witch*—for did any one ever hear of an ordinary woman doing such things? It was too terrible; he could not consent to live with her any longer. We suggested that she might be a somnambulist, but that did not mend matters at all. What arrangements he made with her I do not know, but get rid of her he did, at the expense, I fancy, of a pretty big slice out of his hoarded savings. For two or three years the old man continued a crusty, grumbling solitary. He lived very parsimoniously, and out of his wages (which had by this time been considerably increased) and little extras in the way of *dasturi* (commission) had made a respectable hoard. The rent derived from his little bit of land at Colgong had also been carefully put away. Silver and gold ornaments were the form his savings took, but a bag of rupees was also quietly hid away at the bottom of his old trunk.

My duties next took me to Burdwan, and while there, old Fakeerah found a fourth wife. She was quite a girl, with a frank open face, beautiful large eyes, a neat slim figure and a rather loud voice. She wore only the *sari*, which is a single sheet wound round the waist, brought gracefully over the bosom and then passed over the head, generally leaving the back quite bare. This dress, peculiar to the women of Lower Bengal, when made, as it usually is, of diaphanous material, forms, to say the least, an exceedingly light garment, and used to be an object of special aversion to my old "bearer"; but he had to put up with it now. Instead of being kept down, the Bengalí girl soon got the upper hand of the old man. She would tell him that she was not going to be treated as he had treated his other wives. She would scold him well, and between bullying and wheedling managed to get possession of all his money. I wonder what he would have had to say, after his extensive experience, on the important subject "Is marriage a failure?"

The poor old fellow got very ill, and died, when I was away from home. Loyal to the end, his last words were a touching message to me, expressing his regret at not being able to see me ere he died. The widow, enriched with the spoils she had secured, went off in a few days with a bugler in a native infantry regiment, and we never heard of her again.

I mentioned at the beginning of this paper that the subject of my narrative was a Muhammadan; but I believe he had been born a Hindu and possessed a sort of doubtful belief in the Hindu gods, though, like other renegades, he was disposed to show up his old religion.

His lingering faith in the gods of the Hindu pantheon, as well as his desire to vindicate the supremacy of Islam, may be illustrated by a couple of anecdotes.

I was observing to him one day, that in a certain district of Bengal the women seemed healthier and stronger than the men; to which his immediate reply was, that probably the districts where such was the case were those in which peculiar respect was paid to some female divinity, Kali perhaps, who would of course favour her own sex. The recognition, in this way, by Indian Mussulmans of the power of Hindu deities is by no means uncommon. Islam, originally deeply imbued with superstitions of its own, has acquired a further tincture of the same element from its contact with Hinduism, and from its Hindu converts. So that many an Indian Muslim of the lower classes readily acknowledges the truth of the Hindu legends, assigning a place to their gods amongst the numerous demons and malignant spirits in his calendar, precisely as the early Christians did in respect to the deities held in esteem by the Pagans.

According to Fakeerah, the Hindu god Jagannath, of whose terrible car so much has been written by the missionaries, was originally nothing more nor less than a thievish, lying cook in the service of a Muhammadan Pir. Once Jagannath, tempted by the savoury odour of some delicacy which he was preparing for his master, indulged himself by partaking of a portion of it. The Pir detected the delinquency, and took his servant severely to task for his misconduct. Jagannath protested vehemently that he was innocent of the fault imputed to him. He had not even tasted the dish. The Pir became angry, and, pious man that he was, directed that Jagannath's hands and feet should be cut off as a punishment for his theft and mendacity. In this mutilated state the wretched man (no longer in a condition to help himself) implored his master either to assist him to drag on a weary existence, or else to put an end to his life and his sufferings without delay. The Pir's heart was touched with remorse and pity. He advised his unhappy cook to proceed to a certain place, where he predicted he would be treated with the highest consideration by the Hindus—would, in fact, be venerated by them as a deity. Of course the Pir could not be wrong, and this is the origin of Jagannath the famous divinity of Puree, worshipped by the Hindus under the form of the misshapen torso of a man with mere stumps for arms and legs.

The perpetual rivalry and hatred existing between the Hindus and Muhammadans in India, which has given rise to many a sanguinary scene and many a bitter memory, which even within recent years has caused serious riots, and which at the present moment divides them into two hostile camps, has not been barren of fruits of a less tragic character. Stories holding up one side or the other to ridicule are common. Here is one from a Muhammadan source :

Some Hindu and Muhammadan sepoys were travelling together. At a well the Hindus of the party noticed a *tulasi* plant, and, after performing their usual ablutions, went and paid their respects to it, prostrating themselves on the ground before it. The Muhammadans laughed at them. A dispute arose, and the followers of the Prophet of Mecca, applying the logic so commonly used in such cases to prove the vanity of idolatry, pulled up the plant by the roots, to establish their contention that it was a mere stock and had no power to resent an outrage. The occurrence naturally led to much ill-feeling and strained relations in the little party. The Hindus looked confidently for the vengeance of the offended deity upon the sacrilegious Muslims, but their expectations were not realized. Some days after the incident of the tulasi plant, one of the Muhammadan sepoys prostrated himself with great veneration before some bushes on the wayside. The Hindus noticed this, and coming forward began, by way of retaliation, to tear up the plants which had been the object of his adoration. He warned them that his gods were not so supine as the tulasi plant respected by themselves, but would take speedy revenge for the outrage; and, true enough, they soon had cause to repent of their rashness, for the Muslim wag had got them to handle a lot of stinging-nettles.

III.—Bhujnu and Cherokeeah, or Man and Wife

Far away amongst the lofty pine-trees of cool and pleasant Simla, a woman came to our cottage one summer day to offer herself as *ayah* (lady's maid, or child's nurse) in our household. She was from Kotgurh, a picturesque little village nestling in the valley of the Sutlej, under the shadow of lofty mountains, not many miles from the spot where the river debouches into the plains of Northern India.

When the woman presented herself she was attired in the costume of her country. Her head-dress consisted of a peculiar cap, covering the hair almost entirely, with a band right across the forehead like that worn by certain nuns. She was dressed in a very full skirt gathered in at the waist, a loose bodice, with long sleeves, reaching down to the hips, and a long folded piece of white cloth wrapped round the neck. Her most conspicuous ornament was a huge nose-ring. She looked what she really was, a genuine rustic, with nothing of the smartness or address of the experienced, well-trained ayah about her. But she had a frank, intelligent face, and a certain natural grace which won favour for her and outweighed all her deficiencies. She was duly engaged and put to work, after she had changed her Kotgurh costume for the customary dress of her new occupation.

Bhujnu, for that was her name, made herself very useful, and, being quick of apprehension, turned out an excellent servant. On leaving Simla at the end of the season, my wife promised to re-engage her on our return from Calcutta in the following summer.

At the approach of the hot weather, when coats were becoming a positive encumbrance, and ice and *punkah-wallahs* were in demand, began the usual exodus from Calcutta of the Government establishments. Great and small hurried eagerly to the hills, scornfully regardless of the annually recurring growls of the Calcutta public, and equally indifferent to the economical objections of the Indian press. Overcrowded railway trains carried us 1150 miles to Umballah, and *dak gharries* conveyed us, jolted, dusty, and tired, along thirty-six miles of road to the foot of the Himalayas. But Simla was still a long way off. The luxury of driving rapidly up to the Indian Capua, over fifty miles of good hill-road, was not known at that time. The regular postal route to Simla was by the military station of Kussowlee, and zigzagged over one alpine range and then another, with many a splendid view of mountain scenery, and many a lovely bit of light and shade and colour upon the glorious hills to charm the eye of the appreciative traveller.

The sun was low in the heavens as we were passing along the thickly wooded road which leads into Boileaugunge, the "west end" of Simla, and we were silently admiring the blaze of crimson with which the rhododendrons in full bloom literally lit up the hillsides from base to summit, when two figures in white hurried up to us with low salaams. They were Bhujnu and her husband Cherokeeah, who had been patiently waiting for us, day after day, at this spot. Cherokeeah, who was unknown to us, professed to be a *kitmatgar*, or table servant, and, unrolling a small pocket-handkerchief, produced a few dirty-looking pieces of paper for us to read, which were certificates from former employers. We took the pair into our service, and on reaching our house assigned them an out-office to live in. The man did his work pretty well, the woman very satisfactorily. But they did not live in harmony. There arose constant bickerings and quarrels between them, which sometimes disturbed the quiet of our compound. Annoyed by their conjugal differences, we called the pair before us, and warned them that they would both be summarily dismissed if they allowed their quarrels to trouble us. The man received this warning in silence, and went off quietly to perform his usual duties. Not so the woman, whose heart was too full, or whose tongue was less under control. She seized the opportunity to explain, in detail, how very miserable she was. Her narrative revealed domestic arrangements of so peculiar a kind, and afforded glimpses of ideas and feelings so very unlike those entertained by the Western world, that I thought it worth while to note down her statements, which I now reproduce.

According to Bhujnu's story, she had been married to Cherokeeah for several years, when he took a fancy to her younger sister and induced her also to live with him.[1] Although the new arrangement was not quite to her liking, Bhujnu managed for some months to live amicably with her more favoured sister, and for a while things went on smoothly enough in their little village home, till the younger sister transferred her affections and herself to another man, and now, strange to say, began the discord between the husband and his wife.

Cherokeeah was deeply wounded by the desertion of his favourite, and would have it that his elder wife had either prevailed upon her sister to go away, or had driven her out of the house by unkindness. In moments of vexation

[1] Polygamy is not the general rule amongst the inhabitants of the Himalayas. Polyandry is, if anything, more common. A woman is often married to a whole family of brothers. It is said that fathers object strongly to give their daughters to men who have no brothers, because the death of the single husband would leave the widow without a natural protector. The prevalence of the custom of polyandry in many countries (*e. g.* in Britain in the time of Cæsar) is well known, and its origin has generally been attributed to the poverty of the people, coupled with the habit, so general amongst barbarians, of long absences from home on predatory or other excursions, and the necessity thence arising of a plurality of guardians for the domestic hearth. Touching polyandry, Herbert Spencer says: "Some who have had 'good opportunities of judging' contend that in certain places it is advantageous. It would seem that just as there are habitats in which only inferior forms of animals can exist, so in societies physically conditioned in particular ways, the inferior forms of domestic life survive because they alone are practicable" ("Principles of Sociology," vol. i. p. 677).

he used to draw contrasts between the two sisters, much to the disadvantage of the elder one, likening the younger to an *elephant* in grace and beauty. Under the influence of time, that great healer, the soreness may have gradually passed away, and Cherokeeah may have got reconciled to his lot, but his wounded feelings were periodically irritated by a visit from the younger woman, who had also come to Simla, and saw no reason why she should not be on friendly terms with her elder sister, for apparently there was not the least ill-blood between the two women. Her visits used to stir up old recollections, and revive Cherokeeah's unreasonable anger against his wife. Bitter upbraidings followed each of these unlucky visits, and the squabble usually ended in the woman getting a beating, whereupon she would wisely raise an uproar in order to bring the other servants to her rescue. Sometimes the husband would end the quarrel by refusing to take food, and threatening to commit suicide. If he persisted in abstaining from food for a day or so, the miserable wife would become frantic and fall at his feet, promising to get back her sister. The younger woman, however, was too comfortable in her new companionship to have any wish to return to the old dual arrangement.

Such had been the state of affairs for some months. So weary had the poor woman become of the cat-and-dog life they were leading, that she wished to separate from her husband, and had repeatedly begged of him to set her free. But to this he would not consent. He knew his own interests too well. She was valuable property; she was a source of income to him. Her wages were larger than his. When the question of separation came up between them he never failed to remind her that he had paid *five rupees* for her to her parents, and he protested that he was not going to be done out of his money. I suggested to the woman that, as this purchase money seemed to be the great difficulty in the way of her emancipation, she had better pay the amount and be done with it. With a blank look on her face, she inquired where she was to get the necessary rupees from. I pointed out to her that she earned every month twice as much as her husband claimed on account of purchase money, and might easily pay him the five rupees he gave for her. "Oh, no!" she said, with something like despair in her tone, "don't you see all my earnings are his? I cannot pay him out of what is his own property." It was no use explaining to her that she was a free woman and not a slave. Amongst us, she would say, it is different, for with her the customs and usages of her caste and tribe were everything, let Acts of Parliament and of the Indian Legislature be what they may.

Loth to interfere too actively in a peculiar dispute of this kind, I refrained from pressing the point, and let the matter drop, hoping that the threat of dismissal would keep the badly-yoked pair in order. But further disputes soon arose, followed by applications for my arbitration now that the facts of the case had been made known to me. The course of action generally adopted in such cases by Europeans in India is a very simple one. They haughtily or petulantly decline to listen to the statements of the troublesome disputants; dismiss them at a moment's notice, and engage other servants in their places. This course was open to me, but I hesitated to drop the curtain in this summary fashion upon a little domestic drama so characteristic of Eastern life, and I therefore adopted another plan. To the great joy of the ayah, I offered to pay off the intolerable debt of five rupees which hung like a millstone round her neck. Cherokeeah accepted the offer—not, however, without great reluctance, and only after his claim to all the woman's worldly possessions on that day, including her ornaments and even her very clothes, had been admitted. Willingly did Bhujnu part with all her worldly possessions to be freed from a bondage which had become intolerable to her. The money was paid, and the property handed over to Cherokeeah. Henceforward the two lived apart, and peace reigned in our compound.

At the end of the Simla season, when the time arrived for our return to Calcutta, the woman earnestly begged to be furnished with a written statement, signed by me, to the effect that Cherokeeah had received back, in full, the five rupees he had paid to her parents on the occasion of their marriage. This was a precautionary measure.

She was going for the winter months to her native village, and feared that her late husband would claim her again and deny having received payment. I gave her the paper she wanted, and we had reason to know that, armed with this important document, she was able, without the intervention of any of Her Majesty's divorce courts, to keep herself free from the clutches of her former lord and master, and to enter into other matrimonial arrangements on her own account.

IV.—The Slave Girl

The particulars embodied in the following brief narrative will help the reader to understand the estimation in which women, at any rate those of the lower classes, are held in India.

In the summer of 187–, a young man of the Mehtar[1] caste made overtures for the hand of a young girl with whom, we may suppose, he had fallen in love. Her guardians, distant relations of hers, were willing enough to get her married; but the opportunity was a legitimate one for making a little money, and they were not going to forègo their right to sell the girl whom they had maintained for some years. The young man's proposal was accordingly received with favour, and he was informed that he might take the girl to wife on paying her guardians thirty rupees in hard cash.

Our swain was absolutely penniless, and thirty rupees a large sum in his eyes, seeing that he would probably never at any time of his life earn more than five or six rupees a month; but then he could *borrow*—every native of India knows how to do that, and perhaps some *baniyá* or other would advance the required sum, on the personal security of a friend or two. It is true that the money-lender, handing over good current coin of the realm on such very slender security, would expect and, as far as possible, would screw out exorbitant interest; that, however, was a secondary consideration. To get thirty rupees

[1] The Mehtars are a low caste, mostly employed as sweepers and scavengers. They are a specially intelligent class, strong, plucky, and somewhat quarrelsome.

and the girl of his fancy was all that the lover cared about at the moment: how the money, when borrowed, was to be repaid, with the interest upon it, did not, I feel certain, trouble him at all. He cast about for some one to help him to raise the required amount. A good-natured but improvident friend, named Ghusseetah, who had a large family of his own to support, and only some fifteen rupees a month by way of income—the joint earnings of himself and his wife—was induced to be surety for the ardent young man. An accommodating baníyá advanced the needful sum of money, the girl's guardians received it, and the marriage was duly celebrated.

Bholee took his young wife home, and the girl was, in accordance with time-honoured custom in India, made the drudge and slave of her mother-in-law. For well, indeed, might Indian daughters-in-law exclaim in Shelley's words—

> "Even from our childhood have we learn'd to steep
> The bread of slavery in the tears of woe."

What actually occurred in the little household is unknown to me, but it appears probable that the young wife chafed under the treatment she experienced, and, perhaps, became stiff-necked and obstinate, for eventually her mother-in-law pronounced her incorrigible. Domestic peace being impossible under the circumstances, her husband turned her adrift, leaving Lahore at the same time to avoid being called to account for his conduct by the *panchyat* of his caste.

The baníyá had not been paid a single fraction of the sum originally borrowed from him, though he had managed to extort a respectable amount of money under the name of interest. Ghusseetah, the surety, was warned that as the principal had absconded, he would be required to pay up to the uttermost *cowrie*. Already in the toils of the baníyá on account of other transactions, and often, when short of cash, dependent upon him for the bare necessaries of life, the poor man acknowledged his obligations and humbly promised to pay. But was there no compensation to be had for the loss occasioned by the base ingratitude of his defaulting friend? He pondered the matter, and struck upon the idea of boldly annexing the girl who was the innocent cause of his indebtedness. He told her that as her husband had absconded without paying the money, and had left him solely responsible to the baníyá for the amount wherewith she had been purchased from her guardians, she was now his (Ghusseetah's) property. The argument appeared unanswerable, and, fully persuaded of the justice and lawfulness of this conclusion, the young woman accompanied her new master to his home, and was in due course made over to the tender mercies of his wife. The slave thus acquired—for slave she practically was, be the law of the land what it may—had now to do all the household work of a large and very poor family. In such a position her duties were by no means light. She had to fetch water for domestic purposes, grind corn into flour for the daily consumption of the whole family, prepare the meals, wash the pots and pans, sweep the room and at any rate once a week plaster it over with a mixture of clay and cow-dung, and last, though not least, she had to look after the little ones. Hers was one incessant round of toil, and although recognized as a member of the household and entitled to a share of food, she had to wear rags, to endure the angry vituperation of her mistress, and often the blows of the children, who did not fail to remind her of her servile condition.

When Ghusseetah and his wife entered my service as sweeper and ayah respectively, they were the owners of the slave girl. They took up their abode in a room in my servants' quarters or out-office. The room was about eight or nine feet square. It had one entrance-door, and on the opposite side a little window, with strong wooden bars across it. At this time the family consisted of a son, about eleven years of age, and his child wife; two younger boys, an infant in arms, and the slave, whose age was probably not more than seventeen or eighteen. In my compound the family lived quietly enough, and we had no knowledge of the peculiar position the young woman occupied in the ayah's household. The debt, however, still remained unpaid, and the baníyá threatened legal proceedings.

Although no beauty, the household drudge was young; and youth, clothed even in dirty rags, has its attractions for the opposite sex. A tender feeling for the girl sprang up in the impressionable heart of her master, an elderly grey-headed man, with a rather gaunt appearance. Certain indiscretions on his part aroused ayah's suspicions. She thereupon, unknown to her husband, suggested to the baníyá that he should arrange, if possible, to pass the young woman on to some man or other who would engage to take over the debt. The creditor, who had probably been paid a portion of the interest on the money advanced by him, found a willing bachelor, and arranged the matter satisfactorily. But now a curious difficulty arose—Ghusseetah was not as willing as his wife that the young woman should leave his house. He threw what obstacles he could in the way of the final conclusion of the new arrangement. He did not approve of the future husband, he did not feel sure that the bargain was a safe one. Matters had, however, under his wife's guidance, advanced too far to be easily set aside. The girl was made over to her new lord, who, when he came to conduct her home, brought a gaudy suit of clothes for her. Arrayed in her new finery, and escorted by a small party of friends, she went off cheerfully to her new lord's home, and the fate that might be in store for her there.

On the young woman's departure Ghusseetah broke down completely. He refused to eat or drink, and became reduced to a veritable skeleton. Disconsolate and down-hearted, he wrapped his ex-slave's ragged and dirty sheet about his loins, took a staff in his hand, and wandered forth alone, threatening to go away for ever to some distant land. When he thus cast domestic life behind him and started forth on his tramp, his poor wife and children followed him crying bitterly, and begging of him to come back. The loud lamentations of the deserted family attracted my attention, and from a window I observed the pathetic scene, to which the distraught manner and unusual garb of my generally very sober and orderly servant gave no slight tincture of absurdity. I did not at the moment know what was the matter, and suspected a conjugal difference of a more or less trifling kind. Regardless of the entreaties of his wife and children, Ghusseetah went his way. At night, however, he returned home; but not to eat or to drink. He threw himself down on the bare ground, with only the ex-slave's cast-off rags as a pillow. This display of tender feeling was too much for the long-suffering wife. She snatched up the rags, flung them on the fire and burnt them to ashes, while, in Indian fashion, she heaped curses upon her ex-slave, her parents, grandparents, forefathers, and upon her unborn descendants. Ghusseetah, on his part, refused to be consoled without Subratun, whose name he kept repeating in his sleep. There was no sham about it; the man was evidently quite unhinged. In the day he used to wander about disconsolate; at night he would come home to a restless bed. He gradually got so weak and ill that his family became alarmed for his safety. He told his wife and children that now the end was at hand, all he wished them to do for him was to follow him to the grave, and to deposit in it his favourite hookah and two pounds of good tobacco.

However, he did not die. With time he recovered his senses. He no longer refused food, and gradually got as strong as he had formerly been. But now comes another curious feature of the case. He solemnly averred that he had no recollection of what he had said or done in the matter of Subratun. He protested that he had been bewitched by some enemy, who had given him poison to eat, and had made him ridiculous in the eyes of everybody. He could not be prevailed upon to acknowledge his own responsibility for his sayings and doings; stoutly maintaining that he had been under evil influences and not his own master.

When Ghusseetah got mad—as his wife called it—and could not do his work, I inquired into the circumstances of the case, and then, without any difficulty or cross-questioning, learnt all the particulars detailed above. I was careful to note down immediately the facts as they were communicated to me, for they seemed to afford a glimpse of the inner life of the people which might be as interesting to others as it was to me.

V.—Ganpat's Wedding

Ganpat's father having died years previously, Ganpat's mother selected a bride for her boy, and after the choice had been made and agreed to, the girl was secluded, at least from the eyes of the bridegroom. As they were in humble life the children had seen each other many a time and had probably been playmates.

Funds for the wedding had to be *borrowed*, the whole family being drawn into the transaction as jointly and severally responsible; young Ganpat, in his desire to be married, telling his elderly and reluctant brother-in-law, the fisherman Raghu—at that time one of my punkah-pullers—"Be surety, brother. You won't suffer; *I* will pay the debt off, all of it, and quickly, too." No doubt old Raghu smiled incredulously; but he made himself responsible for the loan, and I know he had afterwards much trouble over the business.

Funds were required to meet many customary payments to the Brahman, the barber and others. Also to provide clothes for the families of the bride and bridegroom; to pay for the wedding feast and the *sharáb* (ardent spirits), about which special stipulations had been made.

With my permission arrangements were made for carrying out the wedding in the *hátha* or courtyard of my servants' quarters, and both families were highly pleased that the *sahib* took an interest in the details of the happy event. Consequently I was freely admitted to view the ceremonies, and eagerly supplied with any information I sought, and indeed even more than I asked for.

When arrangements had been fairly completed for the initial ceremony, I was invited to the *hátha*. A canopy had been put up, and beneath it stood erect a plough having one end fixed in the ground. To this useful, if primitive implement, were tied some grass and leaves and withes of flowering creepers. At its foot was an earthen pot containing water, and over the mouth of this vessel a lighted *cheragh*, though it was eleven o'clock in the forenoon of a bright summer day. There was also at hand a shining brass *tháli* (tray) containing mustard oil and some fresh green grass.

On a wooden stool, not more than four inches high, beautified with a wash of turmeric, sat the youthful bridegroom—a boy of about sixteen years of age—with the least possible quantity of clothing on his person, but adorned with a silver necklet and a silver chain, both borrowed for the occasion. His knees reached almost to his chin as he sat doubled up on the hymeneal stool. Beside the happy boy stood his married sister with one end of her veil over his head. His mother would have performed this duty, but she was debarred from doing so, because she was a *widow*. Several women sat around singing to the accompaniment of a drum. What they sang was mostly of a trivial, childish character. For example, they sang, referring to the bridegroom :

"This is the same Ganpat who was just lately pulling the *punkah*, and now he is on the stool a bridegroom, a Rama.
This is the boy who plays in our lane, and now he is a bridegroom, a bridegroom, a Rama,"

and so on.

While the singing was being carried on certain women went through the ceremony of anointing Ganpat with oil and turmeric. Taking up two tufts of grass, one in each hand, out of the *tháli*, dripping with oil and turmeric, they applied them first to his feet, next to his knees, then to his shoulders and lastly to his head. Five married women (*not* widows) did this in succession, and then while the singing continued they commenced, all together, rubbing the happy bridegroom thoroughly with turmeric and oil. His arms, his legs, his body, his face were all attended to; it being essential that the bridegroom should be thoroughly rubbed all over his person, because any part of him left unanointed would surely become white on the wedding day.

Ganpat sat, during the process I have described, with his two hands before him, each one full of uncooked rice surmounted by a ball of crude sugar.

Throughout this ceremony his married sister kept the end of her *chaddar* on his head, and as soon as the five women had performed their task of anointing him, he

Photo by W. Campbell Oman

GANPAT'S WEDDING

To face page 270

was conducted by her into their cabin, where he was himself to *complete* the anointing of his person and stay there till wanted.

The Brahman, a white-bearded, well-dressed man, with a thick stick tucked under his arm, had looked on, and all I heard him say was: "Don't put so much oil upon the boy; so much oil in this hot weather won't be good for him." But no one seemed to heed his warnings in the least degree.

Of the women who had taken a hand in anointing the bridegroom the most active was, curiously enough, an old Muhammadan woman named Begam, and amongst those who took a minor share in the proceedings were some of the *Mehtar* caste, who I knew attended Sunday-school very regularly, and had some idea of being baptized into the Christian faith, so as to improve their social standing. When old Raghu, the bridegroom's brother-in-law, was asked by me how it was that Begam took an active part in the proceedings, he answered quite simply: "We are one; it is only a matter of eating and drinking." Such apparently being the distinction he drew between Islam and Hinduism. It struck me that quite possibly Begam had belonged to his caste, and may have only recently embraced the faith of Muhammad, but I did not ask the question.

The process of anointing which I have described was repeated on several (six, I think) consecutive days; while the same rite, for such it really was, engaged the attention simultaneously of the little bride's friends, who at her home consecrated her in a similar manner, for her approaching nuptials.

Dancing, in which the women took part, one by one, followed; each performer frisking about according to her own conception of the terpsichorean art. Peculiar and graceful poses, especially admired, were attempted by the more adventurous dancers, but there was no high kicking nor even rising on the tip of the toes, such being quite foreign to Indian dancing. From childhood Indian women are accustomed to drag their feet along the ground to keep their slippers from being left behind, as these articles of footwear are provided with a *sole* and a *vamp*, but no *counter* or back piece. Hence *high action* would never suggest itself to Indian female dancers.

The night before the wedding the bridegroom was carried on the shoulders of a barber to a neighbouring well to have a look into it, and to go through some curious ceremonies. Among others he had to make believe that he was a little child again at his mother's breast as in babyhood, the underlying idea apparently being to awaken tender feelings towards his mother in the boy's heart at this important juncture. Near the well the mother had to pretend that in despair at the thought of her son's marriage she was about to destroy herself. She approached the well, she even sat on the edge of it with her feet dangling over its dangerous depths of thirty or forty feet; but was dissuaded from carrying out her rash intention of suicide by the pleadings of the bridegroom, who assured her that he would work for and support her, and that he only proposed to bring home a *bándi laundi* (a slave girl) to serve her and wait upon her.

When the appointed wedding-day arrived, the little bride—a child of perhaps ten years of age—was brought over to my *hátha* by her friends, with singing and drumming, and a tolerably large company assembled there to eat and to drink at the expense of the bridegroom's mother.

Good kerosene lamps and excellent cotton carpets were lent by the servant of a rich native gentleman, and the affair was conducted with much greater decorum than I could have imagined possible. For music there were drums and tambourines, and there were also professional dancers whose performances were highly appreciated by the guests.

The actual marriage ceremony was simple enough. A little space of ground levelled, swept and smeared over with a wash of cow-dung and fine clay, had been prepared and marked off with a line of dry wheaten flour along its boundary. Around this the boy and girl, with their chaddars knotted together, were made to circle seven times while the officiating Brahman intoned certain Sanskrit texts, unintelligible to every one present and most probably to himself as well. There was no word uttered at the time about conjugal duties and obligations; at any rate no word within the comprehension of the contracting parties or their friends. There was no formal plighting of troth—no marriage vows.

Feasting and revelry, including a good deal of drinking, went on till morning; not the least important part of the entertainment being the *sithni*—" songs of abuse," the common people call them. Sung by women of the party with the greatest gusto and enjoyment, these songs are simply outrageous in their grossness. They are not extemporized, but are so framed that any names may be introduced into them. The singers bring in any names they please, with the result that the persons whose names are inserted find themselves accused before the world, in the most undisguised language, of having committed grossly immoral or even incestuous actions, and possibly the charges may have some truth in them. Men, women and even children listen and laugh, *but no one takes offence*. The singing of these wedding songs is a privilege which is jealously guarded by the women, though some present-day social reformers do inveigh against the practice, and would like to see a discontinuance of it.

I am told that even if there be any metaphor or attempt at poetry in any of these wedding songs, they are still all grossness and shocking indecency.

VI.—Thief-catching

Thief-catching carried out in a thoroughly Indian way has its peculiarities not devoid of interest.

Fifteen rupees had been abstracted out of a box in my study. I called my servants together, made known the loss, and threatened a police investigation. What such an inquiry involved the servants were well aware. The faces of those upon whom, from the nature of their duties, suspicion would naturally fall, showed only too well that their imaginations were already busy, conjuring up the disgraceful scene in which the native constables would endeavour to elicit the truth from them, literally at the point of the baton, dug into their unfortunate sides. The magistrate and his sentence upon the offender are secondary considerations in these cases. It is the preliminary police investigation that is most dreaded. I had not the slightest intention of handing my servants over to the tender mercies of the constables. My threat was merely intended to frighten out a confession, if possible, and I willingly acceded to a proposal, made by one or two of the servants, to investigate the matter themselves.

After performing certain religious ablutions, the cook, a grave Mussulman much respected in the household, produced a shoe, into the inside of which he stuck a shoemaker's awl, and with this instrument proceeded with great solemnity to the detection of the thief. The names of the several servants were written upon separate scraps of paper. The cook and one other man, acting jointly, lifted the shoe, each man applying only one finger under the round head of the handle of the awl. Suspended in this way, the scraps of paper with the servants' names were dropped into the shoe in succession, and it was well understood by all present that when the thief's name was put into the shoe it would turn round in a horizontal plane. It turned very distinctly at the name of a certain servant, and, as might have been expected, the result was received by him with anything but satisfaction. However, he was a Hindu, and affected to believe that this Mussulman mode of thief-catching was not quite fair, at any rate to Hindus, and it was agreed that a reference should be made on the subject to a Brahman in the city, whose verdict would be considered conclusive. Next day the Brahman was appealed to. He went through a form of divination, and then oracularly declared that the thief was a man, not a woman; that he was more than thirty and less than forty years of age, and so on. He very impressively affirmed his ability to lay hands on the thief there and then, but he refrained from doing so, advising the culprit to restore the money within the next two days, otherwise he would expose him and let the law take its course. The Brahman's description of the thief did to some extent tally with that of the man already pointed out by the cook's divining shoe, and confirmed the suspicion against him. Next morning the suspected man came and informed me that the money was in the inner pocket of the broadcloth coat worn by a fellow-servant, a boy of about fourteen years of age. The boy was called, ostensibly to perform some ordinary duty, and upon being suddenly asked what was in his pocket, appeared ready to drop with fear. Seven rupees were found in his pocket, and many were the stories he told in regard to the manner in which he had come into possession of them; but he at last affirmed, and stuck to the assertion, that they had been given to him for safe custody by the suspected man, who declared his intention of replacing them in the box whence he had abstracted them as soon as a favourable opportunity presented itself. Anyhow, between the shoe and the Brahman, the thief or thieves—for I believe the pair were confederates—were detected, and a portion at least of the missing money recovered with little trouble.

VII.—A Youthful Saint

Attracted by the voices of some people passing my window, and especially noticing a high treble voice, like that of a child, speaking in rather more authoritative tones than his years seemed to justify, I looked out and saw a small boy of about twelve years of age, dressed in clean clothes, attended by several of my servants, all apparently most attentive to him. One man, of whom he inquired where his mangoes were, ran off at once, apparently to fetch them, but really to purchase some in the bazaar. The youthful centre of this little group was sauntering in a very leisurely manner towards the gate, conversing with his companions, when suddenly, in the most capricious manner, he turned round and took an opposite direction towards the out-offices at the back of the house. His full face was now in view, and struck me strongly as being very wanting in intelligence, if not bearing visible traces of insanity.

The boy had been living in my out-houses for two or three days. He had come in there of his own accord, and was being feasted and fêted to the full extent of their means by my poor but ever improvident domestics, who were never tired of supplying his wants or humouring his caprices: for, it would seem, the boy was a remarkable person, one especially favoured by Allah.

In his native village near Gujranwallah, his father had recently been engaged in erecting the mud walls of a hut for himself. His humble, if useful, work required a plentiful supply of water, and this the owner of the well hard by absolutely refused to give him. Without water the work could not be carried on. The builder was in great perplexity, when his young son came to his rescue with words of comfort, telling him that what his fellow-man refused Allah would give freely; and so saying, he planted his little foot down vigorously on the ground, out of which a spring of fresh water instantly welled up, and continues flowing to this day. So remarkable an event could not fail to attract attention. The spring became famous all through the neighbourhood. Visitors from near and far flocked to see it. It became a place of pilgrimage. The water was found to have wonderful curative power. Even leprosy was cured by bathing in it, and quantities were stored and carried away for the benefit of sufferers unable to come to the holy spot, where Allah had so remarkably manifested His power and His beneficent remembrance of the wants of the poor. One miserable leper, cured of his disease at the spring, carried away some of the water to Amritsar and sold it there to another sufferer from the same grievous affliction. The purchaser was duly restored to a sound condition by the use of the water; but alas, the mercenary vendor of God's precious, but freely given, gift of healing was attacked again by the hideous malady as a punishment for his avarice.

As suddenly and capriciously as he came, so suddenly and capriciously the boy went away, and I lost all further trace of this interesting little worker of miracles, who, if he has not gone mad, may perhaps have added a new sect or sub-sect to the innumerable ones already flourishing in India.

VIII.—The Daughter-in-Law

Having occasion one cold winter day to pass close to the out-offices occupied by my servants, I noticed a young woman, I may say a girl, lightly clad, sitting outside in the keen frosty air eating her solitary dinner. She was outside, and alone, because, forsooth, she might not eat in the presence of the male members of the family, who were enjoying their dinner, in warmth and comfort, within doors. The woman was the wife of my *dhobi*, or washerman, a Hindu of a low caste. I subsequently ascertained that the rule in this case is sometimes so far relaxed as to allow of the woman's eating with her back turned to her lords and masters. Nor do these rules hold only in the case of the inferior castes or the lower orders. They are of universal application in India. "It is a well-known fact," says a Bengalí writer, "that Hindoo males and females do not take their meals together; . . . it is held highly unbecoming in a grown-up female to be seen eating by a male member of the family. . . . The choicest part of the food is offered in the first instance to the males, and the residue is kept for the females." [1]

A short time after the incident referred to above, my attention was attracted by a woman's voice crying in loud and pitiful tones. In an Indian household such an event would generally be noticed only by a peremptory order to "stop that noise," accompanied by a threat of summary ejectment or worse punishment in the event of a repetition of the nuisance. But having nothing particular on hand, I thought it worth while to go down to the out-offices, which were at some distance from my dwelling-house, and make inquiries into the uproar. As soon as I appeared, the servants began relating a doleful tale of systematic oppression and cruelty. The victim was the girl I had previously seen turned out to eat her dinner in the cold. The oppressor was her mother-in-law. Never a day went, so said the servants, without the young woman being soundly thrashed, with a stick if it were at

[1] "The Hindoos as They Are," by Shib Chunder Bose, pp. 8–9.

hand, or with blows and kicks, as might be convenient. The reasons for these assaults were many and various; no fault, no offence, neglect or oversight, being too trivial to excite the mother-in-law's anger and cause her to become violent. I could not find out what was the real ground for the assault on this particular occasion, but it was quite apparent that the girl had been severely beaten about the face, as it was swollen up, and there was some blood about her person. The mother-in-law was not to be found, and the girl's husband, in a most abject way, tried to explain that the punishment was well merited, as his wife had not performed the tasks which had been allotted her. His fellow-servants stated that the young woman was up every day hours before daylight to grind the corn for the entire household; that she had to sweep the house and lay on a fresh wash of clay over the floor every day; that she had to cook the food, carry it herself two and a half miles to the river where the washermen were engaged, bring back the plates, and cook the evening meal against the return of the dhobís. According to all accounts she worked early and late, but could never please her mother-in-law. I insisted that the old woman should be produced. Her son swore she had gone out; presently, however, I discovered that she was concealed in one of the rooms, and she was brought forward much against her will. The old witch—I had never seen her before—was a wiry woman about fifty years of age, with ill-nature stamped on every feature of her face. I scolded her for her cruelty to the girl; I pointed out that her daughter-in-law was no slave, and that she had no legal right whatever to strike her. But the old hag was not to be put down so easily. She assumed a defiant air, and said she had spent her money in getting the girl and would have her work out of her. To argue with the old termagant was useless. "When a master does not get his work done, doesn't he beat his servants? and when I don't get my work done I shall of course beat the girl." Such was her contention. She insisted that as she had spent her money in getting the girl for her son, she had a clear right to her services. The girl was from a distant village, and possibly her parents had received fifteen or twenty rupees on the occasion of handing her over to her husband, and had, in all likelihood, spent the amount in providing a simple feast of rice and sugar for their rustic friends and neighbours. Yet on the strength of this small sum of money the girl was a real slave to her mother-in-law. I threatened to send for the police, to clear up this point for her, but the old woman was not to be intimidated. The son stood by making apologies with his palms joined together in the most abject manner, but the old witch affirmed boldly, and with a significance not to be mistaken, that whatever the police might do, the *Sirkar* would not take her daughter-in-law away from her. The girl had not a word to say. With her head bowed down and her face almost quite concealed, she sat scrubbing a brass *lotah*, as if afraid that any interruption of her labours would entail further punishment. Without doubt she considered herself a purchased slave, a view in which the bystanders apparently acquiesced, though they thought she ought to be treated with a little less cruelty. And as she sat there, in her coarse, filthy rags, she presented a sad contrast to her mother-in-law in her green and black chintz petticoat, white bodice, and red sheet. The contrast between the two women was so marked, that I began to take note of the appearance of the other members of the family. The men were dressed in clean white clothes, the mother-in-law as already stated, and her own little girl in a nice yellow petticoat, with a white sheet over her head. All looked clean and respectable, except the young wife, the domestic drudge, the slave that had been purchased for so many rupees, silently busy cleaning the brass pot even while her wrongs were being discussed in her presence. I began seriously to regret my interference in the matter. I foresaw that the girl's fate would not be improved by my advocacy. To let the young wife know her legal rights was useless, for her mind, oppressed by the customs of her people, could not rise to a conception of them. She never dreamed of freedom. She was not indignant at, or humiliated by, being abused and ill-treated publicly. She simply cried out when she was beaten, just as a dog might do. The fellow-servants were not outraged at the conduct of the old woman in thrashing her daughter-in-law or exacting task-work from her. That was customary. They merely thought she was rather hard upon the girl.

Had the case been made over to the police, the girl would probably have said she had nothing to complain about, and that the bruise on her face had been caused by a fall.

Month after month the ill-starred girl was beaten and starved by her brutal mother-in-law, without any interference on the part of the husband or other member of the family, and although she did not lay violent hands upon herself,[1] came eventually to an untimely end by neglecting, in times of illness, the sympathetic advice of her neighbours, as well as every precaution which common sense would suggest. Deserted by her husband, and cruelly ill-used by her mother-in-law even when the chill hand of death was unmistakably upon her, the poor girl died as a dog might die, uncared for and *alone*. Often had she been heard to wish herself dead, and to console herself with the thought that she would return as a *choorail* to persecute and destroy her tyrant, relying upon a widely spread superstition, which sometimes has the wholesome effect of restraining, in some degree, the hand of the domestic oppressor. But in the case I am writing about the vengeance of the poor dead woman was completely and effectually guarded against by means of *appropriate ceremonies*. At the various halting places to the grave mustard seed had been scattered about, and a few iron tacks had been driven into the ground with the prayer that the spirit of the deceased might not be permitted to disturb the living. The ghost of the injured woman might haunt the graveyard, but in seeking its

[1] "It is a well-known fact that females who commit suicide in India are generally between the ages of twelve and twenty, and that these acts may almost always be traced to the oppression of cruel mothers-in-law. That the daughter-in-law is, in every Hindoo household, regarded as a servant, is evident from the fact that when the bridegroom is about to proceed to the house of his bride on the occasion of the marriage ceremonies, his mother asks him where he is going to, and he replies with the prescribed formula: 'To bring in your maid-servant.'"—"The Hindoos as They Are," by Shib Chunder Bose, p. 57.

former earthly habitation it would have to retrace the road along which its corpse had been borne. Here it would always find a spiritual garden of mustard plants, and, beguiled into collecting the flowers, would lose the precious hours of the night, and be forced by approaching dawn to hasten back to the land of the dead.

PART IV.—SUPERSTITIONS

I. WITCHCRAFT, DEMONIACAL POSSESSION, AND OTHER SUPERSTITIONS OF THE PEOPLE

II. EXPERIENCES WITH FORTUNE-TELLERS

CHAPTER I

WITCHCRAFT, DEMONIACAL POSSESSION, AND OTHER SUPERSTITIONS OF THE PEOPLE

DURING the intensely hot summer nights at Agra we were obliged to keep nearly every door and window of our *bungalow* open to let in any wandering breeze that might be about, and since thieves (and they abound in that district) might, quite as easily as stray zephyrs, find their way into the house, it was necessary to have a night-watchman, specially entrusted with the guardianship of the premises during the hours of darkness. The *chaukídár*, as this watchman was called, received the sum of five rupees as his monthly wages, and lived in a small outhouse in the compound. All night he was supposed to be on the look-out, taking his rounds and, according to Indian custom, uttering unearthly yells to scare away robbers. But from dawn till dewy eve his time was his own. To sleep away a good portion of the day when the rest of the world was astir, and to walk alone all the quiet night long, was a dull, lonely life, so one day our chaukídár brought home a wife to cheer his solitude and prepare his *roti* (bread). The woman was in rags, and filthy rags too, when she came to live with the chaukídár, but he bought her a new cloth as a nuptial present on the day she joined him. When he made her acquaintance—shall I say fell in love with her?—she was employed in grinding corn for a miller in the bazaar, who provided her with food in return for her labour. For months, perhaps for years, she had laboured for him at the monotonous drudgery of grinding corn in a hand-mill. From morning till evening her duty had been to make the upper revolve upon the nether mill-stone with one hand, while she fed the hopper with the other, but yet she was in the miller's debt to the extent of four rupees. Leave him she could not until she had either paid or worked off the amount, which last was an impossible task, seeing that, according to the miller's calculation, her keep was at best only just covered by the work she did. As the miller's claim to the woman's services was not to be disputed, the chaukídár borrowed the money needed to free her, and, having paid it to the miller, quietly marched her off. But the match was an unfortunate one. The half-starved woman, as soon as she got the opportunity, began to make up for the scanty meals she had so long been forced to live upon. She devoured the chaukídár's provisions in a manner he had not calculated upon, so he told her to go back to her old master, from whom he would claim a refund of the four rupees he had paid on her account. The discarded wife, now a free woman, went her way, but the watchman never got back his purchase money. The matter, however, did not end there. Months went by, and the friends from whom the chaukídár had borrowed the money which he paid to the miller wanted to be settled with. They (a man and his wife) came to demand payment. A dispute arose, abusive language was freely resorted to; the quarrel ended in a fight, in which our watchman came off victorious. The enraged and ill-used creditors beat a hasty retreat, heaping dire curses upon the devoted head of the chaukídár, and threatening that a day of reckoning would soon come. Two or three days after this fracas the victor was struck down by a rather sharp attack of fever. He complained of severe pain in the chest, and declared that when alone at night demons used to come and ride upon his breast. It was pitiful to see the poor man lying upon a scrap of mat, without a pillow for his head, and with only a rag of a quilt to cover him. His cabin contained but a few earthen pots and one brass *lotah* for water, and these were all his earthly possessions. Occasionally a fellow-servant would give him a drop of water, and perhaps, once a day, offer to bake him some bread. As he lay tossing in high fever on his wretched mat, he called to mind the curses that had been hurled at him by his two baffled creditors, and he was convinced that his illness was but the fulfilment of those curses. He was, in fact, according to his own idea, *possessed*, and could not possibly recover unless the curses were withdrawn. He begged piteously that the creditors he had so summarily got rid of only a few days before should be brought to him, and when they came he grovelled at their feet, begging of them to remove the curses. At first they seemed rather surprised, but, profiting by the occasion, they promised to do so, provided he paid them up in full the very next time he received his wages from me. The chaukídár readily consented. Thereupon the woman sat down beside him, sprinkled a little water on him, made several passes over his person in a deliberate manner with a small branch of the *neem* tree, and withdrew the curses that had been piled upon his devoted head. Relieved in mind by this simple ceremony of exorcism, the sick man began to rally rapidly, and in a few days was restored to health and to his round of nightly duty.

* * * * * *

One morning in June my coachman fell down in a fit not far from the door of the room in which I was seated. I went out to see him, and found several natives standing round the prostrate figure, but, with characteristic apathy, simply looking on without attempting to render the slightest assistance. When I suggested that they should splash some water upon his face, all of them objected on the ground that they were not of the same caste as the coachman, and therefore ought not to do it. Amongst the on-lookers was an old woman, who stated in a very positive tone that water was by no means necessary, the proper remedy for the fit being merely to take the man's shoes off his feet and make him smell them. This remedy, although curious, was not so revolting as that recommended for the "falling-sickness" in some old books of medicine, viz. "an ounce or two of the brains of a young man carefully dried over the fire." [1] However, the man was brought round without resorting to the old woman's specific. Inquiring later in the day, I was told that the coachman was not subject to such fits, that

[1] Hugh Miller's "My Schools and Schoolmasters," p. 55.

he had never had one before, and that it was clearly a case of witchcraft. He had been sitting in a *panchayat* (or council) of his caste-people the day before, and the person against whom he had given his vote must have cursed him. Hence these dire results. But subsequently the coachman was struck down on two or three occasions by severe and very sudden fits, and himself attributed them to the spells cast upon him by a wife who had deserted him, and who, I suspect, had not been over well treated by her lord. On my giving him notice of my intention of dispensing with his services, he assured me in the most confident manner that he would not get another fit, as he had, with the assistance of an adept, sent the demon back to take possession of and plague his wicked wife, who was the sole cause of his troubles.

* * * * * *

On another occasion there came to my knowledge the case of a woman who attributed her illness (a severe hemorrhage) to the magic arts of a fellow-servant. According to her story the man concerned had made improper advances to her, and on her repulsing him he vowed vengeance against her. A few days after this she got ill, and found out that her enemy, as we may now call him, had gone to a well with a male companion; that they had carried with them a lemon, which they cut in halves, and, repeating some spells, squeezed out the juice of the fruit into the well, accompanying the act with the expression of a wish that the blood of so and so (naming her) might pour out as the juice had just oozed out of the lemon under the pressure of their hands. The curse, of course, had its effect, and the unfortunate woman was a miserable sufferer for her virtuous conduct. It only remains to be added that the hapless woman learnt the details above given from the wife of the man who aided her enemy and quondam lover in carrying out the mischievous and wicked rites which cost her so dear.

* * * * * *

Not only have the powerful spells of the wicked to be dreaded; the dead are not less capable of resenting any neglect or affront, and when offended have to be duly propitiated by gifts and offerings. A servant of mine at Lahore had been absent from his duties for some days on account of ill-health. Inquiring into his condition and the treatment he had been receiving, I learned that he had, a few days previously, been prostrated by an attack of fever. On the second day of his illness he was, apparently, delirious, and in that state revealed the fact that his fever was due to his having pulled down some branches from a *babool* tree (*Acacia Arabica*) which grew over a Syad's grave just outside my compound. It was a miserable, dilapidated structure this Syad's grave, but the dead occupant was none the less jealous of its honour. According to the sick man the Syad had taken possession of him, and was wreaking his vengeance upon him for having dared to dishonour his shrine. Something had to be done to appease the irate saint, and so the invalid's afflicted wife caused a *mashk* (leather bag) of water to be poured over the Syad's grave, apparently to cool his temper. At the same time a fellow-servant, skilled in such matters, administered a charmed clove to the patient in order to break the spell which had been cast upon him by the indignant saint. But the invalid, instead of improving, became worse, and in his delirium the spirit of the Syad, which had now taken full possession of him, kept uttering through the mouth of the fever-stricken man such contemptuous remarks as these—"Oh, indeed! you have eaten a charmed clove, have you? I will give you a stomach full of charmed cloves!"

The unsuccessful exorcist was called in to try another spell, but as, after the clove episode, the efficacy of his spells appeared somewhat doubtful, the precaution was also taken of endeavouring to pacify the Syad with gifts. He was promised a *cheragh*, or light, upon his tomb, for a certain number of successive Thursday evenings, with an offering of sweetmeats in addition, if he would but forgive the offender. Still the invalid did not mend, and his wife was making up her mind to promise the Syad a more worthy peace-offering (a cock, or a kid) if he would only restore her husband to health, when I became acquainted with the particulars of the case, and recommended her to postpone her vow of a costly offering till she had first tried the effects of sulphate of quinine. I gave her some of the drug with directions how to use it. She followed my instructions, and, to her great satisfaction, found that the bitter white powder had the power either of expelling the spirit or of appeasing it, for her husband quickly rallied, and was able to resume work after a few days. I have reason to believe, however, that, after all, the recovery was attributed more to the spells that had been employed and to the promises made to the saint than to the drug I had administered.

* * * * *

Another interesting case came under my notice at Lahore. A servant, a punkah-puller of the *mehtar* caste, was reported dying in an out-office in my compound. The man had been at work only a few hours before. I went down to see him, and found him stretched out on a low cot with his eyes shut. His weeping wife and son were endeavouring to rouse him, but he could not or would not move, or give any sign of consciousness. A dose of brandy and water, put into his mouth by spoonfuls, followed after a little while by a strong cup of tea, brought him round. On questioning him as to the nature and causes of his illness, he asserted that a Syad took possession of him every now and then, and was persecuting him on account of the non-fulfilment of certain vows. It appeared that three or four months previously his wife was very ill, and while sitting beside her, with some members of the family and a few visitors, the spirit of the Syad took possession of him. He began to be violently agitated, and then spoke, not in his own person, but in that of the spirit that possessed him. He talked about many things, and in his discourse predicted that the sick woman, his wife, would die within a week. This prediction uttered in her hearing so alarmed her that she begged piteously for life, promising, if she were spared, to offer five goats and five cocks on the Syad's grave. She did not die and did not fulfil her vow, so the angry Syad was now victimizing the husband, presumably as the responsible head of the house.

This supposed possession of *mehtars* by the spirits of deceased descendants of the Prophet of Arabia seems to indicate a strange confusion in the religion of the lower castes in India, though the spiritual anarchy in the present case is easily accounted for, being due, most probably, to a growing respect for Islam, a consequent recognition of the potency of the Muslim saints, and an imitation of certain Muhammadan practices to be described later on. But the ordinary Mussulmans of India, almost as deeply tainted by caste prejudices as their Hindu fellow-countrymen, do not take this view of the matter; and when consulted about it, usually aver indignantly that no Syad's spirit would demean itself to enter a *mehtar's* body, but that men of that despicable caste, when possessed, must be under the influence of some BHUT (devil) of their own.

* * * * * *

One morning the dead body of a large and venomous snake, which had been killed near the servants' quarters the night before, was brought to me. It appeared that the cold clammy weight of the horrid reptile upon her neck had roused a woman who was sleeping in the open air at the door of one of the out-houses. Instinctively, she flung the snake off, and immediately called for help. Her brother-in-law, the *dhobi* or washerman, ran to her help, and despatched the intruder with a stick. On the following day the dhobí was taken ill, and his work got into arrears. I wanted to know what was the matter with the man, and found out that his illness was due solely to his having neglected to give the customary funeral feast in memory of his deceased wife, who had died in her native village some months previously. The snake which had visited the servants' quarters was none other than the late wife herself, and had come to wreak her vengeance on the woman, who, it would appear, had stood very much in the way of the funeral feast, and was, moreover, responsible for the neglect which the deceased had experienced during her lifetime. Somehow, and for unknown reasons, the Fates had protected the offending sister-in-law, but the neglectful husband was suffering the punishment of his sins of omission and commission, and it was quite clear that it would go hard with him if he did not very soon make amends for his past misconduct. The first thing to be done was to rescue the sufferer from the vindictive clutches of the spirit of the departed wife. An exorcist was called in, and immediately commenced operations. In the open air, beside the bed of the sick man, he placed a lighted *cheragh*, and just before it, drew on the ground a small circle about three inches across, with two diameters at right angles to each other. He put a couple of cloves at one end of each diameter. Outside the circle he laid a few more cloves and also three small packets, one containing flowers, another camphor, and the third incense. Standing up, with his face turned to the full moon, which was just rising, the exorcist rubbed an open penknife between his hands and kept uttering something which was meant for magical words or incantatory phrases. He then applied the blade to his forehead and sat down, still muttering to himself in a low tone. He next passed the cloves round and over the flame of the lamp. After which he gashed his own arm with the penknife, and collecting the blood on the blade, wet the cloves with it. Next he took all the cloves in his right hand and, closing his fist, passed it, heavily and slowly, over the sick man, beginning from a little above the knee and going gradually up to and round the head, as if drawing or gathering up something towards the top of the head. Whenever the invalid groaned, and he did so pretty often, partly from excitement and partly, no doubt, from the pain experienced under the rough treatment of his physician, the latter expressed his satisfaction, and seemed to coax the spirit to come out. Sometimes the spirit which had taken possession of the sick man would, as it were, struggle under the grasp of the exorcist, and seem as if about to slip away from him. At this the medicine-man's ire would be roused, and, apparently much excited, he would address the enemy in no complimentary terms, while he himself groaned and puffed as if in a severe and exhausting conflict. At length the spirit was safely conducted to the crown of the invalid's head, and was then successfully drawn out of him.

After the completion of this satisfactory operation, the exorcist offered the cloves to the bystanders, but they prudently declined the proffered gifts, objecting to be made the recipients of the sick man's cast-out spirit. After some wrangling, the exorcist determined to retain the cloves himself, and concluded the ceremony by burning some camphor in the flame of the lamp.

The personal appearance of the exorcist was anything but prepossessing. He looked from the very commencement of his proceedings wild and excited, but during his struggles with the refractory spirit he was like a madman.

The reader familiar with the customs of savages, as described by travellers, and reproduced in most modern works on "the primitive condition of man," will at once recognize in our exorcist the *medicine-man* of savage countries, of the wilds of South America, the islands of the Pacific Ocean, of Australia and Africa; but he seems peculiarly out of place in India, in contact with English civilization, and in the broad light of the twentieth century. However, in India he is, and, I doubt not, will long continue there, sharing with native and European drugs the credit of driving away disease and of restoring the sick to health and strength.

* * * * * *

Not only is exorcism commonly practised for the cure of the sick; but also for the relief of sufferers from the effects of snake bites, the bites of dogs or other animals, and the stings of venomous insects.

A female servant attracted my attention one night by her loud cries. She had been stung on the foot by something in the dark—a scorpion she said—and was apparently in great pain. Her first thought was to obtain the assistance of a man who happened to be living in my compound, and was well-skilled in affording relief in such cases. My aid not being required, I did not interfere. The man whose services were in request came as soon as he was summoned, and began making sundry passes over the wound, in order, as he said, "to bring the pain down;" but instead of coming down it went on extending higher up the limb. The woman evidently suffered a good deal. At this stage something like the following colloquy took place :

Woman (sharply) : "What are you about? The pain instead of coming down is going up, higher and higher. Oh dear! oh dear!"

Man : "Wait a bit, mother; be a little patient."

Woman (apparently not relishing the advice) : "Be patient! you say. Be patient! while the pain is extending higher up. Oh! ma : oh! ma-go."

Man : "Yes, mother, yes!"

Woman (testily) : "Why do you say 'yes, yes'? I want the pain to come down."

Man (naïvely) : "Of course, mother; but the pain must first be allowed to go up, and then I'll bring it down."

Woman (fairly enraged) : "Be off, you fool! Bad luck to you," etc., etc. "I'll go and ask the *sahib* for some medicine."

* * * * * *

All the subjects of demoniacal possession referred to in the preceding pages belonged to the lowest castes of the Indian community, which lie practically outside the pale of Hinduism. Amongst them the belief in demoniacal possession is in full force to-day, although it is by no means confined to them, as the following narrative, connected with a respectable Hindu family, will show :

Amongst my informant's relatives was a man who had two sons, both of course married. The elder son's wife died after a lingering illness; her husband seemed to be gradually wasting away and likely to follow his wife to the other world. Friends and relations who had watched the gradual decay and death of the young wife and the critical state of the widower (let us call him W. for convenience), were impressed with the idea that there was foul play at the root of these troubles, and that the power of *witchcraft* had been employed against the dead woman and her suffering husband.

A "wise man" was called in to discover whether a *bhut*—a disembodied spirit—had been set upon these unfortunates to destroy them. In an assembly of relations and intimate friends the wise man went through certain incantations, during the performance of which a little boy of tender years became violently agitated and began to throw himself about. He was doubtless possessed of some spirit or other. "Who are you?" asked the seer or wizard, addressing the *bhut*. "I am A., the son of K.," was the reply—persons quite unknown to the assembled family council. "I died unmarried. My body was burnt to ashes by my father, and these ashes were surreptitiously appropriated by the yogi M., who, by his spells, has taken complete possession of me, and I now obey his behests." This statement created a sensation, because the yogi named was well known in the neighbourhood.

"What are you doing at present?" inquired the wizard, still addressing the *bhut*. "By the yogi's command I have taken possession of W., and am completing his destruction, having already caused the death of his wife," said the *bhut*.

So far, then, the mystery was cleared up—the woman had been destroyed by a *bhut* under the compulsion of a well-known yogi, and her husband was being disposed of in the same cruel way. The yogi who could command the services of disembodied spirits was, of course, too powerful to be brought to book over the affair; but every one naturally desired to know why he dealt so unkindly with the family. It was elicited through the child-medium that W.'s sister-in-law had gone to the famous yogi at dead of night, had given him two valuable gold armlets and four gold earrings, these presents being in exchange for a pinch of the ashes of *A., son of K.*, wherewith to compass the destruction of W. and his wife, whose share of the paternal property she desired for herself and husband. The potent ashes of the unmarried boy (A., son of K.) had been mixed in a dish of *kheer* (milk and rice), which was eaten by the ill-fated pair. With the eating of the ashes the spirit of A. took possession of the couple and gradually reduced one to disease and compassed the death of the other.

It was further ascertained that if a feast were given at the river-side and a fat sheep slaughtered with appropriate ceremonies and if the sick man partook of the feast the spirit would leave him in peace.

Everything was done to satisfy these requirements, and the invalid rallied, but only for a brief space of time, as after a month or so he eventually succumbed to his ailments.

In the household of W. was mourning coupled with anger, suspicion and unavoidable dissensions. The yogi M., who had been named as the perpetrator of the outrage, was, as mentioned before, well known in the neighbourhood, and it was no secret that he received many and many a nocturnal visit from veiled females. But who was there that would have dared to accuse *him* of having a hand in the death of W. and his wife? However, the wicked sister-in-law, who could not produce the gold armlets and earrings which she was said to have presented to the yogi, was chiefly guilty, and had to bear, as well as she could, the reproaches and anger of the family.

Such was the tale told to me. But no very great acumen is necessary to raise the suspicion that this narrative would seem to indicate a family plot to punish a woman who had, in all probability, lost her valuable jewels *with her virtue* in the yogi's company on Ravi side. Yet none the less it throws a strong light upon the ideas and beliefs of the people of even the middle classes. It also shows that in India the air is pervaded by magic and witchcraft. The happiness, the health, the very lives of men, are at the mercy of spells and counter-spells. Aye, and the very gods themselves are not exempt from the influence of magical rites; but must obey the behests of the powerful magician.

Syads, being lineal descendants of the great Prophet of Arabia, have, as we have already seen, special influence on the fate of men, but they by no means enjoy a monopoly of power for good or evil over the living. The disembodied spirit of any man or woman may become troublesome or dangerous. A deceased wife is particularly to be dreaded by her successor.

A female servant, alluding to the death of a man's third wife, remarked to me that such things always occurred amongst the wretched Muhammadans, but that people of her caste avoided dangers of that sort. She explained that the death of the second and subsequent wives was usually caused by the spirit of the first wife, whose jealous spite brought them to an untimely end. To avert danger from this quarter the spirit of the deceased wife had to be propitiated, and it was customary amongst her people to do it in this wise. The likeness of a woman done in silver (known as a *thuppa*) was worn as a locket by the second wife. This image represented the first wife, and had to be constantly propitiated. At every meal the second wife offered a pinch of food to the "thuppa" before she herself began to eat, and when she was about to put on new clothes or ornaments the second wife first offered them in due form to the "thuppa." Appeased and gratified by these attentions, the spirit of the first wife was won over to spare her successor.

* * * * * *

There appears to be a kind of *possession* known amongst the Muhammadans in India. The symptoms are these. Some man, usually one of blameless life and strict habits, is selected by a departed Pir or Syad as the vehicle for conveying his wishes to the living. The entry of the saint's spirit into the body of his chosen vessel is accompanied with violent convulsions. The man possessed of the spirit is thrown into a state of uncontrollable agitation. He foams at the mouth, and usually tosses his head from side to side, or up and down, in a frantic manner. At length he speaks, asserting energetically that he is some Pir or other, and demanding that a certain offering shall be made at his grave, which seems to be all the Pir cares about. The awe-stricken bystanders promise everything required, and the spirit departs, leaving his medium in a state of much physical prostration. I have had personal knowledge of several cases of this kind.

The 24th of November, being a Muhammadan festival, I paid a visit to the shrine of Data Ganj Bakhsh, a saint who settled at Lahore before the Norman conquest of England. Having lived in Lahore for thirty-four years he died there in A.D. 1072. I found a large concourse of people seated near the outer wall of the shrine in the open air. Three musicians, two playing on stringed instruments and one on a drum, were singing away lustily a hymn in praise of the saint. Several greybeards sat in a sort of solemn abstraction close to the wall, while a middle-aged man, dressed in green, with a string of beads round his neck, occupied a prominent position a little in front of the elders. The congregation and onlookers, consisting of two or three hundred persons, sat huddled together on *darís* or cotton carpets in the foreground. As the music went on with a peculiar sort of throb, one here and another there from the midst of the congregation seemed convulsed, as if by galvanic shocks. Presently their movements became more energetic and violent. In one case a man threw himself forward, resting, in a crouching position, on his hands and knees. He swayed his head in a frantic manner from side to side, and it was a marvel to me how it escaped collision with the ground. But escape it did. Exhausted at length by the wild energy of his movements, the man fell in a fit upon the ground. One of his companions now came forward and began to press his limbs, in order, I presume, to calm the excitement of his overwrought nerves. Another man, after the usual premonitory convulsions, writhed on the ground in wild contortions. Two men rushed forward, apparently to prevent him from hurting himself, and holding him up by the waist, allowed him to fling himself backwards and forwards in the wildest manner possible.

Photo by W. Campbell Oman

THE SHRINE OF DATA GANJ BAKSH

To face page 298

Several other men became excited and convulsed under the influence of the Pir, but all the cases of possession I noticed could be referred to one or other of the types I have just described. None of the *convulsionnaires* uttered a single word throughout the proceedings.

On a previous occasion I had visited one of the favourite places for the exhibition of such manifestations. On reaching the ground, I found several persons congregated round a boy of about ten years of age, who appeared to be in a semi-unconscious state. This poor little fellow had been hanging, I don't know for how long, suspended head downwards from the branch of a tree. In this uncomfortable position he had been swaying himself about in a sort of frenzy, and had almost lost consciousness before he was taken down. His father and other friends who were present on the spot assured me that no harm could come to any one taken possession of by the spirit of the *Pir sahib*.

A tailor in my service, a weakly lad with a very queer look about his eyes, used to be a favourite of some Pir or other. He was fond of attending assemblies such as I have described, would readily fall into the ecstatic state, and died very young. As contributions are expected from those who frequent assemblies of the kind just described, it is evident that the guardians of the shrines where they take place reap a substantial advantage, but it is not easy to see what benefit the poor fellows get who may be called the performers on these occasions. They have themselves told me that in the ecstatic state they are unconscious of the world around them, and have the very gates of paradise opened to them.

* * * * * *

In India we live in a world which is accustomed to receive supernatural visitants who associate familiarly with men. We are, indeed, still in the age of the "Arabian Nights." A holy Mussulman faquir, who enjoyed a considerable local reputation, told me of his own experiences with a *Jinn*. The Jinn, in human form, used to visit him, but always came with a green shade over his eyes, as if suffering from sore-eyes. He represented himself as a devotee who, attracted by the fame of my informant, had come to sit at his feet. He was assiduous in his attentions, and one day asked my friend if he knew who he was. On receiving a reply to the effect that the faquir knew nothing about him beyond what he had himself stated, he said he was in reality a Jinn. My friend received the statement with incredulity. Not long after this, being disturbed in his devotions by the noisy chattering of two starlings, my informant asked his disciple, the Jinn, to drive them away, when what was his surprise to find the pretended devotee put forth his hand and catch the birds although they were ten or twelve feet above his head. Another time the Jinn, to oblige him, caught a young fox by simply putting out his foot and placing it upon its neck. The Jinn continued to wear the green shade, because he wished to escape being recognized by that well-known peculiarity of Jinns, their inability to wink. During his sojourn with the faquir the Jinn fell out with one of the persons, a *chaprási*, who was in the habit of visiting the holy man, and having been abused by his adversary caused the death of his children, by literally passing into the poor fellow's house, through closed doors, and strangling his unoffending infants. The mother, in great distress, came and complained to the faquir about the cruel wrong she had suffered. The holy man suggested that she should go for redress to the law courts, but she explained that it was a case of magic, and not one with which the magistrates could deal. On this the faquir reproved the Jinn, and desired him to discontinue his visits; but the Jinn promised better behaviour in future, and, to make amends for the murder he had committed, promised to give the object of his anger—the father of the strangled babes—whatever he asked for, provided he never told any one how he came by it. The aggrieved father looked upon this as *une mauvaise plaisanterie;* but one day being in sore need of four rupees, he held out his cloth and called upon the Jinn to fulfil his promise. Immediately four rupees fell into his cloth. After this he asked for several other things and received them; but one of the prying women of his household having found out how the money came, made a boast of it to some of her friends. The spell was broken. Nothing more was ever received, and the Jinn, enraged at his secret having been made public, destroyed two more members of the *chaprási's* family. At the faquir's very urgent and positive request, the Jinn at length made himself scarce. Every word of this wonderful story the holy faquir assured me was *absolutely true.*

* * * * * *

As a general rule, natives of India of all classes believe in the reality of possession, demoniacal or otherwise. They unhesitatingly admit that some favoured men and women are chosen as the media of communication between departed saints and the human race; but they are not equally ready to recognize the validity of the pretensions of particular individuals. In fact there is often an odd mixture of superstition and shrewd scepticism—or shall I say suspiciousness?—in the Indian character. I well remember a Mussulman telling me, with a good deal of humour and self-satisfaction, the following story. A Pathan from beyond the western border had arrived in his neighbourhood. The rumour went abroad that at times the spirits of certain departed Syads descended upon the Muslim visitor, or, as the native expression is, "got upon" him. He was under the influence now of one and now of another departed saint. Of course he became at once an object of awe and veneration to the people. Every one who longed for the gratification of some cherished desire approached him in his hour of possession, and hoped, by homage and gifts, to obtain the assistance of his controlling spirits. My informant, like others, had his end to gain, and one night, unknown to the members of his own household, stole out to pay his respects to the Pathan. It was warm summer-time, so he went out very lightly clad, and he did not wear the usual turban, in the hope that the absence of this customary head-dress might render him less easily recognizable by any acquaintances he might chance to meet. When he got near the Pathan he found a large number of persons, chiefly females, congregated on the spot. The Pathan, of course, had his satellites and attendants. Some were beating drums, others talking confidentially to the bystanders in praise of their master and acting generally as go-betweens. My informant, who watched the proceedings with keen interest, presently thought he detected manifest signs of imposture, and no longer felt disposed to crave the assistance of the Syads through their Pathan medium. In the little gathering were some persons not unknown to him, at least by sight, and of whose history he had learned something from the gossips of the town. He could, he thought, guess pretty well what they wanted from the saint, and as he felt sure that he was unrecognized by any one present, he was tempted to perpetrate a practical joke. He sat down near one of the drummers, and, by the help of a little silver adroitly handed to him, secured his good offices. Placing a few flowers before himself, he began in the orthodox fashion to toss his head violently from side to side with his face turned downwards, and in a feigned voice repeated over and over again, "I am Syad So-and-so," naming some saint well known to the people of that place. The drummer called attention to this remarkable case of possession, and my informant soon became the centre of attraction. Using his local knowledge and taking advantage of the credulity of the people, he was able to extract for the benefit of his friend the drummer several rupees from his deluded neighbours, giving them in return many promises and a few flowers or cloves. But this opposition business did not suit the Pathan and his more zealous supporters. Angry inquiries were made about the new-comer, and there appeared symptoms of an approaching storm. Collision with the formidable Pathans was not to be lightly risked, so my informant hung his head down and stopped shaking it, thus indicating, by a well-understood sign, that the spirit of the Syad had departed. As he had not pocketed any of the money he had gathered there he was allowed to leave unmolested, and thankfully escaped into the darkness of the night and the intricacies of the lanes with, as he laughingly told me, a confused head and a neck which, unaccustomed to such violent exercise, ached for days and days afterwards.

* * * * * *

A Hindu oracle.—The Muslims, however, have no monopoly in such matters; the Hindus too have their oracles. On an extremely hot and sultry day at the end of June, I learned where one of these augurs might be seen, and I set off in quest of him. I was driven through certain narrow, crowded streets or rather lanes of Amritsar, where evil smells were almost overpowering. Everywhere, in the dirt of the thoroughfares, lay the peels and the seeds of mangoes and the unsightly remnants of musk-melons mingled with the dust, covered with flies and festering in the hot air. As I went along I met a party of policemen with an inspector in charge. They were commissioned to disinfect, with permanganate of potash, certain wells in the city, as a precautionary measure, for deadly cholera had recently made its grim presence felt in that neighbourhood. There had been, that same day, some rough work between the police and the proprietors of these wells before the orders of the *Sarkar* could be carried out.

As I proceeded into the more densely inhabited parts of the town the lanes became narrower, till the carriage could go no further. I had to alight and walk along an alley paved with bricks-on-edge, sloping towards the middle line so as to form an open drain down the centre. In fact, it would not be too much to call the alley, or the floor of it, a surface drain. Fortunately I had now not far to go; perhaps a hundred yards or so.

My destination being reached I had to pass through a door, about three feet wide and six feet high, into a dim chamber about ten feet by fifteen. This it appeared was a sort of temple sacred to Bhairon.

When I arrived with my two companions, Pandit N. S. and the editor of a vernacular newspaper, there was a brisk and very nerve-disturbing tom-toming going on.

My appearance at the door was, to my regret, the reason for several well-dressed women making a hasty departure, some of them through a little window at one side of the room. However, a fairly large number of persons still remained in the chamber, and some who had left it stood at the window and peeped in awaiting developments.

The central figure in the chamber was a tall, sinewy man standing before a shrine of Bhairon, with his right hand resting on the handle of an exceptionally big *mugdar* (Indian club), and twisting his head in a circle to the throb of the drum. I presume he was seeking inspiration, and certainly his neck seemed as supple as a serpent's body. He was, no doubt, a *practised performer*. The room was stifling, but the oracle, under the influence of the presiding divinity and excited by the drum and the singer (for there was one), showed no lack of energy. He was stripped to the waist, and wore only a small loin-cloth. His hair was long enough to fall upon his shoulders. His face was a strong one, and his eyes almost bloodshot. Presently he took up the *mugdar*, and swinging it over his head brought it down repeatedly with a thud upon his bare back. After that he grasped in one hand a bundle of iron spikes fastened together with wire, and in the other a number of short iron chains, and with these he also ill-used himself for a while; then throwing them down he grasped the club again and swung it as before.

This performance went on for quite twenty minutes, and then while he swung his head he inquired whether the *sahib* had come to consult him about the future or only to look on. Being told it was only for the latter object, he continued his performance for a few more minutes and then staggered towards the shrine and rested his head upon the topmost bar of the railing which protected it.

I realized that my presence interfered with, in fact interrupted, the proceedings. No one, it was apparent, would, while I was there, be likely to consult the oracle; so I withdrew, leaving, of course, a present for the augur whose services I was told were in great demand; probably because it was a time of peril, since the dreadful pestilence was stalking around claiming victims from all classes of the community.

* * * * * *

Any one acquainted with the history of the maddening terror which witchcraft in any form inspired in Europe during the Middle Ages, and the horrible, widespread and barbarous persecutions which resulted from it,[1] cannot help noticing, when brought into contact with witchcraft in India, that it stands upon an entirely different footing there. The cause of this is not far to seek. In Christian Europe magicians, necromancers, and witches were regarded as the enemies of God, as monsters in league with Satan and condemned to eternal damnation. They were accordingly destroyed, at the instigation of the clergy, without mercy, and upon the warrant of Holy Scripture. To rid the earth of witches was a religious duty which the priests and ministers (Protestant and Roman Catholic alike) carried out with a burning zeal and a horrid eagerness worthy of a better cause. In India, on the other hand, especially amongst the Hindus, magic and witchcraft are not without a certain respectability. The Brahmans themselves are the possessors of spells (mantras) which even the gods are unable to resist. It is true that in the Vishnu Purana it is said "he who practises magic rites for the harm of others will be punished in the hell called Krimisa" (that of insects).[2] But this threat is neither generally known nor does it practically affect the attitude of the people towards wizards and necromancers. The practisers of the black art in India may be objects of terror to the people, but they do not inspire them with feelings of *religious horror*.

According to popular belief, magicians, sorcerers, and conjurers abound in India. Most of the calamities of life are attributed to them, and it is worth noting that among certain of the aboriginal tribes "even those who are

[1] Lecky's "Rise and Influence of the Spirit of Rationalism in Europe."

[2] Professor H. H. Wilson's translation, bk. ii. chap. iv.

20

accused of being witches do not deny the impeachment, but accept the position readily with all its pains and penalties."[1] Yet the evil is not without a remedy, for sorcerer may be pitted against sorcerer, and the spells of one be nullified by the counter-spells of another. Thus also in Europe, holy water, church ceremonies, consecrated relics, and priestly exorcism were employed against sorcery, witchcraft and demoniacal possession.

* * * * * *

The more powerful conjurers in India inspire dread and command respect. These, therefore, live at ease on the credulity of the many, but occasionally the popular vengeance is wreaked upon some wretched man or woman who is suspected of having caused mischief, and who at the same time is not sufficiently dreaded to hold the rabble in check.

The records of our criminal courts contain many cases of this kind. The following may be cited as an example :

"Wali, an old Bheel woman, about 70 years of age, and her sister Chitri, residents of Deshgaon, Nassick District, were believed by the villagers to be witches possessed of a hidden charm, by which they were supposed to have worked the sorcery to which the deaths of several persons in the village were attributed. . . . A religious mendicant arrived at the village and denounced the sisters as witches, and forthwith the villagers laid hold of Chitri, swung her by a rope to a mango tree, and beat her to extort the hidden charm. She escaped without serious consequences. Wali, the other sister, who had gone to a neighbouring village to beg, was fetched to Deshgaon the same evening, and was the following morning swung by the feet to a tree near the village police-station, was maltreated in the presence and with the connivance of many of the villagers, and was required to disclose the hidden charm by which she and her sister caused deaths in the village. She was removed in a fainting condition to her house, where she died the same day. Three persons were instrumental in causing her death. One, a police constable, swung her to a tree by the feet with a rope and struck her several blows with a hempen thong, another struck her with a shoe, while the third, the police *patel* of the village, superintended the proceedings and instigated violence to the wretched woman. These three persons were tried, and sentenced to rigorous imprisonment."

---

[1] Ball's "Jungle Life in India," p. 115.
[2] "Bombay Gazette," 1881.

If it were not for the protection afforded even to "witches" by the British law, cases of this kind would undoubtedly be multiplied to a very great extent. At the beginning of the last century (1802) a self-constituted native tribunal tried five women at Patna for sorcery, found them guilty, and put them to death. The case attracted the attention of the British authorities, and a proclamation was issued by the Governor-General, declaring that any persons taking upon themselves to act as the members of the irregular Patna tribunal had done, would be considered guilty of murder.[1] There is no reason to doubt that this order has had the effect of saving the lives of a great many women who would otherwise have fallen victims to the popular belief in witches and witchcraft, yet since the date of the proclamation thousands upon thousands must have perished in out-of-the-way places, at the hands of their superstitious countrymen, with the knowledge and connivance of the equally superstitious village police. A few years ago there appeared in the English and Indian newspapers a painful story of the death, under very tragic circumstances, of a woman belonging to a village in Oudh who believed herself to be possessed by an evil spirit. The woman's husband gave out that he had received a divine command to destroy her eyes, which would be miraculously restored. The villagers assembled; the unfortunate woman was held down; and, in the presence of the expectant crowd, the husband gouged out her eyes. As might have been foreseen, the unhappy victim of the barbarous operation died almost immediately.

* * * * * *

The genius of Hinduism is peculiarly favourable to a belief in witchcraft and demoniacal possession, but the modern Hindu thinks that magic with other useful lore

[1] "Medical Jurisprudence for India," by Dr. Norman Chevers, p. 12.

perished, to a great extent, with the men who fell at Kurukshetra, in the war described in the Mahabharata. Muhammadan traditions and literature are also full of records of events brought about by magic arts, but the Indian Muslim holds, like his Hindu countryman, that knowledge of these arts is in a very imperfect condition now.

In ages long gone by there existed a city whose inhabitants had attained, by unlawful and forbidden arts, to a degree of knowledge not inferior to that of the angels. Gabriel was directed to visit this city, and on entering found only children in it. The messenger addressed one of these, inquiring where the elders were, and when they might be expected back. Without replying to the question, the child observed that he himself was quite ready to answer any questions the stranger desired to put. The angel asked where Gabriel was at that time. After a short pause, the boy replied, with a thoughtful expression on his face, "I have scanned the four quarters of the universe, even to the throne of the Almighty, but no Gabriel could I find. Therefore, either I am or you are Gabriel." The messenger departed in astonishment, and carried to heaven a report of his mission; upon which the Almighty decreed that the guilty city, with its inhabitants and its thousands of volumes of unhallowed lore, should be whelmed in one common ruin. A troop of angels was sent to overturn the city from its very foundations, and bury it with its inhabitants for ever. There escaped, however, from the general destruction, a stray leaf or two of the books of divination, and on the imperfect hints derived from these, the modern sciences of magic and astrology have been reared during a succession of ages.

On the superstitions of the people of India volumes might be written; for India is still where Europe was in the Dark Ages, and belief in witchcraft, demoniacal possession, the transmutation of metals, the efficacy of charms, spells, and love-filtres, is quite general amongst all classes of the people. Let me add a few instances to those already given.

A native, referring to the wasting disease (marasmus)

from which an infant seemed to be suffering, assured me that even the shadow of the little child falling upon one in health might prove fatal to the latter. The disease, he said, might in some cases be cured at the expense of the vegetable world; for example, it was well known that if a child suffering from marasmus were taken into a sugar-cane field, there undressed and bathed, and its cast-off clothes left on the ground, the child might recover, but in that case the *sugar-cane would all be blighted.* I subsequently learned another mode of curing the disease. The mother of the sufferer should secure a black dog and decapitate it in the dead of night. She should then boil its head in water, and bathe herself and child in this broth, exactly at the hour of midnight.

* * * * * *

During an excessively dry summer, as I was sitting one evening in the open air, the clouds began gathering rapidly overhead. Every one was anxiously looking out for rain. The sultry heat had caused an outbreak of sickness, and the price of food had gone up considerably. I remarked to a native standing beside me that we would now in all probability have the much-desired rain. He looked up towards the dark overcast sky above, and then, shaking his head doubtfully, expressed his fear that the rascally *baníyás*—vendors of food-grains and other articles of consumption—would not let it rain. The idea was a new one to me. I was familiar with the old Hindu notion that the dark clouds are malicious demons who obstruct or intercept the rainfall, and are only overcome by Indra's flashing thunderbolts, which rend them asunder in the interests of the human race and the parched and gaping earth. But I had never heard that the baníyás were credited with meteorological powers of so very important a character. I pressed the man to explain his remarks. "Don't you know," he said, "that it is to the interest of the baníyás that the prices of all articles of consumption should be as high as possible, and that rain should not fall? Well, to attain their object, they make cakes of wheat-flour and other things, and then deliberately deal with these heaven-sent gifts in such a manner as to offend the gods and make them withhold the rain." He went into details with respect to the proceedings of the baníyás which I need not mention here.

At another time I learned that a baníyá had recourse to a still more effectual method of keeping off the rain. He had a *charkhá*, or spinning-wheel, made out of the bones of dead men. Such an article could only be made very secretly and for a large sum of money, but its action was most potent. Whenever the clouds were gathering the baníyá set his virgin daughter to work the charkhá the *reverse way*, and by that means unwound or unwove the clouds, as it were, thus driving away the rain; and this over and over again, notwithstanding that the young Hindu maidens had gone forth, harnessed themselves to the plough, and with suitable ceremonies and offerings had invoked the gods for rain, while the Muhammadans on their part had assembled in the Musjid and offered up prayers to Allah for the much-needed showers.

* * * * * *

Where credulity abounds, impostors are of course not wanting to take advantage of the credulous, as the following anecdote amusingly illustrates.

A cowherd reported in his village that he often heard a human voice proceeding from the interior of an old neglected grave, demanding to be released. The villagers assembled round the spot indicated. They heard the stifled voice with their own ears, and following the advice of the herdsman, and one or two others in league with him, opened out the dilapidated grave, not, however, without trepidation and many misgivings. As the result of their labour, they exhumed a miserable-looking man in grave-clothes and covered with mud. To the inquiries of the bystanders regarding himself he would give no verbal response, but by means of signs, which were readily interpreted by his confederates, he gave the simple rustics to understand that he had been dead for ever so long a time; that his soul had been in paradise, and had but just returned to reanimate his body, which had been lying in the ground exempt from the influences of decay. The subject of such marvellous experiences was, of course, an object of veneration to the people. The herdsman and one or two others constituted themselves the guardians of the "resurrected" man, and shared with him the gifts and offerings of the credulous peasants.

* * * * * *

As in Europe during the Middle Ages, and much later too,[1] so in India to-day the subject of the transmutation of metals is one which attracts a good deal of attention. As a teacher of science I have frequently been questioned about the practicability of converting copper into silver or gold, and I have found that a very strong and widespread confidence prevails, even amongst the educated, in regard to the existence of a secret art of transmuting metals known to a few adepts. Indeed, some men have assured me that they have seen the process successfully carried out, although they were not admitted into the secret of the art.

* * * * * *

To the many examples of superstitions which I have already instanced I may add what is known in the Punjab as "serpent love" (*már-ashshuq*), at any rate until the facts(?), passing strange, affirmed with respect to it have been scientifically investigated and established.

Serpent love.—A very intelligent Muhammadan once related to me certain peculiar experiences of a near relation of his, a young woman in sound health and easy

[1] "Goethe in Frankfurt was busy with researches after the 'virgin earth.' The philosophers' stone had many eager seekers. In 1787, Semler sent to the Academy of Berlin his discovery that gold grew in a certain atmospheric salt when kept moist and warm."—Lewes's "Life of Goethe," vol. i. p. 319.

circumstances. One unlucky day she was bitten by a snake, and though it was not a deadly serpent she suffered great pain from the bite, and her health was, for a time, much impaired. Before she had satisfactorily recovered from this untoward accident she was again bitten by a snake of the same kind, and again went through great suffering. Time after time, at more or less regular intervals, she was bitten by these reptiles although every precaution was taken to guard her from them.

By great vigilance she might escape one or two of the periodical visitations, but complete immunity seemed impossible of attainment. For a period she escaped her serpent enemies by wearing a portion of the skin of the *markhor*, or mountain goat, about her person, as a sort of amulet; but the charm losing its freshness, she was bitten again. Her health eventually failed entirely under the terror of her position and the venom of her tormentors.

Relating this incident to a well-educated Hindu gentleman—a Master of Arts of the Punjab University—he assured me that stories of *serpent love* are founded on actual fact. He himself had personal knowledge of one case. His people had a servant who was afflicted in this way. Every six months or so the man used to become subject to a strange morbid restlessness, and a mental inquietude *which could only be allayed by his being visited and bitten by a serpent.* Every one looked upon him with repulsion as one strangely allied with such a terrible reptile. He also inspired a sort of awe because of this connection. The man himself was generally unhappy, and when the paroxysms were at hand he was wretched and miserable.

At last the sufferer consulted a wise sádhu, who gave him a *ganda táwiz* (a peculiar *malodorous* amulet). When he had attached this to his person he experienced a sort of nightmare. Serpents seemed to crawl round him, to wind and coil about his limbs, and to hiss and dart at him. Even the ambient air seemed to be peopled with writhing serpent forms. For two hours or so this dreadful vision obsessed him, nearly driving him mad, and then the air cleared, as it were, and the ground at his feet resumed for him its natural appearance. He was cured *for ever;* the mental shadows and the very real serpents passing entirely out of his life.

Both the above cases have peculiarities of their own. In the Muslim family the patient was guarded as much as possible from her serpent visitors, and she died. Whereas the Hindu, labouring periodically under great physical and mental distress, welcomed what may be called the dental attentions of the serpents, and was eventually freed by a wise sádhu from his troubles as well as from the visitations of the uncanny reptiles.

A case somewhat similar to the one relating to the Hindu above mentioned, but without the cure, is described in a book entitled "Thirty-five Years in India" (pp. 140–141), written by Dr. Honigberger, who described himself as physician to the Court of Mahárája Ranjit Singh. Dr. Honigberger's is the only book in which I have found any reference to "serpent love." Writing on this subject, he states as follows:

> "Speaking of serpents, I may mention here a particular disease which they designate at Lahore, Mar-ashakh (serpent-love), and which, according to their statements, occurs only in the Punjab. I have never heard of it in any other place, and I mention it, hoping that the English physicians, particularly those now living in that country, will take the trouble to investigate the subject and ascertain whether this disease is peculiar to the Punjab, and why it occurs only between the Indus and the Sutlej. . . .
>
> "The faqueer, Noor-oo-Din, at Lahore, who at present enjoys great respect from the English for his extended knowledge and eminent merits, was the first who directed my attention to the disease I have mentioned, a short time before my first departure from Lahore in the year 1832, and who introduced to me at that time a patient afflicted with it. It was a laundry man of the age of sixty, although he appeared nearer eighty. He allowed himself to be bitten every month by serpents. He was of short stature and of a cachectical appearance; his perspiration, which I perceived at some distance, was peculiarly offensive, and was similar to that of serpents. He told me he had been troubled with that malady upwards of thirty years; that at the commencement he permitted himself to be bitten once a year, afterwards twice, but at that time once in every month; and that the serpents followed him even into the water. He stated that only four days previously he had been bitten on the upper part of the hand, on which I could perceive a cicatrix, and he showed me numerous scars on his hands and feet, so that I could not doubt the truth of his statement. . . .
>
> "I have seen at least a dozen persons so affected at Lahore, who were all males, and I am told that the number of such patients in the Punjab is very large. The nature of the disease is that the patients at certain periods have an irresistible inclination to be bitten by serpents, which they say does them a great deal of good,

as for a few days previously they are troubled with fainting and dizziness, nausea, want of appetite, disinclination to work, and heaviness in the limbs. These are the symptoms of the disease in question, and at these times the serpents are attracted towards them by the scent; the patients looking upon them as their welcome benefactors."

Besides the cases of "serpent love" mentioned on a previous page, two others were related to me—one by a Kabárí (a seller of old furniture), regarding his son; the other by an Indian gentleman in the Education Department, his sister being the sufferer. From what I have stated it will be seen that there are both Hindus and Muslims in the Punjab who suffer from "serpent love," and that the affection is not confined to males only, as Dr. Honigberger seemed to imply.

In native opinion the explanation of the mystery is this. The snake that inflicts the first bite is a female. The poison she communicates ferments in the blood of the victim, and *periodically* produces in the bitten person the smell of a female snake; the males of the same species are attracted, and, as is the nature of the viper tribe, they bite and run away when they are disappointed. So far the explanation(?) is ingenious enough; but why, under such conditions, *should the bite of the male assuage the mental and physical troubles of the victim*, as described in the cases given above?

As to the efficacy of the flesh or skin of the markhor in such afflictions, it is attributed to the fact that the mountain goat is such an inveterate enemy of snakes that the mere odour of any part of it is enough to frighten the reptiles away.

The whole matter is of such physiological and psychological interest that it is to be hoped that it will be investigated thoroughly by competent medical men, and the results made known outside professional circles.[1]

[1] In his pathetic tale, "Elsie Venner, a Romance of Destiny," Oliver Wendell Holmes has depicted with sympathetic pen the peculiar and deplorable effect upon the character and life-story of poor Elsie, due to her mother having been bitten by a rattlesnake shortly before Elsie's birth. I wonder if Holmes had some Red Indian or negro superstition in his mind when he wrote this *physiological* romance? He does not say so, nor even hint as much.

CHAPTER II

EXPERIENCES WITH FORTUNE-TELLERS

·FORETELLING·THE·FUTURE·

"You cannot doubt the seer's prophetic sight;
Trust me, what he hath said will surely be.
Whatever is uttered by the holy Brahman,
Who is the light divine and manifest,
Must come to pass."
—*Uttara-Rama-Charitra* (Professor H. H. WILSON's Translation).

A WELL-DRESSED man, with a big wallet under his arm and a pamphlet in his hand, presented himself before me as I sat in my verandah, announcing his presence in these words, "*Fartune tailer sar!*" which I believe represented his entire stock of what was meant for English. He was of middle stature, of that clean yellow-brown complexion (which has been compared to the colour of a new saddle) common amongst natives of the better sort in India. His features were well cut, his eyes sharp and intelligent. A white line was neatly painted down the length of his nose, and two other white lines ran along the outer margins of his ears. He wore gold earrings set with pearls, and from his neck hung two strings of beads, the shorter one consisting of alternate pieces of gold and red coral, the longer one of neatly-shaped bits of sweet-scented sandal-wood. There was nothing of the gipsy about this man. Quite the reverse; he looked a person in easy circumstances, enjoying comfortable relations with his neighbours and the world in general.

I asked to see the pamphlet he carried. He handed it to me very readily. It was an astrological almanac for the year, and, after a little chaffering, he sold it to me for six annas, which I afterwards learned was just six times its market value. After buying the pamphlet I told the fortune-teller to go away, but he was by far too experienced in his trade to be got rid of so easily, and immediately had recourse to the old trick so familiar to professors of his art. Without examining my hand he could tell, from the indications given by my face alone, that the fate in store for me was a very good one; but he protested that the pleasant details of the future could only be read in the lines of the open palm. "Just show me your hand," he said, "and I will reveal to you all the secrets ot the future. Yours is a good fate." I still refused. He next tried flattery. Looking straight into my eyes, as if to read me through and through, he affirmed, with much impressiveness, that I was a man of strict probity and one who never broke his word; and this, for reasons which became apparent in the sequel, he reiterated several times. In regard to my past life he hazarded some vague guesses, which in a few cases were fairly correct and in others very wide of the truth. Having prolonged these preliminaries sufficiently for my purpose, which was to draw the fortune-teller out, I resigned my palm to him. After scanning it attentively, he began predicting with much volubility the length of the years, eighty-four, allotted to me; the number of children, thirteen, I was to be father to, and so on. Suddenly he paused in the midst of his vaticinations, as if in some perplexity, and then announced, with every mark of deep and natural concern, that an enemy was endeavouring to cause serious injury to me and mine. "The enemy," he said, speaking slowly and thoughtfully, with a far-off look in his eyes, as if peering into the mystery, "was probably a disappointed servant;" but when pressed on this point, the astrologer admitted that he could not make any positive assertion on the subject. But whoever he might be, the enemy in question had, after the manner of the practisers of the black art in all countries, made tiny images (*putlas*) to represent me and the members of my family, and, invoking a terrible curse upon these *simulacra*, had consumed them with fire.[1] With an appearance of earnestness which would certainly have had considerable effect upon any credulous person, the Brahman revealed to me that the danger hanging over me and mine was death to at least three members of my household, and a long and dangerous illness in my own case. He very prudently did not threaten me with an untimely end, having already announced that I was to live to the advanced age of eighty-four years. Although I tried to betray no signs of incredulity, the Brahman seemed to think that my faith in his knowledge or veracity needed strengthening. "Doubt me not," he said, with uplifted hands and eyes turned heavenwards; "I am a Brahman, and God will strike me blind if I am telling you any untruth. May my strength forsake me, may my very life be the sacrifice, if what I am asserting be false." "Sit

1 "There are districts in Great Britain and America, and many more on the continent of Europe, where spells that waste and destroy are still believed in; where effigies of wax and even onions are labelled with some hated name, and stuck over with pins, and set near fires to be melted or dried up, in full belief that some subject of the charm will be consumed by disease along with the object used."—Conway's "Demonology," vol. i. p. 272.

The same custom was known to Plato and is practised by negroes (Lang's "Myth, Ritual and Religion," i. 98). As every reader of modern English poetry knows, the superstition in question is woven into Dante Gabriel Rossetti's impressive little poem, "Sister Helen," the first stanza of which is:

> "Why did you melt your waxen man,
> Sister Helen?
> To-day is the third since you began!
> The time was long, yet the time ran,
> Little brother.
> (O Mother, Mary Mother,
> Three days to-day, between Hell and Heaven!)"

down here," he added, "and I will make this matter clear to you. I will put it beyond all doubt." He asked for a flower and a basin of water. A rose and a bowl of water were brought. The Brahman made me wash my hands and arms carefully to a little above the wrists, and repeating strange incantations (Sanskrit, *mantras*), he made me close my right hand over the rose and dip both hands, tightly closed, into the vessel of water. I had no idea of what was going to follow, but willing to see and learn, I passively obeyed all the directions of the fortune-teller. After a while he ceased his muttered spells, requested me to take my hands out of the water, and turning up the right sleeve of my coat, showed me—to my surprise, I must confess—a dark mark upon my bare skin just above the wrist, resembling a rudely designed figure with a round head, an oval trunk, arms expanded widely, and legs far apart. Pointing to the mark, the seer said, with bated breath, "The effigies made by your enemy were like that! Do you believe me now? How terrible is the danger that menaces you; but, happily, I can assist you to ward it off."

A metal plate or salver, a little salt, and an iron nail were required at this stage, and were produced. Three pinches of the salt[1] were cast upon the dark portentous mark which still disfigured my arm, and then the Brahman gradually washed it out by rubbing it with the iron nail repeatedly dipped in the water. He next placed the rose on the salver, and after passing it round my head a particular number of times, he made me pour three and a half handfuls of water upon it. From his wallet he produced a bit of old flat iron about three inches long and three-fourths of an inch wide. This he placed in the salver. Still muttering spells and invoking gods and saints (the names of Jesus and Muhammad being strangely blended with the names of the gods and goddesses of the Hindu Pantheon), he asked for some clothes which had been worn by me. The required articles, having been produced, were placed by him under my feet. Next the inevitable

[1] That demons hate or dread salt is an old and widespread superstition. See Conway's "Demonology and Devil-lore," vol. ii. p. 297.

piece of silver was required, and when handed to him was deposited in the salver. I was requested to step over it and back again three times. Now followed more mutterings of spells. The salver was made to rest on both my hands, and the Brahman bid me fix my attention upon the piece of iron lying on it in the water. Speaking after my friend, as I may now call him, I transferred to the lifeless bit of old iron in the tray the curses which had been heaped upon me and mine by our unknown, but not less dangerous foe. While the Brahman muttered his mantras for my preservation, I waited with no very lively curiosity to see what the next proceeding would be. Suddenly I was startled by the scrap of inanimate iron making a lively jump quite out of the salver which was resting on my hands. It fell upon the Brahman's thigh as he sat squat upon the carpet. With well-feigned excitement he interpreted this incident as establishing satisfactorily that the rite we had performed had had the desired effect. The spell cast upon me and mine had been broken.

I thought the business was over, as the Brahman said that the impending evil having been averted by his counter spells, my good fortune would now be very great. Rising above vague generalities, he ventured upon the specific prediction that within three weeks I should receive information of the most gratifying kind, adding that when the happy event occurred he would come to me in person and claim a reward of five rupees. Indeed he was even more explicit in his prediction. A sum of money due to me, the payment of which had been delayed on account of some misunderstanding, would soon be received by me, and I would, probably, before long, leave Lahore for a better appointment elsewhere.

The affair, however, was not quite over yet. It was undoubtedly true that the children and myself were now out of danger, but a special peril still threatened the *Mem Sahib* (the lady). Having averted the danger from myself, surely I would not leave the lady in trouble. Was I sceptical about the risk to which she was still exposed? My doubts could easily be set at rest.

This time a small lump of cotton, dipped in common

olive oil, was required and duly provided. Talking volubly, with great apparent earnestness and many confidential whispers, the fortune-teller made us hold the cotton between our hands, placed one upon the other, palm to palm, and after sundry muttered spells he lifted up the cotton and squeezed the oil from it, quite of a blood-red colour. Of course this was only a token of an impending calamity of some sort, to avert which a piece of clean cotton cloth and some silver were needed. The indispensable articles were brought, and after the appropriate mantras had been uttered, became, I need hardly say, the property of the clever fortune-teller.

The business was at last over ; the Brahman had only to write out two pieces of paper with cabalistic signs, one in the name of my wife and the other in my name. Whilst so employed a little son of mine was standing by with a new inkstand in his hand, one of those ordinary traveller's inkstands shaped like a box, with a spring lid. The Brahman wished to see it, took it in his hand, opened it, observed that there was no ink in it, and quietly placed it just before him on the carpet. He slowly completed his cabalistic papers. One was to be thrown into water the next day, together with some *goor* (crude sugar) and a flower ; the other to be wrapped up in a piece of red cloth, with a clove and a cardamum, and laid under my pillow, until the fulfilment of his prediction that I should receive, within three weeks, good news of a very acceptable kind.

Affirming for the twentieth time the implicit trust that could be placed upon my every word, he now put the empty inkstand into one of my hands and some old clothes in the other, and getting me to repeat certain words after him, the artful Brahman led me, quite easily and without my perceiving exactly what he was about, to make him a formal present of the inkstand, which I really had had no intention of doing.

I now took up and examined the piece of iron which had indicated, in such a lively and demonstrative manner, its willingness to stand vicariously for us. It was a little bit of ordinary flat iron, doubled over at one end to the extent of about one-sixth of an inch. Wedged, but not tightly, in the fold I found a small white bead, which the

Brahman quickly removed when his attention was drawn to it, assuring me that it was only a common bead which must have got in there by accident when the iron was lying, with a lot of other things, in his bag. But the little intruder, I think, betrayed a secret, for, in all probability, by means of it and the help of a long fine hair, the bit of iron had been persuaded into energetic acceptance of the danger threatening us. As to the figure that had appeared upon my arm, it had, of course, been impressed upon my damp skin as the soothsayer was pretending to show me the exact position in which I should hold my hands in the water.

Our friend was packing up now. From the ready way in which we had carried out his instructions, he must—and naturally enough—have concluded that he had credulous dupes to deal with, and so made a last attempt to derive profit either from my superstitious fears or my unwariness. Pointing to the bit of iron which I had replaced in the salver, he requested me to tell him to take that away, together with the dangers which had been threatening us. Too wide-awake this time to be taken in, I lifted the iron out of the salver, and, handing the rusty scrap of metal to him, told him to take it away. This ended the proceedings.

And now for the fulfilment of the prediction of speedy good news. Well, no good news of any kind reached me; but—such is the irony of fate—on the very last day of the three weeks within which I was to receive glad tidings, a letter was handed to me containing the most disappointing piece of intelligence affecting my own prospects which could well have been imagined. In this way were the truthful Brahman's predictions fulfilled. Let him look to it in the next world. For, if we may trust Dante, our Brahman seer, and men of his kind, having presumed to look too far ahead, will for ever wander backwards about the dismal pit with their heads turned round and set the contrary way on their shoulders—and they will richly deserve their punishment.

I cannot hope to have given my reader an adequate idea of the art and power of the crafty Brahman. His earnest and continued appeals to God, his constant and solemn invocations of curses upon his own head if he were departing from the truth, were really very impressive, even to me who had no reason to place the smallest confidence in him. I can well understand how, under ordinary circumstances, such a man could play upon the credulity and fears of ignorant and superstitious Hindus; how weak, impulsive women would be ready dupes of his clever appeals to their hopes and fears, how he would excite their curiosity, how his sleight of hand would impose upon them, and how the respect and awe inspired by his sacred character as a Brahman would complete the delusion of his victims.

* * * * * *

On another occasion I allowed a Brahman fortune-teller to practise his art at my expense. His method of proceeding was somewhat different from that already described. He did not commit himself to any reckless statements in regard to my past life, nor did he venture any very definite predictions about my future. He confined himself to saying that I had a certain object in view, the accomplishment of which I earnestly desired, and that he could easily satisfy me whether I should gain my end or not. After examining my hand, and getting my palm crossed with silver, he made me procure a piece of thread, break it myself into five bits, roll the fragments up together and drop them, hap-hazard, on a strip of cloth covered with various cabalistic signs and figures. The process of dropping the thread on the mystic cloth was repeated several times, the Brahman pretending to take special note of the particular signs upon which the ball of thread fell on each occasion. Once, however, he asked me to separate and count the pieces of thread, in order, as he said, that there might be no mistake about the matter. I did so. At length he handed me the pellet of thread, requesting me to place it in my mouth. I had next to wash my hands and cross them on my breast, solemnly fixing my thoughts on God, and calling to mind any wish I might have specially at heart. I was also to blow five times on the back of my hands as they lay crossed on my breast. While I remained in this position, the Brahman kept repeating various mantras in Sanskrit. He assured me that if a mark appeared on the palm of my left hand, my wish would be fulfilled after the lapse of a considerable time; but that if a mark appeared on the palm of my right hand, I might calculate upon the speedy accomplishment of my hopes. I removed my hands, the left one first. There was no mark on it. But the right hand bore a conspicuous one on the centre of the palm, seeing which the Brahman said that all would be well with me. He then got some more money, which had to be passed over and round my head three times, with the prayer that all my misfortunes might pass away. At this stage the fortune-teller requested me to remove the pellet of thread from my mouth, saying that if the pieces had joined together, then every possible doubt in regard to the fulfilment of my wishes would be removed. I took the thread out of my mouth, and, sure enough, there was but one long piece instead of five little bits. The Brahman now put some salt in my hand, upon the dark mark, and with the rupees and salt rubbed it out, as well as he could, and eventually obliterated it completely, with the aid of five roses, which had been brought for the purpose from my garden. Finally, as a parting admonition, the seer warned me to be very circumspect in what I said; always to keep my own counsel, and not even to relate my dreams to any one. Desiring every soul to quit the room, he whispered into my ear a secret recipe for the preparation of a sweetmeat—I dare not particularize the ingredients—which would possess the strange property of winning for me the sympathy and affection of any person who might partake of it. Seeing my evident surprise at the nature of his prescription, the Brahman told me that I might please myself about making use of the knowledge he had imparted to me, but that I need not fear to act upon his recommendation, for the sin (*goonah*), if any, would be on his head, not mine. Throughout the proceedings the Brahman swore by his sacred thread and by his son, who had accompanied him and was waiting in the verandah outside.

The reader will probably expect me to give an explanation, should I have one to offer, regarding the appearance of the black mark on my hand and the joining up of the five pieces of thread in my mouth. I must confess that, although I was as vigilant as possible, the clever dexterity of the Brahman eluded my suspicious watchfulness over his proceedings, so that I am not in a position to say how his tricks were actually accomplished, though possible explanations have occurred to me. One always fancies that one can unmask the clever juggler, but generally the wish to show him up is stronger than the ability to do so.

It will be evident from the foregoing narrative what a clever, worldly-wise fellow the Indian fortune-teller is. He travels much—I have met the same man at Agra and at Lahore—and he skilfully adapts himself to every age and to all circumstances of life. I remember a Brahman telling me my fortune at Calcutta when I was quite a youth. At that impressionable time of life, what more appropriate road to the purse than the tender passion? So the crafty Brahman solemnly assured me that a married lady, a friend of mine, young and good looking, was madly in love with me, and offered me his assistance to bring us together.

Brahman fortune-tellers are the astrologers who play so important a part in the every-day life of the Hindu. They are consulted, especially by the women, before taking nearly every important or trivial step in life. Is a marriage to be arranged? The astrologer must give his approval and must fix the auspicious day. Is a journey to be undertaken? Is a plundering expedition to be commenced? The astrologer must appoint the day upon which to set off. Has the weather become so hot that people wish to leave their rooms and transfer their beds to the flat terraced roofs of their houses? The astrologer must tell them when this important migration should be carried out. Is the love of a man or a woman desired? The astrologer is again appealed to for charms, spells and love-potions.

Not so long ago a Mahárája in Bengal had spent over twenty lakhs of rupees in the construction and furnishing of a palace for himself, and then left it untenanted because the astrologers said it was not an auspicious house.

Even events of national importance are not beyond the sphere of the astrologer's influence. Is a throne to be ascended? Is a battle to be fought? The astrologer must name the proper time! [1] And these are by no means obsolete functions of a past age; for the astrologer is still an important factor in contemporary Eastern politics. We learn from a well-informed Indian writer that in our time in Kashmir a member of the Raja's family has been led to intrigue against his sovereign through certain predictions of the astrologers in his favour, and that the Raja himself through superstitious dread keeps an astrologer in his service, though he knows the man's loyalty is not to be depended upon.[2]

Pausing one day, just for a minute, by the Bohar gate, near the little bridge over the canal which forms the favourite bathing-place of the people of Multan, a picturesque and interesting scene presented itself to my view. On one side of the bridge the men and on the other the women, very much undraped, were enjoying their morning bath. On the steps leading from the water I noticed a woman in clean new garments whose graceful form attracted my attention. Ascending the flight of steps, she passed through the precincts of a temple of Siva which stood on the bank and deposited a small offering before the *lingam*. An hour afterwards I was at the ancient temple of Prahladpuri, some little distance from the bathing place, and observed, through the wide-open door, the same woman, in close consultation with a Brahman in an adjoining building. The priest was unfolding before her a long roll of astrological paper, and with a look of great apparent sincerity seemed helping her to unveil the secrets of the future. Of what he said or what she wished to learn, I have, of course, no knowledge; but probably an interesting romance was there being worked out under the cunning hands of the wily Brahmans.

[1] Elliot's "Muhammadan Historians of India," edited by Prof. Dowson, vol. v. p. 77. "Voyages de François Bernier," tome i. pp. 213–216. Amsterdam, 1699.

[2] "Cashmire and its Prince," by Jogendra Chandra Bose, M.A., B.L., pp. 37 and 49.

That the Indian fortune-teller can sometimes play a prominent and personal part in the drama of domestic life will appear from the following characteristic story which was related to me by a Muhammadan who knew the parties concerned. A woman whose husband had gone on a journey was very anxious about his prolonged absence from home, as she had received no letter from him since his departure. What more natural than to consult an astrologer? He would surely know what was the matter with the absent man. The reader of secrets was accordingly interviewed very privately. The astrological books were no doubt referred to, and, instructed by the stars, the seer was able to say that at midnight on a certain day of the month her husband would return home; but, for very private and important reasons, would not wish his visit to be known to any one. She was accordingly to keep the matter a dead secret, and on no account to awaken the curiosity or suspicions of her neighbours by any preparations or unusual proceedings. The appointed night arrived, and with it a gentle tap on the door and a low voice asking admission. The woman opened the door of her house with eagerness and admitted her silent and muffled visitor, who, affecting to be very tired, found his way to the little *charpoy* and lay down upon it, inviting the woman to join him. It was not long before she discovered, even in the darkness of the little cabin, that her visitor and her husband were very different persons. What was she to do? Had the wretch who occupied the bed come to murder her for her gold and silver ornaments? Should she call out for help? She was alone and at the mercy of a possibly armed man. Protesting that her lord should not sleep without food after his long journey, she commenced cooking some *poories*, cakes fried in oil. The firelight confirmed her suspicions, and the man in the charpoy, no other than the Brahman astrologer, feeling he was detected, attempted to snatch some ornaments from her person, but she seized the pot and poured the boiling oil over him. His involuntary cries of pain roused the neighbours and led to his apprehension.

Muhammadans also go about pretending to predict

fortunes. They use dice in their divinations, and, if I may judge from those with whom I have come in contact, are but shallow fellows in comparison with their Brahman rivals.

"According to an assertion of the Prophet, what a fortune-teller says may be true; because one of the jinn steals away the truth, and carries it to the magician's ear; for the angels come down to the region next the earth (the lowest heaven), and mention the works that have been pre-ordained in heaven; and the devils (or evil jinn) listen to what the angels say, and hear the orders predestined in heaven and carry them to the fortune-tellers. It is on such occasions that shooting stars are hurled at the devils. It is said that 'the diviner obtains the services of the Sheytan (Shaitan) by magic arts, and by names invoked, and by the burning of perfumes, and he informs him of secret things.'"[1]

As might be expected, it occasionally happens that the predictions of the astrologers turn out correct. In that case the word is carried from mouth to mouth, and the fame of the fulfilled prophecy travels far and wide; but when events do not tally with the declared anticipations of the prophet, the ignorant are readily persuaded that the non-fulfilment of the prediction is due entirely to some want of formality or exactitude in carrying out the ceremonies prescribed by the Brahman.

A very interesting instance of the fulfilment of a Brahmanical prophecy will be found recorded in Colonel Meadows Taylor's Autobiography. A written prediction based upon the horoscope of the Raja of Sholapoor was shown to the Colonel, under a solemn promise of secrecy, many years before the predicted events came to pass. In this document the astrologer had foretold that the Raja would lose both his state and his wife before he attained the age of twenty-four, and the prophecy was verified to the letter under very peculiar circumstances. The story is well told by Colonel Taylor, but from other opinions and statements in his autobiography, there would appear to be reason to believe that the gallant officer was not without a tincture of superstition in his nature, which may have coloured his view and perhaps his narrative of this event. Besides, as horoscopes are consulted in all Hindu families, it is very improbable that the Raja of

[1] Hughes' "Dictionary of Islam," article 'Magic.'

Sholapoor's horoscope was kept so profound a secret as Colonel Taylor imagined. Any way, a lucky hit outweighs a thousand misses, and the world of India goes on, as it has done for ages, consulting the stars in their progress, and easily duped by, but ever trusting with childlike confidence, its astute hereditary priesthood, as, I think, the following extract from a native paper conducted in English will show:

"It is reported from Bombay that a Bania, named Trikamdas, an inhabitant of Ahmedabad, was informed by a Brahman that his death would take place on a certain day in the month of Vaisakh. Thereupon the Bania repaired to the holy shrine of Palitana to perform his funeral rites. But not dying on due date, he returned to Ahmedabad and interviewed the Brahman, who said that he had made a mistake in the calculation, and that Trikamdas would die in the month of Sravan. The devotee has thereupon gone back to Palitana to die!"[1]

Could faith or credulity go further?

India, indeed, is pre-eminently the land of fortune-tellers, and has given to Europe the race of gipsies so well known in story and, to a slighter extent, in real life. But the common-sense of the people often rebels against the pretensions of the soothsayers, as the following story aptly shows. It was related to me by an educated Indian gentleman, who in his infancy had heard it from his grandmother, but he was not able to say from what source the old lady had derived it.

An astrologer once told a Raja who consulted him about the future, that he would assuredly die on a certain date which he named. The Raja took the prediction very much to heart, and when the appointed time was approaching he withdrew from the cares of state, leaving the management of everything to his trusty vazīr (prime minister), and sought solitude in the jungle, where he spent his hours in devotion and fasting. He did this without assigning any reason for his action; but the wise vazīr resolved to find out what motives had prompted his master to abandon his duties as ruler of his kingdom. He sought the Raja in his sylvan retirement, and eventually wormed out of him the secret trouble which was

[1] "Tribune" (Lahore), June 24, 1882.

weighing upon his mind. Then occurred the following dialogue :

"Sire," said the vazīr, "is it possible that your Majesty can put faith in the words of an impostor like that?"

"He is no impostor. He is a learned man, and very pious too."

"Let me convince your Majesty that he is nothing of the kind."

"I don't see how you can do that."

"Permit me to bring him into your Majesty's august presence, and I engage to show you he is but a dull fellow."

"You have my permission."

The next day the vazīr presented himself before the Raja in company with the astrologer. After the usual salutations and obeisances, the vazīr asked the astrologer if it was true that the king would die on the date he had named.

"Alas! sir, such is the decree of Fate," was the reply.

"And oh, learned man," inquired the vazīr, "when will the full measure of your own days be completed?"

"In three years, five months and four days hence. Thus have the stars determined, and who can fight against them?" said the seer.

The words had hardly been uttered when the vazīr, drawing his sword, severed the astrologer's head from his shoulders.

As the startled and horrified king jumped to his feet, the vazīr said :

"Behold, sire, the truthful astrologer. He whom the stars had destined to die three years, five months and four days hence."

The Raja, thus suddenly and dramatically freed from the gloomy apprehensions with which his faith in the astrologer's prescience had oppressed his soul, resumed his duties and lived happily many years thereafter.

INDEX